The Cloudy Mirror

SUNY Series in Chinese Philosophy and Culture
David L. Hall and Roger T. Ames, editors

The Cloudy Mirror

Tension and Conflict
in the Writings of Sima Qian

Stephen W. Durrant

State University of New York Press

Published by
State University of New York Press, Albany

© 1995 State University of New York

Printed in the United States of America

For information, address State University of New York
Press, State University Plaza, Albany, N.Y., 12246

Production by Diane Ganeles
Marketing by Dana Yanulavich

Library of Congress Cataloging-in-Publication Data
Durrant, Stephen W., 1944–
    The cloudy mirror: tension and conflict in the writing of Sima
Qian/Stephen W. Durrant.
        p. cm.— (SUNY series in Chinese philosophy and culture)
    Includes bibliographical references and index.
    ISBN 0-7914-2655-6 (alk. paper).—ISBN 0-7914-2656-4 (pbk.:
alk. paper)
        1. Ssu-ma, Ch' ien, ca. 145–ca. 86 B.C.   2. Historians—China—
Biography. I. Title. II. Series.
DS734.9.S8D87   1995
931.007202—dc20
    [B]   94-43357
                                                                        CIP

10 9 8 7 6 5 4 3 2 1

To my parents
Stewart and Leola Durrant

Contents

Acknowledgments

This book says much about families and the Chinese virtue of *xiao* 孝, which we translate so quaintly as "filial piety." The awkward ring of the term in English reminds us that it is a concept not fully at home in our culture, particularly "at the end of the millennium." Contrary to the injunction of Confucius (*Analects* 4.19), we travel far away from our parents, going wherever the best job and the most money can be found. Many of us may not even fulfill what seems to be one of the minor Confucian requirements of a filial child: to know precisely the age of one's parents, rejoicing if they are still young and being filled with dread if they are aged (*Analects* 4.21). I have not been a particularly filial son and have moved far away from my parents. But at least I know their age, eighty-two at this writing, and this does fill me with dread. So I have dedicated this book to them as a very small way of expressing thanks for their great love and generous support. Sima Qian studied ancient China, he tells us, because it was his family's tradition. I can make no such claim. Still, my mother and father have always encouraged my peculiar intellectual pursuits, even though I am certain they have a difficult time explaining to neighbors in Lehi, Utah just what it is their son actually does.

Many others have helped me in the research and writing of this book—far too many to name here. Two early readers deserve special mention: Professors Stephen West and Joseph Allen. Although each approached the text from a quite different angle and had much critical to say, both encouraged me to push forward and bring this work to completion. I thank them both for their criticism and for their encouragement. For several rainy months, Chiu-mi Lai occupied an office next to mine at the National Central Library in Taiwan. She generously listened to various long-winded monologues on Sima Qian and always responded with great insight and good humor. A teacher at the Inter-University Program in Taiwan, Prof. Chen Shunzheng, was also a wonderful sounding board. Certainly my knowledge of the details of Sima Qian's writings can never approach his. But beyond that, I must say that I never spent an hour in his presence that was other than a complete delight. I also should mention two other teachers, Prof. Gary Williams, who started my wanderings down the sinological path, and Father Paul Serruys, who mentored me through some of the most intellectually exciting and personally challenging years of my life. Finally, another student of Sima Qian, Prof. William Nienhauser, has been extremely generous and helpful to me in recent years. I thank all of these and many others, including my former colleagues at the University of Utah and my current colleagues at the University of Oregon.

Two stints in Taiwan, still a *bao dao* for me, were essential in completing this manuscript. The first was a nine-month stay at the "China Studies Center" of the National Central Library in Taibei under a Fulbright Research Award. The second was six-months at the Inter-University Program (IUP). Each of these stays was comfortable and productive, thanks largely to the staffs of both facilities. I especially thank Liu Xianshu of the library and James Dew of IUP for their support and assistance. I also would like to express appreciation to Diane Ganeles, Production Editor, and the staff at SUNY Press for their assistance and patience during the completion of this manuscript.

Finally, I extend my heartfelt thanks to my immediate family, Kay and my children, who no doubt suffered from the numerous frustrations that accumulated as I worked away on this book during the past several years.

Introduction

Broaden me with literary culture; restrain me with ritual.

—Confucius, *Analects* (*Lun yu*) 6.27[1]

"The history of China, from its origins down to 110 B.C.E., is mixed to one degree or another with the history of one man."[2] So says Jean Levi in the "preamble" to his recent historical novel concerning the great Chinese scholar Sima Qian (145–86? B.C.E.[3]). Levi is right, little can be said of ancient China without turning to Sima Qian's vast, 130-chapter *Records of the Historian* (*Shi ji*), and that text is profoundly shaped by the peculiar "history of one man," its author. But the biographical details of Sima Qian's life are known in too meager detail and derive exclusively from his own hand. In other words, our knowledge of the most influential ancient Chinese historian is autobiographical in nature. Sima Qian begins his final chapter of *Records of the Historian* with a brief family history in which he quotes his father's essay on the strengths and weaknesses of the major philosophical schools. Then he turns to himself: "I, Qian, was born in Dragon Gate (Longmen), where I herded on the southern slopes of the mountains along the Yellow River. At the age of ten I could recite ancient texts."[4]

These autobiographical comments reflect a fundamental tension in Sima Qian's life and work. In the first sentence, Sima Qian draws a pastoral picture: a boy tends animals on the warm slope of a mountain along northern China's greatest river. Dragon Gate, which he identifies as his birthplace, is a spot rich in folklore. Located approximately 120 miles northeast of modern day Xi'an City, Dragon Gate is a place where the southern-flowing Yellow River narrows and cuts through the mountains. The canonical *Ancient Historical Documents* (*Shang shu*) states that Yu, the mythical conqueror of ancient floods, "guided the course of the Yellow River from Jishi on down to Dragon Gate."[5] Other texts claim that the Sage Yu "bored out" Dragon Gate, and later fantastic versions of this story describe how Yu, during his world-saving labors, entered a dark cave at this place, carrying fire on his back, and encountered strange gods, who presented him with the tools to complete his task.[6] To honor the Sage's work, Dragon Gate is sometimes called "The Gate of Yu" (Yumen).

Texts written long after Sima Qian's time say that carp assemble at the bottom of the Dragon Gate rapids and struggle upstream. Almost all fail, "bumping their foreheads and turning back." The few that succeed, who "leap over Dragon Gate," transform into dragons and fly away.[7] Whether this last story was told in Sima Qian's day is impossible to know, but the historian was undoubtedly aware of the story of the great Emperor Yu. In fact, when Sima Qian speaks of his own extensive travels, the first place he says he visited is the "Cave of Yu" at Guiji, where the "borer of Dragon Gate" is supposedly buried.[8]

In the second sentence of his self-description cited above, Sima Qian turns from the romance of herding livestock near Longmen to scholarship: "At the age of ten I could recite ancient texts." Precisely what Sima Qian meant by "ancient texts" is a subject of disagreement. Some commentators believe this is a reference to ancient texts in general or to a specific set of ancient texts, such as those preserved in the pre-Qin script, while others argue that the term is a specific reference to the "old script" version of *Ancient Historical Documents* supposedly transmitted by Kong Anguo (fl. 125 B.C.E.), one of Sima Qian's most respected teachers.[9] It is quite certain, however, that when he began his formal education, Sima Qian was no longer herding livestock on the sunny hills near Dragon Gate but was with his father in the Western Han capital of Chang'an.

More than fifty years earlier, the founder of the Han dynasty, Emperor Gaozu (r. 206–195 B.C.E.), decided to build his capital in the same area that had served as capital during two previous dynasties, the Western Zhou (?1045–771 B.C.E.) and the Qin (221–206 B.C.E.). These earlier capitals had been largely destroyed. Consequently, a new city, known as Chang'an ("Everlasting Peace"), was built on the southern side of the Wei River, an area occupied today by the northwest suburbs of Xi'an. Emperor Gaozu initiated work on two large palaces, with his prime minister Xiao He (d. 193) directing all construction. The walls of the new city, approximately fourteen miles in circumference and enclosing an area of thirteen square miles, were built under Gaozu's successor, Emperor Hui (r. 194–188 B.C.E.). The new capital was finally completed with the addition of several palace complexes during the early years of Emperor Wu's reign (141–87 B.C.E.). Thus, when Sima Qian first visited Chang'an in his early youth, the city was essentially complete and must have been an impressive sight for a youth from the hills near Dragon Gate.[10] A "pivot of the four quarters," an axis uniting heavenly and earthly powers, Chang'an was a symbolic expression of tradition and a focus of order.[11] The walls were oriented to face the cardinal points, the south and east walls running in straight lines for over three miles, while the north and west walls were of irregular shape, perhaps imitating certain stellar constellations. Three gates split each wall, granting access to broad avenues that led directly across the city and were interrupted only by the huge palace complexes. One and one-half centuries after Sima Qian's death, another historian, Ban Gu (32–92), looked back upon the former splendor of Chang'an and wrote:

With its barriers of defense and resistance,
    It is the safest refuge of the empire.
Therefore, its bounty filled the six directions,
And thrice it became the Imperial Domain.
From here the Zhou rose like a dragon,
And Qin leered like a tiger.
When it came time for the great Han to receive the mandate and
    establish their capital:
Above, they perceived the Eastern Well's spiritual essence;
Below, they found the site in harmony with the River Diagram's
    numinous signs.[12]

These two places, Longmen and Chang'an—"Dragon Gate" and "Everlasting Peace"—are geographical symbols we might choose to designate a polarity that sometimes strains and even tears the fabric of Sima Qian's writings. Dragon Gate is a bucolic site of imagination and myth, a place where Sima Qian describes himself as a young herdsman on sunny slopes. Like the creature from which it takes its name, Dragon Gate captures the imagination and generates an endless supply of stories. Chang'an, with a name carrying a wish for quiet stability, is a site of study and order, a place where Sima Qian ingests those "ancient texts" that embody the rituals and traditions of the past.

To analyze Sima Qian's writings in terms of tension and opposition is not new. Li Changzhi's landmark biography, *The Character and Style of Sima Qian* (*Sima Qian zhi renge yu fengge*), posits a tension in the great Han historian's life and writings between the "romantic" spirit of the southern Chinese Chu culture, which was revived in the early Han, and the "classical" culture of Zhou, with the former ultimately prevailing over the latter.[13] Li describes Sima Qian's romanticism as "active, bursting, bold, pursuing the limitless, distressed, and deeply emotional."[14] While Li's analysis inspires and informs my own work, I employ somewhat different terms. His "romantic" is Chinese *langman*, a word that is not a part of the ancient Chinese lexicon but is borrowed from the West. Furthermore, "romantic" is a difficult term that poses problems of ambiguity and misunderstanding I would like to avoid here. Finally, the opposition of "romantic" with "classical" is not a part of Sima Qian's own ancient Chinese tradition but springs from a particular moment in Western history.

Confucius (551–479 B.C.E.), China's "ultimate sage," provides the terms I use to summarize the tension apparent in Sima Qian's writings. Three places in *Analects* (*Lun yu*), the Master places the word *wen* 文 "literary culture" in contrast to *li* 禮 "ritual behavior." A True Gentleman (*junzi*), we are told, is one who achieves a perfect harmony of these two qualities.[15] According to Confucius, *wen* broadens, while *li* restrains and channels energy into appropriate paths. Confucius implies that either of these qualities without the other can bring dangerous excess and threaten the balance upon which civilization depends. Too much *li* leads to empty formalism and spawns a dry proliferation of rites such as arose among some Confucians in the late years of the Zhou dynasty. An excess of *wen* can produce too much feeling and emotion, dissolving correct boundaries and confusing proper discrimination with an ever-broadening circle of aesthetic and literary possibilities. Indeed, tradition might be threatened when *wen* is ascendant not by too little but by too much literature!

Despite the potential conflict between these two principles, the Confucian does not regard *wen* and *li* as antagonistic opposites. Instead, both are essential constituents of the perfect balance that characterizes the True Gentleman. Theodore DeBary's explanation of *Analects* 9.11 addresses this very point: "For Confucius these opposite values [i.e., *wen* and *li*] were both necessary and complimentary. To accept them as such was to accept human life, at its best, as lived in the midst of such tensions trying to strike the

Mean."[16] Certainly *wen*, in its primary meaning of "pattern," is at the foundation of all *li*; and *li* gives visible and appropriate expression to the emotion that is so often a part of *wen*. These two, then, could hardly be locked in a destructive struggle. But aesthetic inclinations and formal demands can produce conflict, and such conflict, I believe, can be seen throughout the course of Chinese civilization. Steven Van Zoeren points to one small corner of such conflict when he notes the existence of "two readings" of *Classic of Poetry* (*Shi jing*), China's most important literary text: "One proper and apologetic; the other secret, pleasurable and dangerous."[17] The first of these readings, to use the contrast I have set up here, is a ritual one, the second is one that follows and conforms to the aesthetic and emotional patterns of *wen*.

The pursuit of *wen*, as I have suggested above, can lead to a dangerous proliferation of texts—that is, to *wen* in its most concrete form. This notion that the circle of literary culture could become too expansive and dangerous seems strange in our day of large libraries and lengthy bibliographies. Consequently, Western sinologists frequently have looked back to the Warring States period (403–221 B.C.E.), when the Various Masters and Hundred Schools (*zhu zi bai jia*) contended and new writings emerged, as a golden era of Chinese thought. However, Chinese scholars of the period from the late Zhou to the early Han saw the elaboration of philosophical schools as further evidence of a collapse of the "Kingly Way" and as another symptom of the decline into political disorder. The thirty-third chapter of *Zhuangzi*, probably written near the end of this period is a typical expression of nostalgia for an earlier era of philosophical unity:

> The empire is in great disorder. The Worthies and Sages are not understood. The way and its virtue are not unified. Many in the empire obtain one aspect [of the Way], examine it, and thereby consider themselves praiseworthy. It is just like the ears, eyes, nose, and mouth; each has its own understanding but is not able to function for the other. This resembles the many skills of the hundred schools. All have their strong points, and at times each is useful. Nevertheless, they are not inclusive, they are not universal.[18]

The *Zhuangzi* essay does not advocate a violent end to the chaos of the time but places hope in a gentle unification of the best of each school, in a new philosophy resembling a whole and healthy body, with eyes, ears, nose, and mouth all functioning harmoniously. This longing for an era of political and philosophical unity, addressed to a war-weary world and projected into the ancient past as a kind of utopia, leads quite logically to the Qin dynasty's effort to control and monopolize texts.

The First Qin Emperor (r. 221–210 B.C.E.) is commonly portrayed in Chinese historical writing as a tyrant who followed his act of political unification with a similarly violent suppression of philosophical diversity. The notorious destruction of books in 213 B.C.E., encouraged by the prime minister Li Si (d. 208 B.C.E.), and the purported execution of 460 literati in the following year are sometimes presented as proof of the Emperor's intolerance for the "disorder" of the Hundred Schools.[19] However, the First Qin Emperor's primary concern was with critics of the new empire and of his own policies, particularly those critics who "studied the past in order to criticize the present." The books singled out for destruction were the "books in the bureau of history" except for "the records of Qin." These records of other states undoubtedly portrayed Qin as a semibarbaric enemy and were particularly distasteful to the new ruler. Furthermore, according to the imperial order, *Classic of Poetry* and *Classic of Historical Documents* (*Shu jing*), as well as the writings of the philosophers, were not to be held by private citizens but were to be preserved only in an official government bureau under the direction of "Scholars of Wide Learning" (*bo shi*; hereafter, simply "academicians"). This interdiction on the writings of the philosophers, as the distinguished modern scholar Qian Mu has noted, was probably directed at the private transmission of learning through "schools," lineages of teachers and students who passed on the traditions of thinkers from the past.[20]

A second critical part of the First Qin Emperor's policy to "control the text," much less frequently discussed than the events of 213 and 212 B.C.E., is the regularization of the Office of Academicians (*bo shi guan*) as a part of the new Qin imperial structure. Several state governments during the Warring States period appointed academicians, and the state of Qi even sponsored an academy, the Jixia Academy, where scholars gathered and debated the issues of the day. The Qin emperor made this institution a part of the new imperial government, perhaps even moving Jixia academicians from the conquered state of Qi to the capital, and consulted with the academicians on several critical issues. But perhaps two of the emperor's critics, the scholars Hou and Lu, recognized what might have been his genuine feeling when they said that "Although there are seventy academicians, their posts are just sinecures, for he (i.e., the emperor) never listens to them."[21]

The sudden rise and even more sudden fall of the Qin dynasty throws a long shadow over the first century of Han rule. Particularly disturbing to men of learning was the First Qin Emperor's attempt to control scholarship. Against such a background, one can regard Sima Qian's historical synthesis as a monumental effort to combat any future control or limitation of textuality; for *Records of the Historian* embraces not just the proliferating texts of the past but the different forms of that vast literature as well. Much of Sima Qian's history, as will be seen in what follows, is drawn directly from other sources, and much more of the text is only slightly rewritten from earlier accounts.

As a great work of synthesis, *Records of the Historian* is very much in keeping with the spirit of consolidation that dominated the Han dynasty. The disunity of the Eastern Zhou (771–221 B.C.E.) and the turmoil of the Qin were a strong inducement to order and security. This led intellectuals toward encyclopedic inclusiveness, toward attempts to incorporate the past in ways that would provide a more sure foundation for the future. In philosophy, such works as *The Master of Huainan (Huainanzi)* and *The Abundant Dew of Spring and Autumn Annals (Chun qiu fan lu)* reflect this new tendency. Even in the field of art, monuments from the Han are works of synthesis fully congruent with the spirit and even the content of *Records of the Historian.*[22]

For all of this spirit of consolidation, there exists in Han dynasty China no grander synthesis than *Records of the Historian.* Sima Qian's passion for *wen*, understood as the texts and styles of the past, induced him to create simultaneously a universal history and a cultural encyclopedia. Such comprehensiveness would seem to make order and coherence impossible, but Sima Qian strove, as he said himself, "to create the words of a single school." His goal was to follow the path of Confucius and present a new order, a new expression congruent with the demands of *li*. Thus, the tension I posit here with the Confucian terms *wen* and *li* can be construed in a variety of different ways: it is the tension between comprehensiveness and coherence, between the storyteller and the philosopher-historian, between the romantic world of Dragon Gate and the ordered world of Chang'an.

My purpose in what follows is to trace several aspects of the tension I have suggested above. In chapter 1 I expand somewhat on my thesis and show how Sima Qian's own sense of failure and frustration stimulated a creative activity that complicated his goal to emulate Confucius and summarize the entire Chinese tradition. Chapter 2 concerns Sima Qian's portrayal of Confucius, the most important single figure of the Chinese past and the most important influence upon the Han historian. Confucius is indeed Sima Qian's model, but he is also an extension of the Han historian himself. It remains almost impossible, even today, to contemplate Confucius without somehow thinking about Sima Qian and his biography of the Sage. That biography, I argue, is a literary work in which the personalities of the Sage and the Han historian are tightly interwoven. In chapter 3, I turn to Sima Qian's portrayal of Confucius as the great transmitter of the past, the historian *par excellence*, and trace the tradition of the Six Classics and Sima Qian's key contribution to the idea of a Confucian canon. I also consider the relationship between one of the most important of those classics, *Spring and Autumn Annals (Chun qiu)*, and Sima Qian's description of his own mission as a historian. In chapters 4 and 5, I examine Sima Qian's adaptation of two highly influential, earlier texts, *Zuo Commentary (Zuo zhuan)* and *Intrigues of the Warring States (Zhanguo ce)*. That adaptation, I argue, reflects Sima Qian's own experience and frustration and provides a key to reading and appreciating other narratives where the historian has not drawn so directly from earlier sources. Finally, in chapter 6, I explore the attempt of subsequent scholars, invited by the claims of the Han historian himself, to find a coherent ideology in *Records of the Historian*. The narrative compulsion, the desire to tell "a good story," I maintain, undermines Sima Qian's pursuit of a unified vision and frustrates all of us who would describe precisely the Han historian's "philosophy of history." In this sixth and last chapter, the tension between *wen* and *li* is put in somewhat different terms, terms perhaps more appropriate to an essentially literary study such as this.

Before proceeding on, several caveats are in order. What follows is not a comprehensive study of the huge and extremely complex *Records of the Historian*. Such a study, particularly one that equals or surpasses the work of earlier scholars is a daunting task and is not attempted here. The reader wanting a more systematic and thorough survey is directed to Watson in English, Chavannes in French, and Li Changzhi or Zhang Dake in Chinese.[23] Instead, my study focuses attention upon relatively few of Sima Qian's numerous narratives and concerns only a limited number of thematic issues. While these issues, I believe, are critical to understanding and appreciating Sima Qian's literary and historiographical art, there are many equally important problems and topics that I ignore entirely.

I also do not attempt to present here a biography of Sima Qian, even though certain biographical details are critical to my arguments. Moreover, my interest in those details centers more upon Sima Qian's self-perception and self-portrayal than on what might have "actually happened," the latter well beyond our scholarly excavations anyway. Nevertheless, to facilitate a clearer comprehension of the sequence of biographical events mentioned here and there in the chapters below, I have included a brief chronology of Sima Qian's life in an appendix. That chronology is not a result of original research but leans almost exclusively upon the pioneering work of Wang Guowei and Zheng Haosheng.[24]

Despite the somewhat narrow scope of the present work, I must turn here to two critical background issues: first, the overall structure of *Records of the Historian*; and second, the question of the authenticity of the received version of Sima Qian's text.

Records of the Historian is divided into five sections. The first section, "Basic Annals" (*ben ji*), contains twelve chapters chronicling the major events of the emperors of China and their governments. The second, "Chronological Charts" (*nian biao*), includes ten chapters that schematically arrange major events and the sequence of rulers, famous ministers, and other noteworthy persons. Each "Chart" is prefaced by a short introduction in which Sima Qian discusses a few of the major issues relevant to the period covered on the chart. These discussions often contain valuable observations about major historical trends and themes. The third section, "Treatises" (*shu*—eight in number), outlines the history and structure of a select number of significant institutions (e.g., "ritual," "music," "the calendar," etc.). The fourth section, "Hereditary Households" (*shi jia*), contains thirty chapters dealing primarily with enfeoffed hereditary households that exercised some sovereignty over portions of China during the Zhou and Han dynasties (see further discussion in chapter 2 below). Finally, there are sixty-nine chapters in a section called in Chinese *lie zhuan*, a term that I translate "Arrayed Traditions" and abbreviate below as "Traditions."[25]

A further word should be said about my translation of the title of this last section. *Lie zhuan* 列傳 has sometimes been translated as "biographies." There are at least two problems with such a translation. First, while most of these chapters concern individuals, others deal with particular groups—for example, "The Xiongnu" (chapter 110), "The Eastern Yue" (chapter 114), and so forth. Second, chapters of this section that do deal with individuals present a highly selective account of events and details obviously meant, in some cases at least, to supplement other sources. Thus, at the conclusion of his accounts of Guanzi and Yanzi (chapter 62), two prime ministers from the Spring and Autumn state of Qi, Sima Qian says, "Many in this generation have their books. Therefore, I do not discuss [what those books contain] but discuss a few neglected episodes concerning them."[26]

A recognition of these problems led Watson to translate *lie zhuan* as "memoirs."[27] While such a translation is acceptable, I have chosen to be more literal. *Zhuan* is, of course, the nominal form of *chuan* "to transmit, to pass down" and means that which has been passed down, often as a canonical commentary appended to a classic.[28] By late Zhou times, *zhuan* seems to have become the name of a literary genre that concerned "traditions" dealing with some person or group.[29] *Lie* means "to arrange, to put in order" and is first used by Sima Qian himself to modify *zhuan*. He does not explain this new term, but one of the most important commentators of *Records of the Historian*, Sima Zhen (fl. 713–742), does: "He put in order (*xulie*) the traces of the lives of subordinates and caused that they be handed down (*chuan*) to later ages. Therefore, it is called 'Arrayed Traditions' (*lie zhuan*)."[30]

The second issue, which concerns the authenticity of certain chapters of *Records of the Historian* , derives from Ban Gu's comment that ten chapters of Sima Qian's work had titles but no text.[31] Zhang Yan's (ca. 250 C.E.) commentary on Ban Gu's passage lists the ten missing chapters as "The Basic Annals of the Filial Emperor Jing" (chapter 11), "The Basic Annals of the Filial Emperor Wu" (chapter 12), "The Chronological Chart of Generals, Prime Ministers, and Famous Officials from the Rise of the Han to the Present Time" (chapter 21), "The Treatise on Ritual" (chapter 23), "The Treatise on Music" (chapter 24), "The Treatise on the Military" (lost as a separate chapter), "The Hereditary Household of the Three Kings" (chapter 30), "The Traditions of Fu, Jin, and [the Marquis] of Kuaitong" (chapter 98), "The Traditions of the Fortune Tellers" (chapter 127), and "The Tortoise and Milfoil Diviners" (chapter 129).[32]

Sima Zhen explains that each of these chapters, with the exception of "The Treatise on the Military," was forged and eventually put back into the text. "The Treatise on the Military," in Sima Zhen's view, was supposedly retitled "The Treatise on the Musical Tubes" and was prefaced by a short text on this subject that was originally broken off from the "Treatise on the Calendar." Both Zhang Yan and Sima Zhen believe the villain in much of this was Chu Shaosun (ca. 35 B.C.E.), who made numerous additions to the text of *Records of the Historian*, many clearly marked.[33]

Certainly portions of Sima Qian's original text have been lost. The current version of "The Basic Annals of the Filial Emperor Wu," to raise one famous example, is merely a copy of "The Treatise on the Feng and Shan Sacrifices," and no longer exists in its original form. Modern scholars have raised questions about other portions of today's text that are not in Zhang Yan's list given above,[34] but Chavannes' conclusion, written after his very careful study of this problem, bears repeating:

> Although the interpolations that are noted in *Records of the Historian* are quite numerous, they do not present a serious attack on the integrity of the work. In fact, the most considerable among them are due to Chu Shaosun; and this writer has almost always taken care to inform us when he is beginning to speak. The result is that it is easy to distinguish between the pages that are his and the rest of the work. As to other additions, one will see, if one counts them, that they are, in sum, an almost negligible quantity. In view of its length and its antiquity, the *Records of the Historian* can be regarded as having come down to us in a remarkable state of preservation.[35]

Those who remain overly concerned with details of authenticity should note, moreover, that my arguments do not rest on those sections of the text most often held in doubt.

Finally, it is well to note that as we step into the world of Sima Qian and the tension in his text I have suggested here, we inevitably enter ancient China. As Jean Levi suggests in the quotation at the beginning of this introduction, it is virtually impossible to think about the Chinese past without somehow being a captive of Sima Qian's categories and themes. He is a creator of the past and hovers over the future as well—later historians in China only rarely escape the patterns he laid down and scholars continually construct themselves within the character categories he portrayed so brilliantly. Indeed, one cannot even read a book about modern China, like Perry Link's engaging *Evening Chats in Beijing*, without hearing Chinese scholars, tragically in this case, repeat a script of personal frustration and agony that the Grand Historian composed so eloquently centuries before them.[36] I do not wish here to minimize the very real and intense suffering of these modern intellectuals, but the stories they tell and the personalities they construct resonate with a tradition that finds its strongest voice in Sima Qian's *Records of the Historian*. In a strange way, Sima Qian mirrors the present day almost as well as he mirrors his own time and the ages that preceded him.

1

The Frustration of the Second Confucius

I transmit and do not create.

—*Analects*, 7.1.

I grieve that my heart has that which it has not completely expressed, and that I might die and my writing not be known to later ages.

—Sima Qian.

Sima Qian not only is ancient China's greatest historian, he also is "the first author of a truly autobiographical self-testimony in China."[1] In fact, when the historian Ban Gu wrote a biography of Sima Qian and included it in his *History of the Han*, he could do little more than quote Sima Qian's own writings.[2] Thus, what we know of Sima Qian derives almost exclusively from his own hand; he creates himself, much as he creates China's past, through his written word. Moreover, the text that is his life and the text that is his history resonate with one another, contain parallel themes, and reflect similar tensions. My attempt to demonstrate this thesis begins with the text that is Sima Qian's life.

Sima Qian speaks extensively of himself in two documents, and these form almost the entire text of Ban Gu's biography: the "Self-Narration of the Gentleman Grand Astrologer" ("Tai shi gong zixu"—hereafter, "Self-Narration"), which is the final chapter of *Records of the Historian*; and "Letter in Response to Ren An" ("Bao Ren An shu"). The first of these is a formal document in which Sima Qian establishes his credentials as a historian, explains why he wrote his monumental history, and summarizes his text's overall structure. The second document is a long letter, probably written in

93 B.C.E. to Ren An, a friend who was in prison under a death sentence and was subsequently cut in two at the waist.[3] This letter focuses almost entirely upon one critical event in Sima Qian's life and is much more personal and emotional than the "Self-Narration." From these two documents, documents quiet different from one another both in purpose and in form, emerges a picture of a profound tension within Sima Qian between a "classical" demand to contain and transmit tradition and a need to vent a prodigious creative energy nurtured by deep personal frustration. This tension can be further explained by a remarkable chapter of *Records of the Historian*, "The Traditions of Bo Yi" (chapter 61), a chapter considered in detail below.

Two figures dominate Sima Qian's "Self-Narration": his father, Sima Tan (d. 110 B.C.E.), and Confucius. Sima Qian presents both as conservative voices, voices of ritual (*li*) and duty (*yi*) that constrain Sima Qian and require him to construct the broad tradition of the past according to a preestablished blueprint. Yet Sima Tan and Confucius, like so many other figures from China's past, are largely creations of Sima Qian's own writing brush and are inextricably woven in the "Self-Narration" into one overwhelming authority figure. As we shall see, Sima Tan invokes the prestige of Confucius, and Confucius, through the principle of filial piety (*xiao*), empowers Sima Tan.

Filial piety, which plays a central role in the "Self-Narration," had become the primary Confucian virtue by Sima Qian's time.[4] During the first century of the Western Han dynasty, the *Classic of Filial Piety* (*Xiao jing*), a text proclaiming filial piety "the root of all virtue," had gained wide circulation, and each Han emperor also had been granted the character *xiao* as a part of his posthumous name. As a result of this promotion of filial piety, Confucius was identified with all fathers, indeed all authority figures. Sima Qian's own acute sense of filial piety is reflected in an interesting passage in *Records of the Historian*, where duty to the father is placed above duty to the state. Although the speaker in the story under question is the viscount of the state of Wei, the quotation has no antecedent in earlier literature, and the distinguished Japanese scholar Takikawa Kametarō argues that Sima Qian is "merely speaking out and recommending his own thoughts":

> The viscount of Wei said, "A father and a son have [a relationship of] flesh and bone, while a minister and a lord are attached by dutifulness. Therefore, if a father is in error, and a son remonstrates

three times but is not heard, then the son complies but cries out for him. If a minister remonstrates three times but is not heard, then dutifulness allows him to depart.[5]

Sima Tan, to whom Sima Qian was attached by a filial relationship he believed transcended even dutifulness to the emperor, served in the Han bureaucracy as Prefect Grand Astrologer (*tai shi ling*), an official position concerned largely with drawing up the calendar and with identifying auspicious and inauspicious days for imperial activities. The Prefect Grand Astrologer seems also to have had the responsibility of keeping records of the correlation between celestial and terrestrial phenomena, a task that made him a recorder of important human events.[6]

Despite the relatively low salary of Sima Tan's official position, his tasks required versatility and a high degree of technical training. At the beginning of his "Self-Narration," Sima Qian writes with obvious pride of his father's educational background and intellect. First, he lists Sima Tan's academic mentors, a highly impressive list, and then he faithfully reproduces his father's lengthy essay entitled "The Essential Meaning of the Six Schools" ("Liu jia yaozhi"). In introducing the essay, Sima Qian notes that his father "served as an official during the *Jian yuan* and *Yuan feng* reign periods (140–110 B.C.E.)." Sima Qian goes on to explain that his father "was distressed that scholars did not elucidate their ideas and that teachers were perverse" and that this is why he wrote "The Essential Meaning of the Six Schools."[7]

Assuredly Sima Tan, as his son's explanation implies, was out of step with the philosophical trends dominating the court of Emperor Wu. Those trends, and Sima Tan's reaction to them, can best be understood against the backdrop of the intellectual developments of the century before Sima Tan's birth. As noted briefly in the introduction, the philosophical variety of the late Zhou, which modern Western scholars are inclined to admire, was usually regarded by ancient Chinese as an unhappy extension of the political disunity of that time. One early Chinese thinker had exclaimed in frustration, "How sad!—the hundred schools going on and on instead of turning back, fated never to join again."[8] The rhetoric of this expression of frustration leans upon a belief, widespread in the late Zhou, Qin, and early Han, that all learning in the halcyon days of the early Zhou was "official learning" and hence completely unified.[9]

The political and intellectual conflict of the last centuries of the

Zhou, which contrasts so starkly with the legendary unity of an
earlier and "happier" era, stimulated a search for new order both in
the world of government and in the world of thought. This search,
I believe, produced two groups: those who sought unity in intellectual conquest, usually in conjunction with political conquest; and
those who sought unity in philosophical synthesis. The line between these two groups, of course, is not always clear. Certainly
advocates of conquest were touched themselves by the spirit of
synthesis, and advocates of synthesis were not entirely free of a
more aggressive side.[10]

Two late Zhou treatises, both stylistic forerunners to Sima
Tan's evaluation of the "Six Schools," allow us to see the distinction between advocates of conquest and advocates of synthesis. The
first of these treatises is found in the writings of the great Confucian
master Xunzi (?340–?245 B.C.E.) and is entitled "Against the Twelve
Masters" ("Fei shi er zi").[11] Xunzi launches strenuous attacks in his
treatise on twelve late Zhou masters, who represent various intellectual positions. His criticisms are directed both at teachings and at
personalities. Indeed, the only compliment Xunzi can pay his philosophical opponents is to admit, somewhat grudgingly, that "what
they support seems reasonable," at least "sufficiently so as to de-
ceive and mislead the ignorant multitude."[12] In his eyes, none of
these teachers, nor their teachings, could contribute to the unified
kingdom that Xunzi wanted—his own brand of Confucianism was
the only hope for the future. Although Xunzi's famous students,
the Legalists Li Si and Hanfeizi (d. 233 B.C.E.), may have deviated
from the Confucianism of their master, they do resemble him in
advocating an aggressive unification based primarily upon a single
philosophy.

The second treatise, also an evaluation of other philosophers, is
found in one of the later chapters of *Zhuangzi*.[13] Unlike Xunzi, who
could find no value outside of the Confucian tradition, the author of
this treatise discovers genuine merit in all of the "Hundred Schools"
and believes that the Taoism of Laozi is sufficiently broad to allow
a collection of those precious fragments of truth that had been so
widely scattered throughout the philosophical world. Entire works
written in the late Zhou and early Han dynasties strove for precisely
the type of eclecticism reflected in the *Zhuangzi* treatise. These
works gathered teachings and principles from a variety of schools
and brought them together into a broad synthesis that has often
been labelled "Taoist." One of the most noteworthy of these texts,
The Spring and Autumn Annals of Master Lü (*Lü shi chun qiu*), can

be seen as the Qin Minister Lü Buwei's (d. 235 B.C.E.) attempt to combat the movement toward belligerent narrowness dominating the court of Qin and represented by such figures as Li Si and Hanfeizi.[14] The goal of Lü Buwei's encyclopedic text was, in the words of Sima Qian, "to complete the affairs of heaven and earth, of the ten thousand things, and of both antiquity and modernity."[15] *Huainanzi*, a later work somewhat reminiscent in its eclecticism of *The Spring and Autumn Annals of Master Lü*, is the outstanding example of intellectual synthesis in the first century of the Han dynasty. In fact, *Huainanzi* perhaps represents a last gasp of Taoist eclecticism before such doctrines, prominent during the reigns of the Han emperors Wen (r. 180–157 B.C.E.) and Jing (r. 157–141 B.C.E.), were supplanted at court by Emperor Wu's sponsorship of Confucianism.[16]

Sima Tan's treatise fits very much into the spirit of synthesis typified by the second of these groups, and it comes, like *Huainanzi*, at a time when that other spirit, the spirit of philosophical conquest advanced by such a formidable figure as Dong Zhongshu (?179–?104 B.C.E.), was ascendant at court. It is impossible to date Sima Tan's treatise precisely, but it was most likely written in the thirty-year period between Dong Zhongshu's memorial to Emperor Wu in 140 B.C.E. (?), advocating that "all not within . . . the arts of Confucius . . . be cut short," and Tan's death in 110 B.C.E. If this is so, Sima Tan and Dong Zhongshu may indeed have been archrivals, as Zhang Dake and other modern scholars have suggested.[17]

Sima Tan, like his contemporary Liu An (179–122 B.C.E.), gathers his eclecticism under the philosophical rubric of Taoism. In fact, Taoism is the only one of the six schools discussed in Sima Tan's essay to receive an entirely positive evaluation: "Taoism . . . changes with the times, responds to the transformations of things . . . is economical in doctrine and easy to carry out. Its duties are few but its merits many."[18] Sima Tan's criticisms of the other five schools largely center either upon their troublesome proliferation of rules and prohibitions (Confucianism and the Yin-yang School) or upon their excessive and unreasonable harshness (Mohism and Legalism).

Such Taoist sympathies plainly belong to the early decades of the Han dynasty when Taoism had become the basis of an imperial policy of "non-action." Whether or not the reigns of the Han emperors Wen and Jing, during which Sima Tan must have grown up and matured as a scholar, were as quiescent as sometimes portrayed is a subject of some dispute.[19] Nevertheless, it is certain that these decades were a period of consolidation in which Taoism was often invoked to justify essentially laissez-fair policies. With Emperor Wu's accession in 141 B.C.E. and the death in 135 B.C.E. of Empress Dou, an ardent advocate of Taoism, this all changed. Emperor Wu was an activist who wanted to expand both the boundaries of the empire and the government's economic powers. He was also profoundly influenced by the recommendations of the Confucian scholar Dong Zhongshu, who called for a thorough reorganization of intellectual life around the traditional "Six Arts."[20]

One might conclude from reading Sima Tan's "Treatise" that he was a tolerant Taoist thinker completely disaffected with the Confucian trends of his time. Such a reading is complicated somewhat by Sima Qian's memory of his father's deathbed admonition. In the most dramatic section of Sima Qian's "Self-Narration," Sima Tan claims that his family's "ancestors were Grand Astrologers for the house of Zhou." After expressing concern that his family has declined, Sima Tan continues declaiming to his son in the most emotional terms: "Will it end with me? ... When I die, you must become Grand Astrologer. When you are Grand Astrologer, do not forget what I have desired to evaluate and to write!"

Next, Sima Tan quotes *Classic of Filial Piety* to reinforce the plea that his son must continue the family tradition and bring glory to both himself and his ancestors: "Filial piety begins in serving parents, matures in serving the ruler, and ends in establishing oneself. To raise one's name in later generations and thereby glorify one's parents, this is the greatest expression of filial piety."[21]

A passage like this, from a text of such extraordinary status and authority, could hardly fail to make a powerful impression on any devoted son. Moreover, Sima Tan immediately follows his quotation from *Classic of Filial Piety* with a summary of the great labors of the Duke of Zhou and Confucius, who heroically preserved and illuminated the past. He himself would continue the work of those earlier sages, but his own time has run out, and so the heavy task must be given to his son:

> From the capture of the unicorn on down has been more than four-hundred years ... Today Han has arisen and the whole empire is united. But as to enlightened lords, worthy rulers, loyal officials, and gentlemen who died for duty, I have been Grand Astrologer and have not evaluated and recorded them. The loss of the empire's historical documents is what I deeply fear. I hope you will think of this![22]

Sima Tan's deathbed reference to the time that has passed since the capture of the unicorn is clarified somewhat by another statement that Sima Qian attributes to his father and includes elsewhere in his "Self-Narration:"

> My father used to say: "From the death of the Duke of Zhou, five hundred years passed, and there was Confucius. After the death of Confucius down to the present time, there have been five hundred years. If one could only link up with the enlightened generations and put in order *Changes* (*Yi*), continue *Spring and Autumn Annals*, and take as basis *Poetry, Historical Documents, Ritual* (*Li*) and *Music* (*Yue*)!"[23]

Sima Tan, as quoted by his son, alludes here to Mencius' theory, picked up in the early Han by Jia Yi (201–169 B.C.E.), that a sage arises every 500 years.[24] His arithmetic, surprisingly inaccurate for a Prefect Grand Astrologer who has as one of his duties the calculation of the calendar, leads to the conclusion that another sage is due. The presence of the previous sage, Confucius, was signalled by the capture of a unicorn, an event reported quite soberly for the year 481 B.C.E. in the very last entry of *Spring and Autumn Annals*.[25] If another sage is due, then so is another unicorn; and the mythical beast, as we shall see, will indeed wander onto the pages of history once again!

The words of Sima Tan, dying in frustration near Luoyang, hardly remind us of the author of "The Essential Meaning of the Six Schools." The Taoist syncretic, Sima Tan, who advocates in his essay a path that is neither harsh nor troublesome, suddenly appears, in Sima Qian's account of his final words, filled with anxiety about the preservation of tradition, a tradition linked with the Duke of Zhou and Confucius. Indeed, Sima Tan presents Confucius as the model his son must follow in order to prevent the past from slipping into darkness forever. Sima Qian, in the words of a father who elsewhere praises Taoist "non-action," must "not forget," he must "think of this." Whatever moderation he may have advocated in his "Essay," Sima Tan conveys to his son an ostensibly un-Taoist and very "troublesome" anxiety in his final paternal injunction.

Sima Qian responds to this admonition as we might expect from a filial son: "I, Qian, bowed my head and, with flowing tears, said, 'I the small child, am not clever, but I request in all cases to elucidate the old accounts that you, father, have put in order. I would not dare to be deficient!'"[26] Sima Qian's response to his father's speech on the five-hundred-year succession of sages is similar: "How could I, the small child, dare yield this task to others!"[27]

How do we explain the apparent discrepancy between Sima Tan, the Taoist author of "The Essential Meaning of the Six Schools," and Sima Tan, the stern voice of Confucian responsibility speaking to his son in the "Self-Narration?" Part of the explanation may be sought in a critical feature of Sima Qian's style as a compiler of the past. *Records of the Historian*, as subsequent chapters of this study will attempt to demonstrate in some detail, is a vast collection of diverse texts and conflicting voices. Sima Qian sometimes adapts older texts, bringing them into general compliance with his own language and narrative style, while other texts are edited in a somewhat cursory fashion, and still others are quoted verbatim. Although there is no second source of Sima Tan's treatise on the Six Schools, I believe that it belongs to the last of these categories—it is a direct and faithful reproduction of Sima Tan's actual essay. Elsewhere, Sima Qian shows no inclination to write this type of extended philosophical piece, and the voice speaking in the treatise, both in its pro-Taoist content, and its somewhat dispassionate, impersonal style, does not resemble that of Sima Qian. So far as I know, no one has suggested that this piece is anything other than what it purports to be—an authentic treatise by Sima Tan, accurately reproduced by his son.

Sima Tan's deathbed admonitions are quite another matter; these closely resemble the dramatic speeches delivered at crucial moments throughout the pages of *Records of the Historian*. Sima Qian, we know, wrote his "Self-Narration" as a postface to *Records of the Historian* after he had virtually completed his vast study. Thus, it was written approximately twenty years following his father's death. Consequently, Sima Qian's memory of that event is inevitably molded by his own intervening experience, and that experience demands that he provide the strongest conceivable justification for being alive and speaking out at all. The suggestion that Sima Qian's record of his father's final words might be distorted requires us to consider the crucial event standing between the death of Sima Qian's father and his own record of that death. That event was, of course, his tragic involvement in the Li Ling affair and his subsequent imprisonment and castration. The story of this episode in Han history has been told in detail elsewhere and need only be summarized here.[28]

In 99 B.C.E., Li Ling, a young and somewhat impetuous general, led a small army of five-thousand infantry against the Xiongnu, a non-Chinese people who had posed a problem to the Han leaders for much of the previous century. Although Li Ling's small army fought with great courage and inflicted heavy casualties upon the enemy, it was eventually defeated, and Li Ling was captured alive. When news of these events reached court, an explosion of criticism was directed at the young general. Only Sima Qian defended Li Ling before the emperor, but his defense was "misunderstood," and he was turned over to the court, where he was sentenced to death for "defaming the emperor." The punishment could have been commuted by paying a sum of money, but his family's wealth was insufficient, and no friends nor relatives came forth to help or "speak a single word" on his behalf. Eventually, perhaps as a result of his own plea, the punishment was reduced to castration, which Sima Qian suffered in the notorious "Silkworm Hall."[29]

The terrible trauma of Silkworm Hall and of his subsequent life as a eunuch is powerfully described in the second document in which Sima Qian discusses his own experience, the famous "Letter in Response to Ren An." This letter will be explored in greater detail below; it suffices here to note that as Sima Qian sat to compose a letter to his condemned friend Ren An, the specter of his father, now posthumously dishonored by his son's castration, rose before him:

> Because of the words of my mouth, I have encountered this calamity, am deeply ridiculed in my native village, and have thereby dishonored my father. With what face can I again ascend the grave mound of my parents? Although a hundred generations pile up, my disgrace will only multiply![30]

Mutilated, "a remnant of saw and blade," as he calls himself, Sima Qian has violated one of the most critical demands of filial piety—to return the body received from one's parents to the grave whole.[31] In addition, his reputation, not yet properly established, cannot bring the honor his father demanded as he lay dying. Instead, Sima Qian claims that he is ridiculed, just like the other eunuchs he catalogues in his letter.[32] Faced by such overwhelming shame and disgrace, Sima Qian must present a compelling justification for rejecting suicide and continuing to live. Just such a justification is found in the dying voice of his father commanding him to complete the record, to summarize the tradition, and to become another Confucius. The stain on his father's and his own name cannot be removed by the noble path of suicide but only by remaining alive and piously heeding a father's call to duty.

To digress briefly into a somewhat more speculative interpretative arena, it seems to me that one can identify in Sima Qian's description of his castration and of his subsequent memory of his father's words, a curious "family romance." Sima Tan, as the voice recreated in his son's own mind, becomes the agent of castration, keeping his son alive as a pitiful "remnant of saw and blade." That voice, as I have noted elsewhere, would trim and shape his son's creative powers around the authoritative presence of Confucius. But Sima Qian, as we shall see, will confront the anxiety of his father's invocation of the Master by producing a history so comprehensive and complete as to defy simple reduction into any Confucian categories, as well as radically to overstep even his father's own modest treatise as an exercise in broad and creative synthesis.

I am not necessarily claiming that Sima Tan's words, heard through a filter of twenty years and an extremely traumatic event, are entirely his son's fiction. What I am arguing is that Sima Qian remembers his own past and reinterprets that past, like all human beings, through a haze of subsequent events, and that in this case memory inevitably reflects the pain and internal conflict of those terrible events. Thus, the voice of Sima Qian's father, dying near Luoyang, unlike the voice of his philosophical treatise, is at least partially Sima Qian's own voice. The stern, demanding Sima Tan may be at least partly a creation Sima Qian can utilize to justify living on in shame and humiliation.

Still another reason for the apparent disharmony between the Sima Tan of the treatise and the Sima Tan who speaks to his son from his deathbed leads us toward Confucius, the second dominating figure of the "Self-Narration." Sima Qian, we must remember, was the child of an age quite different from that in which his father had grown up. To him, Confucius is clearly the ultimate authority, and he quotes the Sage repeatedly in *Records of the Historian*. Li Changzhi may be quite correct in labelling Sima Qian "the second most loyal follower of Confucius, the first being Mencius."[33] But Sima Qian must strive to be more than just a loyal follower, for his father has enjoined him to become a second Confucius. Such a lofty, perhaps even vain ambition is not without dangers. First, it can hardly be considered modest, in an age when Confucius is proclaimed as "the ultimate Sage" (zhi sheng), to announce oneself as his successor. Second, Confucius' life and the texts that he produced were regarded in the Han as necessary to correct the terrible political chaos of his time. Thus, for Sima Qian to present himself as "a second Confucius" is to imply a correspondence between his own time and the time of the Sage, a correspondence that the arrogant Emperor Wu would hardly find pleasing. Sima Qian plainly anticipates and attempts to allay these vexing issues. Making use of a rhetorical strategy common in ancient Chinese prose, Sima Qian creates an interlocutor, in this case "the high official Hu Sui," who asks "questions" and thereby provides Sima Qian with an opportunity to defuse potential objections. Hu Sui, sensing the parallel Sima Qian is drawing between himself and Confucius, asks:

> In the time of Confucius, there was no enlightened ruler above, and he was unable to obtain employment below. Therefore, he wrote *Spring and Autumn Annals*, handing down theoretical words to determine ritual and dutifulness and to constitute the law of a true king. Now, you, sir, encounter an enlightened Son of Heaven above and manage to hold office below. Since all business is complete and everything is ordered to its advantage, what do you, sir, wish to illustrate with your writings?[34]

In a rather tangled response to this question, Sima Qian asserts that he is only trying to proclaim fully the virtue of Emperor Wu, the "enlightened sage" who is on the throne. The current age, he claims, is not at all the same as the chaotic age of Confucius.[35] Indeed, Sima Qian argues that his very purpose is to prevent the loss of a proper record of all those worthy and meritorious men who have contributed to his own age of peace. Far from detracting from his age, he would only immortalize its true glory! Then Sima Qian concludes his argument with the following fascinating statement, "What I am referring to is transmitting ancient matters and arranging traditions passed down through the ages. This is not what can be called 'creating.' For you, lord, to compare it to *Spring and Autumn Annals* is mistaken indeed!"[36]

In this final passage, Sima Qian goes beyond rejecting a likeness between his own age and that of Confucius and seems even to deny that his historical work is in any way equivalent to the Sage's work, for he, unlike Confucius, is only a transmitter and not a creator at all! However, Sima Qian, great scholar that he is, knows full well that Confucius himself said, "I transmit and do not create."[37] By stating that he only transmits and does not create, Sima Qian appears humbly to reject, the comparison with Confucius, but he is in reality only affirming it.

One need not look far for additional evidence of Sima Qian's attempt to present himself as the next link in the 500-year "sage-

cycle," the true inheritor of the tradition of the Duke of Zhou and
Confucius. As noted previously, a unicorn was supposedly captured
in 481 B.C.E. The report of this mysterious event concludes *Spring
and Autumn Annals*, the paradigmatic history attributed to
Confucius. The *Gongyang Commentary* (*Gongyang zhuan*), one of
three ancient texts that have been transmitted as authoritative
commentaries to *Spring and Autumn Annals*, explains that "If there
is a true king, then [the unicorn] comes."[38] Assuredly a true king was
not in a position of political power during the chaotic years in which
Confucius lived. That true king, according to an early Han interpretation, was the "uncrowned king"—Confucius himself. Sima Qian
reports that in 122 B.C.E. another unicorn was captured, and he
further characterizes his own history as covering the period from the
mythical Taotang "on down to the unicorn."[39] This event could, of
course, signal Heaven's approval of the reign of Emperor Wu, or it
could signal the appearance of another uncrowned king who, like
Confucius before him, would present to posterity a definitive summary of tradition.

   Furthermore, at the end of *Gongyang Commentary*, just after a
comment on the significance of the unicorn that appeared in
Confucius' age, this influential exegesis of *Spring and Autumn
Annals* concludes with the words of Confucius himself: "I have put
in order the principles of *Spring and Autumn Annals* and thereby
await a later sage." By means of these final words, *Gongyang Commentary* indicates that another sage will come who will fully understand the real meaning of Confucius' subtle history. Sima Qian ends
his *Records of the Historian* with a similar note, which overtly
unites his own text to the earlier *Spring and Autumn Annals*: "I
have stored one copy [of *Records of the Historian*] in a famous
mountain and a second at the capital. I await a sage, a true gentleman, of later generations."[40]

   A much fuller explanation of the relationship between
Confucius, the Confucian tradition, and Sima Qian will be found in
chapters two and three below. It is important here only to realize
that Sima Tan's charge to his son "to be another Confucius," and
the specter of the uncrowned king summoned through those words,
exercised a restraint upon our historian, defined a particular task,
and empowered him with the authority of the past. Sima Tan and
Confucius speak to Sima Qian as voices of duty and responsibility.
Moreover, the Confucian restraint and moderation those voices urge
is not just ideological, it is also verbal; for the Ultimate Sage, as a
historian, is also noted for his remarkable verbal economy. When he

composed his masterwork, *Spring and Autumn Annals*, Sima Qian claims that Confucius "made the words economical but the meaning broad."[41]

Despite this compelling Confucian model of restraint, the power of Sima Qian's *Records of the Historian* derives neither from containment of emotion nor from economy of words. The powerful forces of ritual duty and tradition represented by Sima Tan and Confucius are balanced and frequently overwhelmed by Sima Qian's compulsion to expand his work and digest all that has gone before him. As the great Han historian's temporal and textual horizons broadened to include all of the past and its manifold texts, the possibility of conflict and dilemma increased. Furthermore, the very power of Sima Qian's text, as I hope to show below, derives from such conflict and not from terseness or ritual order.

In addition to the problem of scope mentioned above, Sima Qian's own theory of literary creativity was certain to subvert the model of restraint and economy presented by *Spring and Autumn Annals*. According to Sima Qian, literary power springs from a prodigious, frustrated energy that makes constraint and control all but impossible. In one of his most important passages, and the only extended passage he repeats virtually verbatim in both the "Self-Narration" and the "Letter," Sima Qian explains the origin of creative energy in the following words:

> In former times the Count of the West was arrested at Qiangli and developed *Changes of Zhou* (*Zhou yi*). Confucius was in distress in the region of Chen and Cai and created *Spring and Autumn Annals*. Qu Yuan was banished and wrote "Encountering Sorrow" ("Li sao"). Zuo Qiuming lost his sight, and then there was *Discourses of the States* (*Guo yu*). Master Sun had his legs amputated at the knees and elucidated *Military Tactics* (*Bing fa*). Buwei was removed to Shu and generations have passed down his "Overviews of Lü" ("Lü lan"). Hanfei was imprisoned in Qin and we have "The Difficulties of Persuasion" ("Shuo nan") and "The Frustrations of Standing Alone" ("Ku fen"). The three hundred pieces of *Poetry* were, for the most part, written as a result of worthies and sages expressing frustration. In all these cases, men had ideas that were stifled. They could not manage to communicate their doctrines [in their generation]. Therefore, they narrated past events and thought of people to come.[42]

Great literary works, according to this theory, result from extreme human conditions such as rejection, imprisonment, frustration, and the pain of mutilation and death. Literature, then, is displaced energy—unable to express ideas in the immediate political world, which should be the concern of all good Confucians, the writer withdraws, ponders "past events" and speaks his heart to an audience yet unborn. In the model Sima Qian elaborates above, the writer dies to his own generation to be reborn through the text he creates in another, juster age. One might even say that the frustrated scholar becomes a "textual" shaman who speaks for the dead in a later generation. And as the scholar-historian bestows immortality on others, he garners the same precious gift for himself.

The perspective reflected in Sima Qian's theory of literary production spawns in China a whole body of literature containing what Hellmut Wilhelm has called "the theme of the scholar's frustration."[43] In such literary works the author typically bemoans the fact that he is born out of his time and therefore must live unappreciated. He lays his case for fame and understanding before an audience that is yet to come—his readership in future generations. It is correct, I think, to regard *Records of the Historian* as one of the great fountainheads of this important Chinese literary theme. One can, of course, point to earlier figures, Confucius and the poet Qu Yuan (?343–?277 B.C.E.) among them, whose lives exemplify the "scholar's frustration," but we know of these figures and become aware of their unhappy obstruction precisely because of the way they are portrayed in *Records of the Historian*. In other words, these paradigmatic representatives of frustration are in large measure Sima Qian's creations!

It is interesting to note, in this connection, that Sima Qian has left one significant piece of literature other than his massive *Records of the Historian* and his "Letter in Response to Ren An," and that also exemplifies the theme of frustration. A rhapsody (*fu*) entitled "A Lament for Unemployed Gentlemen" ("Bei shi bu yu"), it speaks of unappreciated talent:

In truth his endowment is adequate, but his time is out of joint.
Endlessly he toils up to the very verge of death.
Though possessed of [pleasing] form, he goes unnoticed,
While capable, he cannot demonstrate his ability.[44]

The deep frustration described in this rhapsody must issue forth—it is the wellspring of a great literary work. Elsewhere, Sima Qian uses the term *fa fen* 發憤 to describe an extreme outpouring of such repressed emotion. Most of the poems of the highly esteemed

Classic of Poetry, Sima Qian claims, are the results of *fa fen*, which I have translated in the passage cited earlier as "expressing frustration."[45] Sima Qian also uses this same term to describe the extreme release of emotion that led to his father's death. He writes that when the Emperor Wu first performed the Feng sacrifice in 110 B.C.E. to proclaim formally to Heaven the succession of the Han, the Duke Grand Astrologer, Sima Qian's father, was left behind in Zhounan and was unable to attend. Saddened at his exclusion from the sacred ceremony, Sima Tan "expressed frustration" (*fa fen*) and drew near to death."[46] This term, which appears elsewhere in Sima Qian to describe a release of energy in some good cause, obviously cannot be covered adequately by a single English word and needs further explanation.[47]

 Fa fen is a verb-object compound. The verbal element, *fa*, means simply "to release, to shoot forth (as an arrow), to express." The object, *fen*, is etymologically a part of a whole family of words associated with being "filled up," usually, but not always, with "vexation" (*fan* 煩), "resentment" (*men* 悶), or "anger" (*fen* 忿).[48] Elsewhere, Sima Qian uses the word *yuan* 怨, which may be a more distant member of the same word family, to express the emotion that so often leads to literary production and/or death. The critical point is that the term connotes a damming and subsequent release of energy. This intense release, an eruption of pent-up frustration, quite naturally inclines towards excess and cannot be easily contained within discrete ritual categories.

 Sima Qian's theory of literary production, as described above and encapsulated in the term *fa fen*, evokes one of the fundamental contradictions of his life. Confucius, the representative of restraint and economy, stands before him as the model cited in the recollected words of his father, and such a model, it would seem, should moderate both Sima Qian's language and his emotion. But his frustration, validated and enhanced by mutilation that left him "a remnant of saw and blade," fights against containment. Indeed, his own historical work, in direct opposition to the subtle understatement of Confucius' *Spring and Autumn Annals* becomes a virtual catalogue of excess.

 I do not mean to imply here that Confucius was without his own frustrations. Indeed, his life, at least as Sima Qian presents it, is a study in frustration (see chapter 2). But Confucius' response to political failure, for the most part, is one of restraint. The Sage never falls into the extremes of frenzy and self-destruction typical of so many other characters portrayed in *Records of the Historian*. Chief among this latter character type, and perhaps Sima Qian's strongest contrast to the restraint and caution of Confucius, is Qu Yuan, sometimes called "the father of Chinese poetry." As is so often the case with figures from China's ancient past, Qu Yuan is primarily Sima Qian's creation, and the historian presents the story in a way that directly links Qu Yuan's poetry to political frustration. In the narrative of Qu Yuan's life, more clearly than anywhere else, Sima Qian ties together the theme of annihilation in one's own time with the theme of literary production, which guarantees a reputation in some later age.

The story is a famous one that has become firmly embedded in the consciousness of both the educated elite and the commoner as well. Qu Yuan warns the king of his native state of Chu against any alliance with Qin, the ominous power developing in the northwest. For his anti-Qin advice, he is traduced by officials, estranged from the king, and finally exiled. Sima Qian describes Qu Yuan's tragic demise in the most extreme terms.

> Qu Yuan was a man of undeviating duty who devoted all his loyalty and all his knowledge to the service of his prince; yet he was traduced by false witness. Well might he be called "afflicted." He was faithful, yet was disbelieved; loyal and yet calumniated. Is it any wonder that he was resentful (*yuan*)? It was the sense of wrong that inspired Qu Yuan's composition of "Encountering Sorrow." . . . [After further estrangement and banishment] Qu Yuan came to the banks of the river. With his hair hanging down in disarray, he wandered by the water's edge, singing as he went. . . . Then he composed the poem "Embracing the Sand." . . . Then, clasping a stone to his bosom, he threw himself into the Milo River and perished.[49]

While the admonition of his father may turn Sima Qian towards Confucius, his own experience with "calumny" and "estrangement" assuredly summons the memory of Qu Yuan.[50] Sima Qian's description of his personal experience, as written in his impassioned "Letter in Response to Ren An," is no less emotional nor more restrained than his tale of Qu Yuan, the "afflicted" poet of "disarray" and suicide. Indeed, the prose of Sima Qian's famous letter is so filled with frustration, pathos, and self-denigration that it is almost unbearable to read.

Why Sima Qian chose to write such a piece to a man who was himself condemned to death is a difficult question. Chavannes thinks that the ultimate intent of the letter to Ren An is to convince his friend to commit suicide and avoid the humiliation of imprisonment and execution.[51] This is a more charitable interpretation of Sima Qian's intentions than I can provide. Many scholars argue that Ren An had asked his friend in a letter to intervene with the emperor on his behalf and that this request motivated Sima Qian's response. However, a careful reading of the letter leads to a somewhat different conclusion. Ren An, at an earlier date, and in somewhat happier times, may have written a high-minded letter admonishing Sima Qian "to recommend and advance qualified persons." Sima Qian did not respond for a rather long period of time and in the interval Ren An fell under a shadow himself. Thus, Sima Qian saw his letter as a last chance to communicate with Ren An. I believe, contrary to Chavannes, that Sima Qian is not trying to convince Ren An of any particular course of action. Instead, he uses the fact that he is speaking to someone who will soon be dead himself as an opportunity to express his own terrible frustration. Ren An's rather pedantic advice is immediately brushed aside by Sima Qian's observation that he himself is only a pathetic eunuch and quite powerless to recommend anyone for advancement; certainly he cannot assist Ren An in his hour of extreme need. After this brief justification for inaction, Sima Qian shifts the focus of the letter from Ren An's predicament to his own unhappy experience. Perhaps the letter, which eventually found its way into the *History of the Han* was never intended simply as a private communication but was written as a final testament to posterity in which Sima Qian allowed himself to be much more direct and emotional than was appropriate in a more formal document like his "Self-Narration," which, after all, constituted the concluding section of his vast history of China.

Whatever Sima Qian's intentions in writing to Ren An, the topic of blocked-up energy, so central to his theory of literary production, appears repeatedly in his letter. He would try to help Ren An, but "When I move I meet with censure." Powerless in the face of the government, Sima Qian claims that he is "despondent and has no one with whom I can speak." The last sentence, incidently, is a quotation from Qu Yuan, indicating how strongly he identifies with the great poet.[52] Sima Qian goes on in his letter to say that there is no disgrace "greater than castration." A punishment of this type, in his opinion, permanently prevents him from having any immediate political impact, keeps him blocked up: "Although the present court lacks [men of talent], how could it allow a remnant of saw and blade to recommend the talented and heroic?" Sima Qian describes himself as "a mutilated slave who sweeps paths," one who dwells amidst "trash"—and here again the theme of blocked language appears—"Alas, alas, can one like me still speak?"[53]

As Sima Qian narrates the details of the Li Ling episode, which led to his imprisonment and punishment, he turns to the subject of suicide and tries to explain why he did not choose this "noble" alternative. The term he uses for suicide is the somewhat unusual *yin jue* 引決, which means something like "to draw forth and decide," with the two syllables of the compound literally meaning "to draw open" and "to open up a channel."[54]

As a literal reading of the term *yin jue* indicates, suicide is one means to alleviate intense pressure, one way to open a channel whereby frustration is finally released. Suicide appears frequently in the pages of *Records of the Historian*, and the characters who are led to "open up" this particular channel inspire some of Sima Qian's most powerful narratives. There is the marvelous example of Xiang Yu, who actually has been called in later times the "Frustrated King" (*fen wang*). Surrounded and facing certain defeat, and insisting to the end that it is no fault of his own but heaven that has defeated him, Xiang Yu sees a former associate in the opposing army and calls out, "I hear that Han has offered for my head a thousand pieces of gold and a fief of ten thousand households. I will do you a favor." He then draws a sword and slits his own throat.[55] Or there is the case of the grandfather of Sima Qian's friend Li Ling, General Li Guang, whose great strength and passion is typified in the famous episode where he mistakes a rock for a tiger and shoots an arrow deep into the hard stone. Late in his life, General Li made a critical mistake and was consequently ordered to stand trial for incompetence. The moment for his decision arrived: "I, Guang, am more than sixty years of age. I will never again respond to petty scribes!" He then "drew his knife and slit his own throat."[56] Or there is General Fan, who had fled the state of Qin and was living in frustration in Yan, hoping always to gain revenge against the king of Qin for the murder of his family. Told that if his own head was presented as a gift, an assassin could get close enough to kill the king, General Fan was overjoyed: " 'Day and night I have been gnashing my teeth and growing more deeply distressed over this. Now I have been able to hear your instructions.' He thereupon slit his own throat."[57]

All of these heroes, and many others not listed here, open up the final channel to relieve frustration, and their names are firmly established, their reputations assured, in that moment when they summon the courage to take a last dramatic step. But Sima Qian explains to Ren An, with considerable anguish and self-loathing, that he himself did not choose suicide. Here too, his explanation conjures up the familiar image of blockage: recalling the violence and terror of his jailers, Sima Qian says that "An accumulation of acts of intimidation gradually restrained me."[58]

Still, the main reason Sima Qian chose to stay alive, at least the main explanation he offers to Ren An, was that he had not yet completed his history of the past. In his case, frustration and humiliation accumulated in the world of action would not be expressed in suicide. Sima Qian, unlike the military heroes he describes with such narrative power, was a man of the written word who would transfer his frustration into the world of literature: "When my draft was not yet complete, I met with this calamity. Therefore, I proceeded to the extreme penalty with no appearance of rancor."[59] His rancor, in complete accord with his own theory of creativity, is sublimated into a text that would exonerate him posthumously just as it would exonerate others: "I grieve that my heart has that which it has not completely expressed, and that I might die and my writing not be known to later ages. The wealthy and honored of antiquity who have completely perished are too numerous to name."[60] Sima Qian cannot allow his own name to disappear, just as he cannot allow others to fade unknown into the past. Thus, he concludes his letter by saying that if only his completed history "is passed down to others, penetrating villages and great cities, then although I should receive ten thousand humiliating punishments, what regret would I have."[61]

Records of the Historian, like so many of the works Sima Qian admires, is born of frustration. It is a literary effusion, the scholar's equivalent to the violent suicides of heroes like Xiang Yu, General Li, and General Fan. Such an interpretation, I should note, does not imply that all of *Records of the Historian* was written after the Li Ling episode and reflects the pathos of that event; to determine precisely when each chapter of this complex work was actually written is impossible.[62] But one thing is certain, the same spirit that explains and rationalizes his behavior in the "Letter in Response to Ren An" fills many of Sima Qian's historical narratives and leads the great Lu Xun (1881–1936) to describe *Records of the Historian* as "the ultimate lyric of the historian, a rhymeless 'Encountering Sorrow.'"[63] This, "ultimate lyric," born of frustration and passion, casts a net of narrative much more widely than had ever been cast before. The tremendous release of energy, *fa fen*, that produced *Records of the Historian* could not easily be restrained within the boundaries of tradition nor within the tight limits of a sparing text like *Spring and Autumn Annals*.

Sima Qian's comprehensive and fervent treatment of the past

inevitably leads the historian to a profound and self-tortured questioning of all boundaries. This questioning is illustrated most directly in the "Traditions of Bo Yi" (chapter 61), an extremely important chapter that stands at the head of the "Traditions" section, the longest and most literarily significant section of Sima Qian's text. In his "Self-Narration," Sima Qian explains why the chapter on Bo Yi is given such an important position:

> In latter ages people struggled for advantage. Only these [Bo Yi and his brother Shu Qi] pursued duty, yielded the state and died of starvation. All under Heaven praise them. [Therefore] I have written "The Traditions of Bo Yi" and have placed it first [in this section].[64]

The chapter on Bo Yi is completely unlike any other of the "Traditions" in at least two ways. First, all other chapters in this section deal with figures who lived during the Eastern Zhou, the Qin, or the Han dynasties (that is, after 771 B.C.E.). This one chapter alone concerns a figure from an earlier period, and it is significantly earlier, the last years of the Yin and the earliest years of the Zhou (ca. 1040 B.C.E.). The anomaly has not gone unnoticed—the Tang historiographer Liu Zhiji (661–721 C.E.), one of Sima Qian's most perceptive critics, wonders why Sima Qian does not include other pre-Eastern Zhou figures. After suggesting several possibilities, Liu says, "Why not select one of these and compile [a chapter] for him?"[65] Second, the chapter on Bo Yi is stylistically unique. In the typical chapter of this section, Sima Qian narrates the traditions concerning an individual or a group with very few direct comments of his own. Both in the "Traditions" and in the other sections of *Records of the Historian*, Sima Qian reserves his evaluations and comments for the conclusion of the chapter, a "judgment" that is always introduced by the phrase "the Duke Grand Astrologer says." However, in this particular "Traditions" chapter, the actual account of the story of Bo Yi fills less than one-third of the text, while Sima Qian's direct evaluation and discussion of the story occupies the other two-thirds. A judgment at the end of this chapter is unnecessary precisely because the entire chapter is a judgment. The Ming scholar Chen Renxi (1579–1634) is correct in asserting that this chapter "rather seems like an essay and not like a biography."[66] Whatever great virtues Bo Yi and his brother Shu Qi might have possessed, this chapter clearly is placed at the head of the "Traditions" to serve as an introduction to the entire section. As such, it concerns issues very similar to those of both the "Self-Narration," which stands at the end of the "Traditions" section, and the "Letter to Ren An."[67]

The chapter on Bo Yi begins by stating a principle that guides much of Sima Qian's "formal" thought: "Now, the writings recorded by scholars are extremely vast, but one still tests reliability on the basis of the Six Arts."[68] Nevertheless, as soon as Sima Qian states this principle, a principle popular in the early Han, he questions it. Accounts in non-canonical sources claim that the sage-emperor Yao ceded the empire to a certain Xu You and that other worthies named Bian Sui and Wu Guang also declined the throne in the Xia Dynasty.[69] Moreover, Sima Qian affirms the historicity of Xu You by noting that he personally has ascended Ji Mountain and has seen this worthy's grave. Confucius, quite inexplicably, has ignored these earlier paragons of deferential behavior:

> Confucius ranks the humane, sagacious and worthy men of antiquity, and such people as Wu Taibo and Bo Yi are discussed in great detail. From what I have heard, [Xu] You and [Wu] Guang were men of the highest dutifulness. But not even a small number of words concerning them appears [in the classics]; why is that?[70]

Sima Qian implies here that the standard of reliability provided by the Six Arts, which in his time had become identified with the Six Classics, might not be complete, that preservation of one's name within the canon might be partly a matter of chance and not the result of the Sage's thorough sifting of the historical record.

Sima Qian will return to the critical role of chance in historical writing, but first he turns to the Sage himself; for it is Confucius, after all, who has guaranteed Bo Yi's and Shu Qi's immortality through the very act of speaking their names. Confucius said, "Bo Yi and Shu Qi did not remember old insults. Their resentments, therefore, were few. They sought humaneness and obtained humaneness. So what would they resent?"[71] The biography of these figures, as preserved in earlier sources, should exemplify the moral judgment of Confucius: Bo Yi and Shu Qi should appear as models of equanimity who respond to crisis with exemplary moderation. But Sima Qian immediately points to the problem, "I grieve at the intentions of Bo Yi. But when I look at the 'neglected poem,' there is something I find unusual in it."[72]

To indicate precisely what it is that he finds "unusual," Sima Qian must retell the story of Bo Yi and Shu Qi. It is an old tale that appears with considerable variation in texts predating *Records of the Historian*.[73] Sima Qian's version is as follows:

Bo Yi and Shu Qi were the two sons of the Ruler of Gu Zhu. Their father wished to establish Shu Qi as successor, but when the father died, Shu Qi yielded the throne to Bo Yi. Bo Yi said, "It was father's command," and thereupon fled. Shu Qi also was unwilling to ascend the throne and fled the state. The people of the state established a middle brother as successor.

Thereupon, Bo Yi and Shu Qi heard that Chang, the Earl of the West, was fond of nourishing the old. "Why not go over to him?" When they arrived, the Earl of the West had died. King Wu was carrying the wooden ancestral tablet, had given [the Earl of the West] the posthumous name "King Wen," and was attacking King Zhou to the east. Bo Yi and Shu Qi detained his horse and rebuked King Wu, saying, "When your father is dead but not buried, can it be called filial to take up shield and spear? Can it be called humane for a minister to kill a ruler?" [King Wu's] retainers wished to put them to the sword, but Duke Tai said, "These are dutiful men." So, helping them along, they sent them away.

When King Wu had pacified the disorder of Yin, the empire was united in Zhou. But Bo Yi and Shu Qi were ashamed of this and by principle would not eat the grain of Zhou. They hid at Shou Yang Mountain, picked ferns and ate them. When they were starving and about to die, they wrote a song. Its words are,

"We ascend this western mountain and eat its ferns.
With violence he replaces violence and does not know it is wrong.
Shen Nong, Yu, and Xia have suddenly departed, where can we go?
Alas, it is over; the mandate has been lost."[74]

This story raises some very troublesome political problems. Perhaps the most obvious of these is the whole issue of the succession of dynasties. Regicide is the most serious crime, and yet all the great dynastic founders, cultural heroes such as the Zhou Dynasty King Wu included, have been guilty of this most heinous deed. The Confucian philosopher Mencius once discussed this problem and insisted that killing an undutiful king was not really "regicide" at all but merely punishing a "common criminal."[75] Mencius' rather easy solution notwithstanding, the issue lived on into the Han and was debated before Emperor Jing just a few years before Sima Qian's birth.[76]

However, the troubling political implications in the story of Bo Yi and Shu Qi are not Sima Qian's primary concern. Instead, he pursues another problem: "When we examine this story, are they (i.e., Bo Yi and Shu Qi) resentful or are they not resentful?" There can be little doubt what answer Sima Qian expects to this rhetorical question. As the commentator Sima Zhen puts it, with a caution that may indicate his own discomfort with the ramifications, "The Duke Grand Astrologer is saying that he had already examined the sentiment of this poem, and it seems that it does perhaps contain some resentment."[77]

The disharmony between the received tradition of Bo Yi and Shu Qi and Confucius' description of these heroes obviously troubles Sima Qian. How could Confucius have said that the two Yin loyalists died without resentment? Thus, Sima Qian implies, not only are the Six Arts incomplete, but Confucius himself is fallible—Sima Qian's doubt deepens as he fails to find justification for the judgment of the Sage. But instead of pursuing this issue further, the historian turns quite suddenly to a much larger problem and leaves behind, for a time, the issue of the classical record's completeness and accuracy. He introduces that larger problem by quoting what must have been an old and widely accepted adage: "The way of heaven has no favorites. It constantly associates with the good."[78] Unfortunately, Sima Qian's reading of the facts of history does not support such a naive proclamation of heaven's fairness, for paragons of morality, like Bo Yi and Shu Qi, starved to death, and Yan Yuan the only disciple Confucius could heartily recommend, died young, while the evil Robber Zhi lived to a ripe and happy old age. Faced with such distressing examples, Sima Qian becomes increasingly troubled: "I am extremely confused by this. If this is what we call 'the way of heaven,' then is it right or is it wrong?"[79]

At this critical juncture in his presentation, when the foundations of historical and moral evaluation are crumbling beneath him, Sima Qian's prose dissolves into a welter of quotations. It almost appears as if he is rummaging through an inventory of past wisdom and stringing together every relevant passage in a futile attempt to find some escape from his own persistent doubt. First, he quotes three successive passages from *Analects* without providing any commentary or explanation:

> The Master said, "Since their ways differ, they cannot make plans for one another. Each follows his own intentions."[80]
>
> If wealth and nobility could be sought out, then although I were a knight who holds a whip, I would do it. But if they cannot be sought out, then I will follow what I like.[81]
>
> Only after the year gets cold [do you know] that the pines and the cypresses lose their leaves last.[82]

The wisdom of the Sage is then followed immediately by another ancient Chinese adage: "When all the world is turbid, the pure gentleman appears."[83]

Precisely what is the argument inherent in this string of quotations? Sima Qian provides no answer. Perhaps the historian is implying that since human destiny is uncertain, all one can do is follow his own inclinations and hope for the best—no guarantee of fairness is possible. Besides, only at very rare moments, particularly difficult moments, are men of true worth revealed. Thus, many deserving gentlemen, confined to a period of time or to a situation where there is little chance to display great merit, labor and die in obscurity. No one, it seems, can count on fame.

After this rather disconnected series of quotations, Sima Qian poses a rhetorical question that has become the most disputed passage in the entire chapter. The grammar and lexicon of the question are clear, but the possible antecedents of two critical demonstrative pronouns leave considerable margin for interpretation. Literally, "How could we (or "they") consider it as heavily (i.e., serious) as that, and we (or "they") consider it as lightly as this?"[84]

The commentator Sima Zhen believes the antecedent of "that" in the passage above to be Bo Yi's act of yielding the throne to Shu Qi, and the antecedent of "this" to be his plucking ferns and starving to death. According to this interpretation, the passage is an expression of surprise at the priorities and the resolve of our heroes: "How could they have considered yielding the throne to be so serious and starving to death to be so easy?"[85] The great Ming-Qing scholar Gu Yanwu (1613–82), in an opinion supported by the modern scholar Wang Shumin, believes that the understood subject of each clause, which I have translated as "we" above, should be taken in the third person and given a different antecedent in each clause. In the first clause the antecedent is "the common man," and in the second it is "the true gentleman." The possessive pronoun *qi* (my "its"), he believes, refers to "wealth and honor." Thus, we would translate, "How could the common man consider wealth and honor as heavily as that, and the pure gentleman consider wealth and honor as lightly as this?"[86]

Neither the interpretation of Sima Zhen nor that of Gu Yanwu addresses the immediate context—a series of authoritative quotations from the past. I believe that the enigmatic statement focuses directly on the dilemma of heaven's fairness that has troubled Sima Qian in the previous sentences: "How could we consider it (i.e., the situation) as seriously as that" refers to the less immediate context, precisely what we would expect from the demonstrative *bi* "that over there"—in other words, the story of Bo Yi and the further examples of Yan Yuan and Robber Zhi. And "how could we consider it as lightly as this" refers to the lines just before the rhetorical question—the "easy" answers given by the sages of ancient times. A somewhat more liberal translation would be, "How could the examples of injustice be so extreme, so terrible, but the whole problem be dismissed so easily." The quotations that Sima Qian dredges up and strings together cannot and do not remove the frustration and confusion inherent in the historical record; the wisdom of the past provides only facile and almost ridiculous answers to this grave question. Sima Qian, I believe, is expressing extreme dissatisfaction—he finds no magic antidote in the words of either Confucius or Laozi to cure the fierce doubt that plagues him.

Sima Qian is, however, a historian, an office he holds in fulfillment of his father's wish. As the "Traditions of Bo Yi" continues, he attempts to reconstruct himself and his filial responsibility around another Confucian: "The True Gentleman detests that he will die and his name not be praised."[87] This is reinforced with a quotation from Jia Yi, a paragon of virtue who served earlier Han emperors and was not fully appreciated: "The covetous man seeks wealth; the outstanding gentleman seeks a name."[88] This would seem to sanctify the role of the historian, who not only seeks to establish his own name but the names of other "outstanding gentlemen" as well.

Sima Qian goes on to quote still another text, *Classic of Changes*: "The same lights illumine one another; things of the same category seek out one another."[89] Thus, Confucius illumined Bo Yi, Shu Qi, and Yan Yuan. By praising them, he guaranteed their immortality; they attached themselves to him like "flies to the tail of a racehorse." The historian thereby becomes the savior, those attached to him are saved, living on through the power of his writing brush. Such a quasi-religious conception of the role of the historian is in part a remnant of an earlier era when astrologer-annalists managed divination, offered prayers, and performed a whole host of pious tasks.[90]

But at Sima Qian's moment of regenerated self-confidence, in which the historian assumes the loftiest of roles, doubt rises again: "There are gentlemen of rocky caves whose behavior is timely. How sad it is that the names of those in this category perish like smoke!"[91] Thus, Sima Qian knows his work, like that of Confucius, will be imperfect—injustice will remain. The historian must try to make up for the unfairness of heaven, but he, like heaven, will fail . . . though he, having less power, perhaps deserves less blame!

The "Traditions of Bo Yi," located near the center of Sima Qian's vast work and at the beginning of its most literarily important section, is a radical questioning of the entire endeavor in which the historian is engaged and of the moral world in which that endeavor is embedded. It is, in a sense, an announcement of failure, an apology for the incompleteness of his compendious history, and a defense of inadequacy that points to the deficiencies of Confucius' record and to the even more glaring injustices of heaven itself. Plainly, his father's charge is an impossible one. The energies of history cannot be bound up into a neat, new synthesis. Sima Qian has found too many margins of doubt, too many loose ends, that defy containment.

The problem, viewed from a perspective that returns us to our original terms, is that when Sima Tan supposedly bestowed upon his son the mission to be a second Confucius, he gave to him a herculean task. The first Confucius had an easier mission than our second Confucius, for the literary tradition, the spread of textuality, was not so overwhelming in the mid-Zhou as it was in the early Han. Most Chinese scholars have accepted the traditional notion that learning in the Western Zhou was monopolized by government offices and that in the time of Confucius this old monopoly had disappeared. Confucius responded to the growing chaos by attempting to bring order both to the disintegrating political world and also to the fragmentary textual world. To earlier Han scholars, who longed for a recovery of that ancient, more orderly age, Confucius was the transmitter of the Six Arts, the distilled truth from the past. But the "unified" tradition contained in the Six Arts continued to break down despite Confucius' efforts, and the Warring States period witnessed a proliferation of literary culture such as had never occurred in China before. The hundred schools contended, and a vast assortment of new texts appeared. The tradition became more diffuse and more difficult to contain. As Sima Qian surveyed the past, particularly from the beginning of the Warring States period to his own age, he must have felt considerable confusion and self-doubt, feelings recorded so dramatically in the "Traditions of Bo Yi." The past, to put it simply and directly, had become too large. So many years of disunity and textual proliferation vastly complicated his attempt to range across the past and create "a single school."[92] But Sima Qian's search for a containment and order such as that of the Six Arts, and his attempt to become a second Confucius, is complicated by more than just a proliferation of texts. His story of the past is also driven forward by a need to break through a blockage that, as we have seen, he mentions time and again in his tragic reply to Ren An. His creative impulse, and he is assuredly a creator and not just a transmitter, will burst forth, driven by an overwhelming frustration and passion, the very forces that he himself believes forever set the most powerful writing brushes into motion. Sima Qian's own brush ranges with astonishing energy across a burgeoning past, but that past, enlivened by his intense emotion, cannot be contained within neat boundaries. His attempt to organize the tradition into a clean Confucian unity fails, and his later readers, as they try to comprehend his brilliant text, frequently fall into befuddlement, the same type of befuddlement, perhaps, that Sima Qian sometimes felt as he himself tried to make sense of the accounts before him.

2

Sima Qian's Confucius

[Confucius] can indeed be called "the ultimate sage."

— *Records of the Historian*

Sima Qian lived in a world of constraints, a world of ritual and tradition. If deep personal frustration drove him at times to question and challenge those constraints, we still cannot regard him as an opponent of tradition, for Sima Qian himself is largely responsible for constructing that tradition. Concern with the Chinese tradition necessarily entails careful attention to the values, principles, and patterns of *Records of the Historian;* and at the very center of Sima Qian's construction of the past stands the towering figure of Confucius, "the ultimate sage," who Sima Tan admonished his son to emulate. Confucius, I believe, is the central character in *Records of the Historian*. Moreover, Sima Qian's sense of self and mission, as indicated in the previous chapter, is tightly entwined with his concept of Confucius. Although a rich trove of stories and traditions about Confucius already existed in Sima Qian's time, no one had yet attempted to organize these into a "life." Thus, chapter 47 of *Records of the Historian*, entitled the "Hereditary Household of Confucius" ("Kongzi shi jia"), is the first effort in Chinese history to write a biography of the Master and thereby occupies an important place not only in Sima Qian's text but in Chinese cultural history as well. According to some critics, Sima Qian's biography of Confucius is a spectacular failure. Indeed, both the form and the content of the "Hereditary Household of Confucius" have been the target of harsh criticism. Critics concerned with formal questions ask why the account of Confucius is placed in the "Hereditary Households" section rather than in "Traditions." The former section, they argue, should only include accounts of families that held some measure of

29

political autonomy over a fief for a succession of generations. Wang Anshi (1021–86), the great Song literatus, argues that Confucius "was a traveller . . . without the authority of a single inch of land." He goes on to suggest that he should be included in the "Traditions" and asks, "Why is he among the `Hereditary Households?'"[1]

The great Qing scholar Zhao Yi (1727–1814) answers Wang Anshi's question by suggesting that Sima Qian wished to honor Confucius and consequently set him apart from other lesser masters.[2] Although this is almost certainly true, there may be more to the problem of the historian's classification of Confucius than Zhao Yi's simple answer would indicate. In the first place, Sima Qian's own definition of those included in his "Hereditary Households" section, contrary to the assumption of many later scholars, stresses neither possession of land nor hereditary succession:

> The twenty-eight constellations revolve around the north star. Thirty spokes share a single hub. They circle endlessly. Top-level ministers, the arms and legs of the ruler, are the same as these. They loyally and sincerely carry out the true doctrine and thereby serve the ruler. [Therefore], I make thirty "Hereditary Households."[3]

This powerful image of the constellations and the North Star is drawn from a statement of Confucius himself, while the image of thirty spokes and a single hub comes from *Laozi*.[4] The important fact, however, is that the emphasis in Sima Qian's definition is not upon holding a hereditary fief but upon serving the throne. Such a definition appears to conflict with the very name of the section; and certainly most of the chapters do precisely what that name implies—that is, trace in chronological fashion the major events in the history of an enfeoffed hereditary family. But Sima Qian's definition does leave room for figures such as Confucius or, for that matter, Chen She (chapter 48), a rebel leader who did not receive a hereditary fief but served the Han emperor by helping to sweep away the previous dynasty. Indeed, one scholar, Liao Dengting, argues that "power" is the basic criterion for inclusion in "Basic Annals" and "duration" in "Hereditary Households." Liao's interpretation might lead us to conclude that what has been translated here and elsewhere as "Hereditary Household" could be more exactly rendered as "Families (or Schools) that Endure through Time."[5]

In Sima Qian's view, to whom did Confucius make his great contribution? Wherein did he become "the arms and legs of a ruler?"

Certainly Confucius' primary service was not in the state of Lu, where he served only a brief term in government. The answers to these questions are found in Sima Qian's "Self-Narration," where he tells us that "Confucius fashioned a standard for the empire and passed down the governing principles of the Six Arts to later generations."[6] Thus, Confucius' service leaps across the chaos of the Zhou dynasty and profoundly shapes the imperial world of the Western Han. The Master provides the Han dynasty, and all subsequent dynasties for that matter, with a political foundation.[7] Since this is the highest service any minister could ever render, Confucius becomes the most glorious constellation circling the North Star and deserves, by this logic, to be included in "Hereditary Households."

The second criticism of Sima Qian's account of the Master, and a much more serious one, focuses on content. The Qing scholar Cui Shu (1740–1816), who undertook a detailed and extremely learned study of the "Hereditary Household of Confucius," calls the biography "seventy to eighty percent slander," and notes elsewhere that "the errors of 'The Hereditary Household of Confucius' are so numerous that they cannot be completely counted."[8] Sima Qian's account is even more distressing to H. G. Creel, the best-known English biographer of Confucius. Creel calls chapter 47 "a slipshod performance" and adds further that

> There is little motivation and almost no development of a consistent character for Confucius. It [the chapter] consists, in fact, of a series of incidents gathered from Confucian, Taoist, and Legalist sources, thrown together in what is alleged to be a chronological order with very little criticism or harmonization. The result is that Confucius moves through the story like a puppet. Anachronisms are not exceptional but almost the rule.[9]

Creel notes, with considerable dismay, that the work "has been received for two thousand years as the definitive portrayal of Confucius." He then adds that it is in actuality "a piece of carefully veiled satire" concocted by the "pro-Taoist" Sima Qian who saw Confucians in general, and Confucius in particular as "mealy-mouthed" and "hypocritical."[10] Creel's argument, if it is in fact correct, would seriously undermine the thesis I have advanced above—that is, Sima Qian not only profoundly admires Confucius but would emulate the Master and assume a place beside him in the sacred succession of sages.

Scholars such as Cui Shu, Qian Mu, and Edouard Chavannes have so amply discussed and documented the errors in Sima Qian's account of Confucius, that we can no longer deny its many problems and general confusion.[11] But these scholars have said little, except in a summary fashion, concerning such issues as the nature of the problem facing Sima Qian as he sat to pen his life of Confucius, the principles that seem to have shaped his account of the Master, and what those principles reveal about the Han historian himself. In other words, before applauding Creel's harsh judgment, we should ask not just historical questions but literary questions as well.

By the end of the first century of the Han dynasty, when Sima Qian attempted to provide some coherence to the story of the Master, the available sources were contradictory, and confusing. Four basic sources can be identified: (1) *Analects*, (2) historical texts such as *Zuo Commentary* (which Sima Qian always calls "*Zuo shi chun qiu*" [*The Spring and Autumn Annals of Mr. Zuo*]) and *Discourses of the States*, (3) the writings of Warring States' and early Han masters such as *Zhuangzi, Xunzi*, and others, and (4) oral tradition. The first of these sources, *Analects*, is a collection of sayings, brief dialogues, and reports of the actions of Confucius and his immediate disciples presumably based on collections made by a second or third generation of Confucius' followers. The text of *Analects* available in Sima Qian's time was probably close in both content and form to today's version.[12] Fifty-six different sections, approximately one-fifth of the text of *Analects*, are cited in Sima Qian's biography of the Master, making it by far Sima Qian's most important single source. As readers of *Analects* all recognize, the sayings and dialogues in this work are extremely brief and cry out for historical context. By referring to other written sources at his disposal, by utilizing oral traditions, or by supplying his own conjecture, Sima Qian provides a biographical context for the *Analects* passages he includes in his study of Confucius. For example, in one famous passage in *Analects*, Confucius simply says, "If only someone would use me, in a full year it [i.e., the government] would be acceptable, and in three years it would be complete."[13] Sima Qian places this comment in a specific historical situation: Confucius is living in Wei and hopes to serve the duke, but the duke "was old and neglected government." Frustrated at not being allowed to serve, Confucius tells his disciples, in the passage quoted above, how quickly his own policies could have political impact.[14] In fact, by providing so many passages with a situational context, Sima

Qian has had a profound influence on subsequent readings of this "classic."[15]

Zuo Commentary and *Discourses of the States*, the two most important works on the history of the period in which Confucius lived, provide a second critical source for Sima Qian's biography of the Master. Despite the ostensibly close relationship between these two texts, an issue to be considered in a later chapter, each portrays Confucius somewhat differently from the other. In *Zuo Commentary* the Master is perhaps slightly mythologized, but he is still generally presented as a capable, wise, and quite human figure. Confucius' greatness is forecast in *Zuo Commentary* by Meng Xizi, a type of event common in the "life of the hero."[16] Later in *Zuo Commentary*, Confucius oversees the reconstruction of Duke Zhao's tomb,[17] participates in the Jiagu meeting between Qi and Lu,[18] orders an attack on Bi,[19] and dissuades Wenzi from an attack upon the Younger Brother Ji of Wei.[20] He also comments frequently in *Zuo Commentary* upon major events of his era, such as the death of the famous minister Zichan and the decline of the state of Jin,[21] and identifies as a "unicorn" the one-horned beast, which appears at the end of the Spring and Autumn Period.[22]

In *Discourses of the States*, by contrast, Confucius consistently displays superhuman perspicacity: he understands an obscure prodigy, delivers a lecture on mysterious spirits, and shows a miraculous grasp of recondite historical information.[23] Thus, *Discourses of the States* provides the first unambiguous evidence of the gradual apotheosis of Confucius that continues into and throughout the Han dynasty. It is possible, as the Japanese scholar Honda Shigeyuki has suggested, that *Zuo Commentary* and *Discourses of the States* represent two different views of Confucius that already existed among the earliest disciples.[24]

The works of late Zhou masters (the so-called *zhuzi*) provide Sima Qian with a third source of Confucius stories. These texts emerge from the intense intellectual competition and controversy in the final century of the Warring States period, and Confucius, by this time, had become a powerful voice to appropriate or a provocative target to ridicule. The Taoist text *Zhuangzi* provides an excellent, if extreme example of the way Confucius was sometimes used in the works of the masters. On page after page of this famous Taoist text, Confucius appears alternately as a spokesman for Taoist values and as a target of the most extreme and often humorous ridicule. For example, in the beginning of chapter 4, the Master is portrayed as a model Taoist who enunciates Zhuangzi's code for successful behavior, while his beloved disciple Yan Hui (?521–?490 B.C.E.) articulates the standard Confucian position.[25] Elsewhere, the roles are reversed—Yan Hui is the insightful Taoist and Confucius is the dull disciple.[26] While Sima Qian is generally cautious about using material drawn from the texts of the Zhou masters, there are several episodes in his account of Confucius that are conspicuously taken from such sources.[27]

Oral tradition must have provided Sima Qian with a fourth source of material concerning Confucius. To determine precisely what Sima Qian might have drawn from an exclusively oral source and what might be based upon some now lost text is impossible. However, Confucius lore found in late Zhou and early Han dynasty texts shows the type of variation that often characterizes oral transmission. For example, while Confucius is visiting the state of Chen, as Sima Qian tells the story, he hears that there has been a fire in an ancestral temple in Lu. Confucius quite mysteriously announces that the fire was undoubtedly in the temples of dukes Huan and Li.[28] In the account of this event found in *Garden of Sayings (Shuo yuan)*, a somewhat later Han text by Liu Xiang (77–6 B.C.E.), Confucius is sitting with Duke Jing of Qi and hears of a fire in a Zhou temple. Immediately, he declares that the fire is in the temple of Xi of Zhou (r. 680–675).[29] In both versions his announcement is revealed to be accurate and is given as proof that the Master possesses mysterious sensitivity. A second example of such variation appears when Laozi, in Sima Qian's account, sees Confucius off and prefaces his final advice with the following words, "I have heard that the rich and noble send one off with goods. The humane man sends one off with words." This same comment is ascribed in *Xunzi* to the famous prime minister Yanzi as he is seeing off Confucius' disciple Zengzi at the borders of Qi.[30] In both of these cases the differences in the versions are not ideological, such as we might expect from variations embedded in contending philosophical texts, but are merely variations of detail and attribution, precisely the sort of differences frequently encountered in oral transmission.

We can gain a good idea of the complexity of the materials available to Sima Qian by examining the *Collected Sayings of Confucius (Kongzi jiyu)*, a work assembled by the Qing dynasty philologist and collator Sun Xingyan (1753–1818). This work of seventeen chapters, or 330 double-sided Chinese pages, arranges all the passages concerning Confucius available in early Chinese texts other than *Analects*. Much of the material in Sun's collection appears in works later than Sima Qian (*Shuo yuan, Lun heng,* etc.), but at least half is from texts earlier than *Records of the Historian* and was thereby available to Sima Qian. The Han historian's difficult task was to sift through and make some sense from this body of material as well as other materials that might have been in his possession but lost in the long years before Sun Xingyan's compilation. At any rate, a survey of the *Collected Sayings of Confucius* reveals that the vast textual material concerning the Master is filled with conflicting information and reflects a variety of philosophical prejudices.

As noted earlier, Sima Qian's attempt to bring factual coherence to his Confucius biography, if such was indeed his purpose, is not entirely successful, and several later scholars have reshuffled the available material into more plausible patterns. Nevertheless, the critical issue, and an issue rarely discussed in the scholarly literature, is the general picture of the sage that emerges from Sima Qian's writing brush. Precisely who is his Confucius? What are the thematic principles according to which Sima Qian has selected and arranged episodes included in chapter 47? Such questions are not only critical in any attempt to understand Confucius, but, more importantly for our study here, to understand Sima Qian.

Bearing in mind his father's injunction to be a second Confucius, a task Sima Qian says sustained him through his years of shame, and given the prominent place of Confucius in the "Hereditary Household" section, I cannot accept Professor Creel's claim that Sima Qian's Confucius is the target of "veiled satire." On the contrary, I believe that Sima Qian portrays Confucius as a heroic figure and is entirely sincere in proclaiming him "the ultimate sage."[31] That Sima Qian made chronological errors in his treatment of Confucius and that he is sufficiently faithful to his disparate sources to include some episodes treating Confucius ambiguously, or even negatively, should not blind us to the fact that his overall goal is to honor the Master he believed to have consolidated and transmitted the culture of the past. To substantiate such a claim and demonstrate the literary coherence of Sima Qian's account of Confucius requires a detailed examination of chapter 47, a biography, I must emphasize once again, that has influenced all subsequent discussion of the Master.

Sima Qian's Confucius, while not yet the fantastic, divine figure of later Han apocryphal texts,[32] has many features associated with heroes elsewhere in world literature: his birth is the result of an unnatural union; he possesses an unusual physical feature—the top of his head is indented and the sides raised into a natural, regal crown; his father dies shortly after his birth; his childhood behavior gives evidence that he is extraordinary; and there is a "prophecy" of his future greatness.[33] Furthermore, Sima Qian's account of Confucius' life, in general outline, follows the mythic-heroic pattern of exile and return and can be analyzed in terms of four basic themes: (1) early and brilliant service, (2) departure, (3) trial and wandering, and (4) return.

Near the beginning of his account of Confucius, Sima Qian points towards the four fundamental themes listed above as he anticipates and epitomizes the central events in the life he will describe: "Confucius became minister of works. Quitting, he left the state of Lu. He was banished from Qi, driven from Song and Wei, and in distress in the region of Chen and Cai. Thereupon, he returned to Lu."[34] Since this passage speaks of events that will not be fully described until much later in the narrative, some commentators consider it to be misplaced.[35] However, each of the four basic themes, which I have listed above, is reflected in this epitome and provides a framework upon which Sima Qian suspends the remainder of his narrative. Service, departure, trial, and return constitute the essential features of Sima Qian's life of Confucius and will be considered in order below.

Sima Qian, drawing upon old sources, describes Confucius' early political service in the state of Lu as exemplary.[36] Duke Ding of Lu (r. 508–495 B.C.E.) appoints Confucius governor of Zhongdu, and "after one year, all in the four quarters took him as a model."[37] As a result of this success, he is promoted to minister of public works and then to chief of justice. Sima Qian lists a number of benefits that resulted from his service in these posts: the price of meat was not raised, men and women remained separated on the streets, there was no theft, and so on. But, according to Sima Qian's account, the Sage's most noteworthy contribution to the state of Lu was rendered at the famous meeting at Jiagu, where feudal leaders of the states of Lu and Qi assembled in 500 B.C.E. to negotiate a treaty. This particular episode not only illustrates the great power of Confucius' political service, but also exemplifies the way Sima Qian reshapes an earlier and highly prestigious source, *Zuo Commentary*, in order to emphasize or enhance certain themes.

Zuo Commentary reports that in 500 B.C.E., Duke Ding of Lu met with the marquis from the state of Qi at a place called Jiagu, located in modern Shandong province. Confucius attended the meeting as an assistant (perhaps a "minister") to the Duke of Lu and provided critical advice that turned the meeting to Lu's advantage.[38] First, Confucius uses his knowledge of correct ritual to humiliate Qi into abandoning an attempt to intimidate the Lu delegation with non-Chinese soldiers. Second, he cleverly adds a provision to the alliance oath between the two participants, which requires Qi to return previously seized Lu lands. Third, he rejects a Qi feast and entertainment, again claiming that proper ritual forbids such pleasures. In short, the story in *Zuo Commentary* portrays Confucius as a hero who uses his knowledge of correct ritual behavior to assist his lord in a dangerous negotiation with Qi.[39]

The account of this event in the "Hereditary Household of Confucius" is not only much fuller than the *Zuo Commentary* account, somewhat unusual for one of Sima Qian's adaptations of this particular historical source, as we shall see in chapter 4 below, but it also reports the event in a significantly altered way. In general, Sima Qian's version, much more than that of *Zuo Commentary*, emphasizes and glorifies the critical role Confucius plays at the Jiagu meeting. First of all, Duke Jing of Qi anticipates that Confucius' participation in the meeting constitutes a serious threat to Qi. Consequently, Confucius advises his own duke to make appropriate military preparations in order to secure their delegation's safety at the meeting: "Those who have cultural business must have military preparations," he warns. Second, in Sima Qian's version, the duke of Qi clearly wishes to avail himself of the musical clamor and confusion to seize or threaten Duke Ding of Lu, a plan made even more explicit in other accounts of this episode.[40] Faced with this grave danger, Confucius acts dramatically to save his duke's life. Finally, in Sima Qian's account, the famous Qi minister Yanzi is present. It is highly unlikely that Yanzi could have attended the Jiagu meeting, if such a meeting was ever actually held,[41] but by including him and enabling Confucius to get the best of the aged prime minister of Qi, Sima Qian both enhances the significance of Confucius' achievement and also allows him to gain revenge against an old nemesis.[42]

The skilled tactics that the Master employs at the Jiagu meeting, as reported in *Records of the Historian*, result in an enormous political victory for the state of Lu—Qi returns seized lands, an outcome only implied in the *Zuo Commentary* but made explicit in *Records of the Historian*. Furthermore, Confucius' actions shame the marquis of Qi, Lu's powerful neighbor, and illustrate the power and culture of the Master's principles.

One of the most controversial items in Sima Qian's life of Confucius appears in the episode under discussion. Just before the Qi delegation departs from the Jiagu meeting, Sima Qian reports that

[A] Qi official rushed forward and said, "I request to perform palace music." Duke Jing agreed and the jesters and dwarfs came forth to perform. Confucius hurried forward and ascended the steps. But when he had not yet gotten to the last level, he said, "When a commoner throws feudal lords into confusion, the crime deserves execution. I request that you so order the official." The official applied the law to them, and their hands and feet were in different places [supposedly a emphemism for being cut in two at the waist].[43]

This cruel execution of the musical performers, an episode that does not appear in *Zuo Commentary* at all, is also reported in *Guliang Commentary (Guliang zhuan)*[44] and is one of two executions Sima Qian's Confucius orders. Scholars who would like a gentler Master reject both episodes as historically unfounded.[45] However, Sima Qian's portrayal of Confucius as a stern leader perhaps prepares the reader for the Master's ultimate contribution, the completion of a work of history, *Spring and Autumn Annals*, which will not be at all gentle in its impact but will make "disorderly ministers . . . frightened."[46]

By placing such emphasis upon the political skill and power of Confucius, Sima Qian forces the reader to ask how someone as politically capable as the Master of the Jiagu meeting, the minister who brought about Qi's voluntary return of occupied Lu lands, could fail to advance to the loftiest political position. In a period of intense competition to recruit talent, how could Confucius not become the object of the fiercest bidding? The answer to this question is found in the second great theme of chapter 47: Confucius is forced to leave the state of Lu and is denied the opportunity to serve elsewhere because he is repeatedly and unfairly maligned. In fact, one Chinese scholar, Chen Renxi, has quite correctly observed that the entire chapter "takes the two words 'not used' as hinge."[47] Confucius, despite the remarkable talent illustrated during his years of service in the state of Lu, is not used. His great potential as a government official is frequently recognized, but misunderstanding and jealousy repeatedly block the Master's advance.

Confucius' initial departure from the state of Lu, after the spectacular political service described above, is precipitated by conspiracy: "The men of Qi heard [of Confucius' successes in Lu] and were afraid. They said, 'If Confucius acts in government, then Lu will surely become hegemon.'" The conspirators proceed to divert Duke Ding's attention from government by sending eighty beautiful dancing girls to the state of Lu as a gift. Disgusted that Duke Ding becomes obsessed with these "gifts" and is so easily distracted from affairs of state, Confucius departs.[48] On another occasion, the famous Duke Jing of Qi considers granting Confucius a fief, but "the grandees of Qi wanted to harm him." The duke, who has previously heard Yanzi's slanderous attack against the Master, is influenced by the grandees and says, "I am old. I cannot use him."[49] In this particular episode, as elsewhere, the feudal lords fear that if Confucius acquires power in any state, he will pose a serious threat to all other states. Later, Confucius is slandered in Wei,[50] blocked once again from serving in his home state of Lu,[51] and is subsequently rejected in Chu. In the last case, just as earlier in Lu, the rejection comes from conspirators who fear that Confucius is so talented he might "become a king" if he controls any land at all.[52]

A certain cynicism rests at the bottom of Sima Qian's portrayal of the repeated rejection of Confucius. No one was ever worthier of political respect and employment than the Master, and yet he was not used. Talent, Sima Qian implies, does not ease one's way but only attracts jealousy and rejection. While Sima Qian is perhaps consoling himself as he writes of Confucius, his portrayal of the slander received by the greatest figure of the past will provide salve for the wounds of countless generations of frustrated Chinese scholars, noble in their own sight, who were spurned by government leaders.

Constant buffeting and rejection leave Sima Qian's Confucius deeply frustrated: "There is no one who knows and appreciates me," he says. And when his favorite disciple dies, he cries out, "Heaven is destroying me!"[53] On one occasion, a stranger describes the Master as "despondent like a dog in a house of mourning," a description that Confucius, at least in Sima Qian's version, accepts with good humor.[54] The Master's intense ambition enhances his dejection. "If only someone would use me . . . in three years there would be success," he says after one instance of traducement.[55] In fact, if Sima Qian's Confucius possesses any flaw at all it is excessive ambition. On at least three occasions he shows too much eagerness to serve and is "reined in" by those around him.[56]

This problem of ambition becomes an issue in the most famous verbal attack against Confucius in Sima Qian's account, an attack that comes from Laozi, his best known contemporary philosopher:

> Confucius . . . went to Zhou to inquire about ritual. It seems that he saw Laozi.[57] When he had taken leave and was departing, Laozi, who was seeing him off, said, "I have heard that the rich and noble

see others off with riches. People of humanity see others off with words. I am not rich and noble, so I usurp the title of a man of humanity and see you off with words: That which is intelligent and deeply perceptive but draws one near to death is a fondness for evaluating others. What is vastly discriminating and great but endangers one's body is to expose the faults of others."[58]

This is only one of two accounts found in *Records of the Historian* describing the famous meeting between Laozi and Confucius. The second version appears in Sima Qian's "Traditions of Laozi" (chapter 63) and is much harsher in its treatment of Confucius than the version quoted above. In that second version, the aged Laozi tells the upstart Confucius to "get rid of your haughty air and many desires, your superior attitude and excessive ambition. These all are of no benefit to you."[59]

Considerable criticism has been levelled at Sima Qian for including such episodes in his work at all; but by the Han dynasty this story, which apparently originates with anti-Confucian Taoists, was widespread.[60] Indeed, the canonical Confucian *Record of Ritual* (Li ji) contains records of four discussions between Laozi and Confucius on ritual, and the later *Family Sayings of Confucius*, very Confucian in its overall point of view, has expanded versions of the Laozi-Confucius discussions.[61] The admonition of Laozi, even in its stronger version, finds echoes elsewhere in *Records of the Historian* where other voices beckon away from a life of duty and constant self-improvement toward another, quieter path.[62] Such voices are found even in *Analects*, the most Confucian of texts, and in those cases too, are often considered evidence of anti-Confucian tampering.[63] However, the eremitic ideal has been deeply embedded in Chinese culture from the earliest times and was always presented as an alternative to the dangers of active social and political life. Certainly to all those engaged in the exhausting Confucian quest for sagehood, such voices must have carried occasional appeal. In the case of Sima Qian, they echo the vision of a father who had, after all, written an essay criticizing Confucianism as "laborious." But the plurality of voices in the "Hereditary Household of Confucius" no more makes this chapter anti-Confucian or "veiled satire" than the plurality of voices in *Analects* turns it into an anti-Confucian tract. It may be a somewhat naive approach to the texts of ancient China to demand a consistency or uniformity that texts in any tradition rarely possess.[64]

Still, as I have implied above, the voices that speak in the Laozi episode and address the general problem of ambition, reflect the tension between the eclectic Taoist vision of Sima Tan and the enormous ambition that he transmitted to his son. On one level, Laozi's voice may be speaking to the meddlesome Sima Qian who defended Li Ling in an honest and thoroughly Confucian way and, thereby, "endangered his body." On a deeper level, Laozi is perhaps also speaking to a man who has defined himself in terms of the strenuous task of writing a comprehensive history of the past and can only find personal redemption in the completion of that task. Sima Qian labored to the end of his life, much of the time in shame and disgrace, because of overwhelming ambition to be another Confucius. The words of Laozi, spoken to the first Confucius, must frequently have resounded in the heart of the toilworn and deeply humiliated Sima Qian!

However extreme his ambition, Sima Qian's Confucius is consistently frustrated in his desire to serve. The strongest voices of his age, Laozi and Yanzi, attack him for not giving up, not pulling back into the quieter world of contemplation. But rather than renouncing ambition, Confucius becomes a vagabond, endlessly searching for the lord who would employ him. Wandering and trial constitute the third great theme of the chapter, one intimately interwoven with the second theme discussed above. Rejection, of course, is one kind of trial, a test of resolve, but the Master must pass through more dangerous trials than this. Perhaps the most important test, and one occupying a central place in Sima Qian's vision of Confucius, is the famous "distress in the region of Chen and Cai." References to this event are found in such texts as *Analects, Mozi, Xunzi, Zhuangzi,* and *Spring and Autumn Annals of Master Lü.*[65] According to Sima Qian's account, which is quite different from these earlier versions, when Confucius is in the region of Chen and Cai,[66] he receives an invitation from the state of Chu. As he is about to depart,

> the grandees of Chen and Cai conspired, saying, "Confucius is a worthy man. All his criticism perfectly addresses the faults of the feudal lords. Now, for a long time he has been in the region of Chen and Cai, and all the policies of the various grandees have met Confucius' disapproval. Chu is a great state and has come to invite him. If Confucius is utilized by Chu, then the grandees who handle matters in Chen and Cai will be endangered!"

Chen and Cai then join together and dispatch soldiers to surround Confucius and his party in the countryside so as to prevent them from travelling to Chu. The small party's provisions dwindle, and Confucius' followers become ill, but "Confucius lectured, chanted, strummed, and sang, and did not become discouraged." Reduced to such difficult circumstances, the disciples become resentful against their Master. Sima Qian's account continues with conversations between Confucius and three of his most important followers:

Confucius . . . summoned Zilu and said, "*Poetry* says,

> 'I am not a rhinoceros, I am not a tiger,
> But I am led into this barren wild.'

"Is my doctrine perhaps in error? How could I come to this?"

Zilu said, "I think perhaps we are not yet humane, and people do not trust us. I think perhaps we are not yet wise, and people do not allow us to act."[70]

Confucius said, "Is this so? Yu [Zilu's personal name], if, by way of example, the humane were certainly to be trusted, then how could there be Bo Yi and Shu Qi? If the wise were certain to be allowed to act, how could there be Prince Bigan."[68]

Zilu left and Zigong entered and saw Confucius, who said, "*Poetry* says,

> 'I am not a rhinoceros, I am not a tiger,
> But I am led into this barren wild.'

"Is my doctrine perhaps in error? How could I come to this?"

Zigong said, "The Master's doctrine is supremely great. Therefore, there are none in the empire able to accept you, Master. Why don't you diminish it somewhat?"

Confucius said, "Ci [Zigong's personal name], a good farmer can sow, but he cannot be sure to harvest. A good artisan can be skilled, but he cannot be sure to please. A True Gentleman can cultivate his doctrine, summarizing and arranging it, consolidating and organizing it, but he cannot be sure to be accepted. Now, you do not cultivate your doctrine but seek to be accepted. Ci, your ambition is not far-reaching!" Zigong went out.

Yan Hui went in and saw Confucius, who said, "Hui, *Poetry* says,

> 'I am not a rhinoceros, I am not a tiger,
> But I am led into this barren wild.'

"Is my doctrine perhaps in error? How could I come to this?"

Yan Hui said, "The Master's doctrine is supremely great. Therefore, there are none in the empire able to accept you. Even though this is so, you, Master, should persist and carry it out. What is the harm if they do not accept you? Although they do not accept you, later on they will see that you are a True Gentleman. If the doctrine is not cultivated, then that would be our abomination. But if the doctrine is already greatly cultivated, but not utilized, that is the abomination of those who rule. What is the harm if they do not accept you? Although they do not accept you, later on they will see that you are a True Gentleman."

Confucius was pleased, laughed, and said, "It is thus, indeed. If, son of the Yan clan, it were caused that you had much wealth, then I would administer it for you."

Thereupon, Confucius sent Zigong to Chu. King Zhao of Chu raised troops to meet Confucius. Only then did he manage to escape.

The account, quoted at length above, differs markedly from other accounts of the distress in Chen and Cai in two important ways. First, Confucius' difficulty is precipitated by fear in Chen and Cai that he would use his political genius to assist Chu. This unites Sima Qian's theme of trial to that of jealousy and slander. Second, Sima Qian's report of the Master's conversations with his three disciples allows an exploration of possible responses to personal trial and frustration.

In the account of this famous event found in *Mencius*, Confucius fell into distress in the region of Chen and Cai "because he had no friends at court."[71] In other accounts, no reason is given for the Master's difficulty, but no serious political complications or troops are mentioned. Cui Shu, who believes that there must be some factual basis for this event, points out quite convincingly that, whatever actually happened, it could not have involved the political complications Sima Qian describes. Cui Shu concludes that the event was much less dramatic than Sima Qian's description and probably involved little more than a natural depletion of supplies in a region notorious for its bad roads![72] Certainly Sima Qian's version makes the trial more pronounced—it involves high-level fears, the political machinations of three feudal states, and puts Confucius in considerable danger.

The distress in Chen and Cai is not the only passage in Sima Qian's account where the Sage's life is imperiled. Elsewhere, Huan Tui, an officer in the state of Song, tries to kill Confucius by felling a tree on him.[73] Several years before this attempt on his life, Confucius is arrested and held for five days because he is mistaken for the notorious rebel Yang Hu.[74] And on another occasion, when he is detained in Pu, Gongliang Ru, a mysterious figure mentioned nowhere else in *Records of the Historian*, saves him with his martial skill.[75] However dramatic and dangerous Confucius' life may actually have been, it is apparent that Sima Qian, always a connoisseur of the dramatic, considerably enhanced those events.

Confucius' conversations with his three followers during the distress in Chen and Cai, each using the same format, provides a pattern of possible response to repeated frustration and adversity. The first possibility, broached by Zilu, is that Confucius himself is not worthy and still must strive to achieve the humanity and wisdom he preaches. If Confucius really possessed these virtues in their fullness, then success would open before him. Zilu assumes that there is absolute justice in the world and that the sufficiently worthy will indeed succeed. The second possibility, articulated by Zigong, is that Confucian doctrines are too lofty and must be adjusted to reality. Zigong thus appears as the compromising pragmatist who would pitch Confucian doctrine to a less worthy audience. The third possibility, presented by Yan Hui, ever the paragon of insightful discipleship, is that there is no deficiency in the Master and there should be no diluting the doctrine. The prescient Yan Hui argues in favor of pushing forward and expresses confidence that one day the Master will be seen for what he is, a "True Gentleman." Confucius responds favorably to the third alternative. There can be no compromise, one must persist in duty and look forward to the judgment of history, for "later on they will see that you are a True Gentleman." Sima Qian awaits precisely this type of redemption: "I await a sage, a True Gentleman of later generations," he says at the conclusion of his "Self-Narration."[76]

But Confucius' supreme moment of trial and resolve is still to come, and Sima Qian locates in that moment the seed of the Master's literary power, the power that will make him known in later generations. Freed from "the distress in Chen and Cai," Confucius returns to his home state of Lu. The return is initiated by a team of emissaries who are sent with gifts to welcome him to Lu. Confucius accepts the invitation, returns, and immediately encounters a hopeful sign: Duke Ai (r. 494–467 B.C.E.) asks him about government. At this point, the reader expects final success, a triumphant return, "the return of the king." But this is not to happen: "Nevertheless, Lu to the very end was unable to use Confucius." Here is the final rejection, the last time the refrain "not used" will sound in Sima Qian's narrative, for Confucius this time responds to rejection in an entirely new fashion: "And Confucius also *did not seek* position" (emphasis mine).[77] The Master, as Sima Qian creates him, now turns away from the immediate political world and begins the work that will be his most important contribution, the summary of an entire tradition in the form of the Six Arts. His ambition thwarted, Confucius weaves his own frustration into the Confucian classical tradition, the warp of all subsequent Chinese culture. Thus, the great contribution of "the ultimate sage," in Sima Qian's view, comes through the act of editing and writing. Joseph Campbell has shown how the quest of the mythic hero always requires that he bring back the prize, "the Golden Fleece," so as to "redound to the renewing of the community."[78] Sima Qian's Confucius does just this—he returns to his native state with the necessary wisdom to complete a work that will shape an entire tradition. In this most bookish of all cultures, the True King returns not in splendid military garb to claim his rightful throne but in the written characters he silently etches on bamboo or strokes on silk, characters that have acquired power in the furnace of personal frustration.

To disentangle Sima Qian from Confucius in this narrative of rejection and final redemption is impossible. Sima Qian, enjoined to be another Confucius, presents to us an image of the Master as he would have him. The issues of the life he presents are, time and again, the issues of his own life, and all those issues, in the final analysis, point toward the production of texts, the last and only hope for the frustrated scholar. Everything that Sima Qian's Confucius does before his return to Lu is a preface to the real work that is to follow.

Sima Qian, too, has his real work, and his rejection of suicide is justified only if he can finally duplicate the contribution of the "ultimate sage" and weave personal frustration into a new synthesis of all that has preceded him. "The distress in Chen and Cai," which Sima Qian mentions in his own summary of the life of Confucius, and upon which he dwells at such great length in the biography itself, is an emblem of all those instances of rejection and frustration that must precede the cultural production of a sage. In his short account of Mencius, Sima Qian notes that the second great Confucian "was in difficult straits in Qi and Liang," and he calls attention to the parallel with Confucius.[79] It should not surprise us, then, that in the account of his own travels, Sima Qian reports that "he was in distress and difficult straits in Po, Xue, and Pengcheng."[80] His trials bear a striking likeness to those of the Master and fully qualify him as Confucius' successor in the heritage of sages.

3

Sima Qian, the Six Arts, and Spring and Autumn Annals

Confucius completed *Spring and Autumn Annals,* and disorderly ministers and violent sons were frightened.

—*Mencius* 6:14a (3B:9)

As we have seen in the previous chapter, Sima Qian's portrayal of the life of Confucius follows the heroic cycle of exile, wandering, trial, and return, and culminates in the compilation and authorship of texts. Through this "textual labor," completed in the last years of his life, Confucius becomes the prototype of the "conservative" Chinese scholar, who summarizes the past so as to lay a sure foundation for the future. Here, too, Sima Qian's contribution to our interpretation of the past is critical, for he first imparts a clear historical shape to Confucius' work upon the classics, and in that shape we once again discover the peculiar contours of Sima Qian himself. The Han historian's crucial role in constructing the Chinese conception of the classics must be seen against the backdrop of a process of growing textual authority and canonization that had been going on for several centuries. However, before turning to a short history of that process, which will enable us to understand Sima Qian's unique contribution more precisely, a brief explanatory word is in order concerning the classics themselves.

When scholars of the early Han spoke of the classics, they often used the term "Six Arts" (*liu yi*). In an earlier period of time, Six Arts described six fields in which the sons of Zhou aristocrats were supposed to be educated: ritual, music, archery, charioteering, writing, and arithmetic.[1] The Han reorganization of the notion of the Six Arts around the Confucian classical canon was the culmination of a very significant educational reform, a "curriculum change," that was to have a profound influence on the course of Chinese civiliza-

47

tion. After this reform, "Six Arts" no longer referred to "concrete, practical skills or patterns of behavior" but to "specific, classical texts."[2]

The term "Six Classics" is itself somewhat problematic. Indeed, during the first century of the Han dynasty, it was more common to refer to "Five Classics." These were:

1. *Classic of Historical Documents (Shu jing)*, a collection of historical documents that purportedly come from the Xia, Shang, and early Zhou dynasties.

2. *Classic of Poetry (Shi jing)*, an anthology of poems, originally sung, that derive from roughly the first five centuries of the Zhou period.

3. *Classic of Changes (Yi jing)*. A divination text organized around sixty-four "hexagrams" (all possible combinations of broken and unbroken lines in six places) and a series of divinatory and philosophical texts elucidating these hexagrams.

4. *Ritual (Li)*, a series of texts supposedly preserving the ritual of the Zhou aristocracy.[3]

5. *Spring and Autumn Annals (Chun qiu)*, a brief chronological record of major events occurring in the feudal state of Lu and its neighbor states between 722 and 481 B.C.E.

The classic missing from this list, the work excluded from the "five" but included among the "six," is the *Classic of Music (Yue jing)*. Whether or not such a text ever existed is a difficult question. Some Chinese scholars, often associated with the later "New Script" (jin wen) school, believe that there never was such a book and that the "skill" of music was embedded in the musical tradition that once accompanied the transmission of the *Classic of Poetry*. Other scholars, usually identified as partisans of the "Old Script" (gu wen) school, argue that a *Classic of Music* once did exist but was destroyed in the First Qin Emperor's famous book-burning of 213 B.C.E.

By Sima Qian's time, these texts had become an educational canon. Moreover, Sima Qian, as we shall see in detail presently, added to the prestige of the canon by claiming that Confucius was responsible for the content of each of these texts. According to Sima Qian, the Master "put in order" *Ritual, Music, Documents, Changes,* and *Poetry* and "produced" *Spring and Autumn Annals*. How had these texts come to be identified with the sacred name of Confucius and achieved canonical status? How had they gained the authority that not only attracted Sima Qian's attention but led him to enhance and further shape the tradition surrounding them? This story, which must be told here all too briefly, should perhaps begin with *Analects*, the text usually regarded as most accurately reflecting the earliest Confucian teachings.[4]

Analects clearly indicates that poetry, ritual, and music were central concerns of the Master. On one occasion, for example, Confucius said, "I am excited by poetry, established by ritual, and perfected by music."[5] Although *Analects* even speaks of a specific text of "three hundred poems," it never says, as Sima Qian later asserts, that Confucius edited or compiled *Poetry*.[6] *Analects* also refers to "historical documents" (*shu*) as authoritative texts, and elsewhere quotes Confucius saying that if he had sufficient years of life left, he would use them to "study changes," a passage that often has been understood to reflect the Master's interest in an early redaction of *Classic of Changes*.[7] But nowhere in *Analects* is there any indication that Confucius was an editor of these texts, if indeed full texts and not just miscellaneous documents existed at that time. Furthermore, no reference can be found in *Analects* to *Spring and Autumn Annals*, the work Sima Qian claims was Confucius' greatest contribution to humanity. In fact, the closest *Analects* comes to associating Confucius with editing or writing "classics" at all is a somewhat ambiguous reference to his work upon music and poetry: "Only after I returned to Lu from Wei was the music put in order; and the 'ya' and 'song' each obtained its proper place."[8] If Confucius was indeed preoccupied in the latter part of his life with editing manuscripts and creating definitive historical annals, it is curious that no notice of such an endeavor would find its way into *Analects*, which supposedly was compiled by second- or third-generation disciples of the Master himself.

Zuo Commentary, a history perhaps written in the late fourth century B.C.E. and transmitted as a commentary on *Spring and Autumn Annals*, provides ample evidence that the subjects of poetry, historical documents, ritual, and music were central to the education of the mid-Zhou aristocracy, perhaps already supplanting the older and more martial Six Arts.[9] A passage in *Zuo Commentary*, describing an event that took place in 634 B.C.E., quotes an official from the state of Song who claims that "poetry (*shi*) and historical documents (*shu*) are repositories of propriety," and "ritual (*li*) and music (*yue*) are models for virtue."[10] Furthermore, *Poetry* and *Historical Documents*, as well as *Changes*, are quoted throughout *Zuo Commentary* and were obviously regarded as authoritative texts by the time of the compilation of this work.[11]

In spite of the fact that *Zuo Commentary* has usually been

considered as a commentary to *Spring and Autumn Annals*, it
nowhere *explicitly* states that Confucius is the author of the latter
text.[12] An event dated in *Zuo Commentary* to 540 B.C.E., refers to
the *Spring and Autumn Annals of Lu* and quotes a Jin state official
as claiming that "the ritual of Zhou is completely extant in Lu."[13]
Here, it would seem, is an ideal place for *Zuo Commentary* to
describe the relationship between Confucius, who is frequently
mentioned throughout this text, and the esteemed *Annals of Lu* (*Lu
chun qiu*), which is usually presumed to be the antecedent of the
Master's own *Annals*. *Zuo Commentary*, however, remains silent
on this issue.

With Mencius, the second great Confucian master, the picture
changes considerably. In fact, Mencius is the first important link in
a chain of interpreters of the classical tradition that leads directly to
Sima Qian. Mencius quotes *Poetry* a total of thirty-four times and
makes reference to *Historical Documents* sixteen times, but he does
not say Confucius edited either of these texts. Mencius' major
contribution to the formation of the Confucian canon, however, is
that he first associates *Spring and Autumn Annals* with Confucius
and, in fact, claims that *Annals* is the Master's greatest gift to
humanity. Mencius articulates a grand theory of history in which
Spring and Autumn Annals plays a central role. According to his
theory, the world fluctuates between periods of order and disorder.
The mythical flood of high antiquity was a time of disorder, and the
primary contribution of the sage-kings Yao, Shun, and Yu was to
control the flood and usher in an era of peace. Then, "after the death
of Yao and Shun, the doctrine of the sages declined and violent
rulers arose one after another." This disorder continued until King
Wu and the Duke of Zhou, "the sages of middle antiquity," brought
peace and order to China once again. But this period of peace was
short-lived:

> The world declined, the true doctrine grew weak, and perverse
> theories and violent acts arose. There were even cases where min-
> isters killed their rulers and sons their fathers. Confucius was
> frightened and produced *Spring and Autumn Annals*. A "Spring
> and Autumn Annals" is the business of a king. Therefore,
> Confucius said, "Those who know me, I expect will be on account
> of *Spring and Autumn Annals*, and those who blame me will be on
> account of *Spring and Autumn Annals*."[14]

Here, Mencius indicates that Confucius' *Spring and Autumn
Annals* was only one of a whole group of such texts, a fact we can

confirm from references in the philosophical text *Mozi* to "Spring and Autumn Annals" from the states of Zhou, Yan, Song, and Qi.[15] These texts were all written, it seems, as official endeavors (i.e., "the business of a king"), while Confucius supposedly produced his text outside of an official context and, in addition, made it a repository of his loftiest political doctrines. Ample ground is found in *Mencius* not only to build the theory, so prominent in Han times, that *Spring and Autumn Annals* is Confucius' primary contribution to mankind but also to argue that Confucius is, in some figurative sense, a "king," or at least establishing a standard for kings.[16] In a somewhat briefer repetition of the genealogy of sage-kings summarized above, Mencius reiterates the profound political impact of the Master's great text:

> Anciently Yu controlled the flooding waters and the empire was at peace. The Duke of Zhou joined the barbarians to China, drove away wild beasts, and the people were secure. Confucius completed *Spring and Autumn Annals*, and disorderly ministers and violent sons were frightened.[17]

Thus, Confucius, as a result of his completion of *Spring and Autumn Annals*, stands in a line of sages whose primary influence was political. Mencius notes that once again the world has fallen into disorder, and that men of wisdom in his age await a new Confucius; but, "sage-kings do not arise." The strong political slant that he imparts to the Master's mission places Mencius in a lineage of interpreters that is to have profound impact on Han thinkers in general and Sima Qian in particular.

Despite Mencius' concern with *Spring and Autumn Annals*, a concern extremely important in eventually drawing that work into the canon, and his frequent references to *Poetry* and *Historical Documents*, the second great Confucian does not use the term "classic" (*jing*), nor does he provide a specific grouping of texts or Arts. Thus, although Mencius obviously regards certain texts as authoritative, he provides no evidence that a formal canon yet existed in his day. Such evidence appears only with the next great link in our chain, that forged by the Confucian Xunzi and his disciples.

If we accept the filiation of scholars presented in Sima Qian's "Traditions of a Forest of Confucians" (chapter 121), and supplement it with various information found in other texts, we are led to the conclusion that Xunzi profoundly shaped the entire classical tradition. Each of the classics, and the Han interpretations of those classics, was apparently transmitted and strongly influenced by this towering figure.[18] Moreover, the text *Xunzi* first groups *Spring and Autumn Annals* together with *Poetry, Historical Documents, Ritual,* and *Music,* establishing a set group of five canonical disciplines. Xunzi also attempts to organize these authoritative texts into a coherent curriculum and to articulate the didactic essence of each classic, an obsession that will continue into the Han:

> The words of *Poetry* give the appropriate inclinations; the words of *Historical Documents* the appropriate official business. The words of *Ritual* give the appropriate behavior; the words of *Music* the appropriate harmony; the words of *Spring and Autumn Annals* the appropriate subtlety.[19]

While *Changes* is not mentioned here and seems not to have played a major role in Xunzi's philosophy, it is quoted several times in his work as a definitive text.[20] Moreover, *Changes* is included in a grouping of canonical works that appears in *Record of Ritual,* a collection of texts concerning the Art of Ritual that may have taken shape through the work of Xunzi's disciples during the early Han.[21] The *Record of Ritual* passage under discussion here is of critical significance in a history of the formation of the canon and possibly reflects the earlier teachings of Xunzi, for it too presents the classics as an ideal educational curriculum:

> Confucius said, "When I enter someone's country, its teachings can be known. If the people's behavior is warm and sincere, then it is because of the teaching of *Poetry.* If they are perceptive and understand things far off, then it is because of the teaching of *Historical Documents.* If they are broad-minded and at ease, then it is because of the teaching of *Music.* If they are pure and subtle, then it is because of the teaching of *Changes.* If they are respectful and imposing, then it is because of the teaching of *Ritual.* If their words are the same as their actions, then it is because of the teaching of *Spring and Autumn Annals.* Therefore, the neglect of *Poetry* brings stupidity, a neglect of *Historical Documents* delusion, a neglect of *Music* profligacy, a neglect of *Changes* violence, a neglect of *Ritual* vexatiousness, and a neglect of *Spring and Autumn Annals* disorder.[22]

Despite the attention given to the classical tradition in both *Xunzi* and *Record of Ritual,* neither claims that Confucius is the editor of any of the classics nor that he wrote *Spring and Autumn*

Annals. This is particularly surprising when we consider the emphasis Xunzi's immediate Confucian predecessor Mencius gave to the connection between Confucius and *Annals*.[23]

One of the most definitive statements about the canon, and quite possibly the first case where the terms "Five Classics" and "Six Arts" appear, is in the writings of the early Han politician and philosopher Lu Jia (fl. 200 B.C.E.). According to traditional accounts, Lu Jia was a vocal advocate of *Poetry* and *Historical Documents*, who, when challenged by Emperor Gaozu to show the practical value of these texts, wrote a lengthy response entitled *New Sayings* (*Xin yu*).[24] In the first chapter of the latter work, Lu Jia sets forth a theory of three eras of "sages." A sage who lived in the last of these eras "established the Five Classics and elucidated the Six Arts . . . he united earth and established the subtleties of government affairs." This "latter sage," according to Lu Jia, "put in order chapters and literary compositions to pass down to coming generations . . . in order to correct decline and disorder."[25] Although Confucius is not mentioned here by name, he is, of course, the "latter sage," for elsewhere in *New Sayings*, Lu Jia notes that Confucius defended against disorder with "classics" and "arts." Furthermore, Lu Jia is explicit in naming the classics, and he notes that *Spring and Autumn Annals* used "humaneness and propriety to censure and renounce."[26]

Lu Jia had a strong political agenda and used his position of influence with Emperor Gaozu to advance a particular collection of texts as the best defense against another decline into disorder and chaos. Of course, Lu Jia makes it clear that the lofty principles of the texts he promotes are so subtle as to require the "divination" of specialists like himself. Indeed, throughout *New Sayings* one can discern a persistent attempt to resuscitate the status of specialists in the oldest and most revered ancient texts—those scholars who had suffered so greatly under the First Qin Emperor in the previous two decades. As a result of his regard for classics and scholars, Lu Jia lays a strong foundation for the canon in the early Han, and he also continues in the Mencian tradition of imparting to the classics a distinctively political hue.

The great strength and wide influence of the concept of the Six Arts in the early decades of the Han is also reflected in the writings of the young literary genius Jia Yi (201–169 B.C.E.),[27] who not only sees the Six Arts as defining a fixed curriculum but also tries to correlate this group with other sacred sextets so as to fashion a grand harmony based on the number six:

Nevertheless, although a man has Six Actions, they are subtle and difficult to recognize. Only the former kings were able to discern these. Since the commoner cannot of himself reach this discernment, he must await the Six Teachings of the former kings in order to know what to do. Therefore, the former kings established teachings for the empire. They relied upon what man possessed [by nature] and made these into instructions; they respected the emotions of man, and made these their truth. Therefore, within they took as model the Six Regulations, and without they embodied the Six Actions. Thus, they gave rise to the methods of the six, *Historical Documents, Poetry, Changes, Spring and Autumn Annals, Ritual,* and *Music,* and took these as their great principle, calling them the "Six Arts."[28]

While Jia Yi's strange and complex philosophy blends elements of Legalism and Taoism with Confucianism, he continues the older emphasis upon the educational importance of the Six Arts, and he ascribes the great principles contained in the classics to the wisdom of former kings.[29]

The inclination in the first century of the Han dynasty to canonize certain texts and valorize the educational traditions based upon those texts is reflected in the way government-sponsored education under Han Emperor Wu gradually solidified around "academicians" (*bo shi*) who were specialists selected strictly on the basis of their mastery of particular classics. The Han dynasty institution of academicians probably derived from the Jixia Academy, a haven of free philosophical debate founded in the state of Qi towards the end of the fourth century B.C.E.[30] After the First Qin Emperor unified the empire and ascended the throne in 221 B.C.E., he visited the former state of Qi and first encountered the Jixia masters, who apparently numbered seventy at that time. Shortly thereafter, we read of seventy academicians at the imperial court in Xianyang, which suggests that the entire Jixia academy, or at least a nucleus of prominent scholars from that academy, had been transported to the new capital, where they had become the core of a new Qin institution.[31]

The *History of the Han* indicates that academicians were originally officials "who understood both the ancient and the modern, and who reviewed the old and understood the new."[32] These early academicians were truly "Masters of Broad Learning," as a literal reading of the Chinese-language official title *bo shi* would imply, and were not necessarily identified with a particular body of texts or a specific philosophical orthodoxy. Such breadth continued to characterize the academicians until the early years of Emperor Wu.

However, he restructured the institution around a Confucian canon, a policy that probably resulted from one of a series of three memorials the scholar-official Dong Zhongshu submitted sometime during the first years of Emperor Wu's reign.[33] The critical recommendation, which was to have far-reaching impact, comes toward the end of the third of Dong's memorials and is an extraordinary attempt to limit official discourse to the confines of a Confucian canon:

> The teachers of today have diverse standards, men have diverse doctrines, and each of the philosophical schools has its own particular position and differs in the ideas it teaches. Hence it is that the rulers possess nothing whereby they may effect general unification, the government statutes having often been changed; while the ruled do not know what to cling to. I, your ignorant servitor, hold that all not within the field of the Six Arts, or the teachings of Confucius, should be cut short and not allowed to progress further. Evil and licentious talk should be stopped. Only after this can there be a general unification and can the laws be made distinct so that the people may known what they are to follow.[34]

The youthful Emperor Wu heeded Dong Zhongshu's advice. In 136 B.C.E., he drastically reduced the number of academicians and began appointing scholars who were specialists in a single classic.[35] Thereafter, the academicians were identified in terms of the particular classic they taught and transmitted to their disciples. Xu Fuguan, a distinguished twentieth-century specialist on Han thought, has given a very perceptive summary of the twofold impact of this change in the Office of Academicians. First, the learning of the academicians, who had earlier represented breadth and diversity, now narrowed to an official duty entailing the interpretation of individual classics. These new academicians were specialists more equipped to explicate particular texts and perhaps less equipped to participate in wide-ranging political discussion. Second, the Five Classics, which had previously been freely evaluated by private individuals and by society in general, now acquired the status of a legal authority that only government officials could properly interpret.[36] This was a decisive moment in Chinese history. A canon had been formally established and placed at the center of a government-controlled educational establishment, and much of the subsequent intellectual history of the Han dynasty concerns attempts by various schools of classic-interpretation to gain access to the power that came with government recognition and sponsorship.[37]

While Dong Zhongshu's most immediate and significant contribution to the history of the classics might have come through his
political recommendation that teaching and study be restricted to
the Six Arts, his more general ideas about the classics deserve closer
scrutiny. Like Lu Jia before him, Dong Zhongshu believed that the
Han leaders needed to effect a wholesale transformation of "criminal" Qin policies.[38] Almost seventy years had passed since the
founding of the Han, but despite the urging of scholars such as Lu
Jia, Dong Zhongshu felt that the necessary transformation had not
yet taken place: "Han has not changed what it ought to have
changed," he said in dismay.[39]

Dong Zhongshu's political agenda, advanced in his three memorials to Emperor Wu, is elaborated considerably in his lengthy
philosophical work, *Abundant Dew of Spring and Autumn Annals*
(*Chun qiu fan lu*), a highly important text that has not yet been fully
translated into a Western language.[40] Briefly stated, Dong Zhongshu
wished to subordinate imperial authority to purposive cosmological
forces. As the emperor controls subjects, reasoned Dong, so heaven
should control the emperor. Indeed, an elaborate system of correla-
tions between heaven and earth means that the emperor must constantly beware; for any misrule will result in inauspicious portents
and natural disasters. The emperor fulfills his sacred mandate and
thereby averts calamity by overseeing the moral education of the
people.[41] To assist him in this enormous task, he must diligently
seek men of talent. In fact, according to Dong Zhongshu's recitation
of history, the primary characteristic of the rule of sages is their wise
use of talent.[42] "If you previously have not supported scholars, but
wish to seek out worthies," he tells Emperor Wu, "then that is just
like not polishing jade but seeking beautiful patterns."[43]

Like all good Confucians, Dong believed that the Six Classics
were the very foundation of the True Gentleman's educational
nourishment. In *Abundant Dew of Spring and Autumn Annals*,
much in the fashion of Xunzi and *Record of Ritual*, Dong
Zhongshu sets forth his theory of the peculiar transforming
power of each of the Six Arts, and his account, as we shall see,
finds clear echoes in the writing of his younger contemporary,
Sima Qian:

> The True Gentleman knows that one in a position of authority
> cannot use evil to subordinate others. For that reason, he selects
> the Six Arts in order to support and nourish subordinates. *Poetry*
> and *Historical Documents* express one's desires; *Ritual* and *Music*

purify one's beauty; *Changes* and *Spring and Autumn Annals* clarify one's understanding. The Six Arts are all important, but each has its particular strength. Since *Poetry* speaks of desires, it is strongest with regard to physical substances. Since *Ritual* establishes restraints, it is strongest with regard to aesthetic culture. Since *Music* sings of virtue, it is strongest with regard to education. Since *Historical Documents* records merits, it is strongest with regard to official business. Since *Changes* is based upon heaven and earth, it is strongest with regard to calculations. Since *Spring and Autumn Annals* establishes a correct standard for right and wrong, it is strongest with regard to ruling others.[44]

While each of the Arts has its proper function, *Spring and Autumn Annals*, in Dong Zhongshu's view, is the most useful Art for "ruling others." Thus, he builds upon Mencius' notion that this work has a distinctively political message. As we might expect, he also accepts the claim of Mencius that Confucius produced *Annals* and that it is the Sage's single greatest achievement. Dong Zhongshu even goes one step beyond Mencius and states that Confucius produced his famous historical text in direct response to the command of heaven as that command was revealed through the capture of the unicorn in 481 B.C.E.[45]

According to Dong Zhongshu, *Spring and Autumn Annals* is "the greatest expression of justice" and is a constitution for all time.[46] Most of Dong Zhongshu's intellectual career was devoted to this one classic, and his studies led him to conclude that *Spring and Autumn Annals* is a mysterious text that utilizes a highly subtle system of "praise" and "blame" to evaluate the figures and events of the past. Such a theory derives from a tradition of *Spring and Autumn* exegesis that is reflected most powerfully in *Gongyang Commentary*, a text Sima Qian directly links to Dong Zhongshu. Indeed, Sima Qian says that in his age "only Dong Zhongshu had a reputation for understanding *Spring and Autumn Annals*" and that "he transmitted the traditions of Mr. Gongyang."[47]

The origin and transmission of *Gongyang Commentary* is unclear and has generated considerable controversy. Dai Hong (ca. 150 C.E.), who wrote a preface to the text, claims that it was first written down in the reign of Emperor Jing and existed only as an oral tradition before that time. If this is true, then Dong Zhongshu, who was active during the reigns of emperors Jing and Wu and was known as a transmitter of the *Gongyang* tradition, could have either been involved with the actual writing of the text or was at least close to other scholars who were so involved.[48]

In spite of the critical role Dong Zhongshu plays in the transmission of the *Gongyang Commentary*, and the impact of this particular tradition on his own work, Dong's theory of *Spring and Autumn Annals* goes beyond the *Gongyang Commentary* in at least three important ways: first, he not only interprets the words of *Spring and Autumn Annals* in a fashion reminiscent of the *Gongyang* tradition, but he also repeatedly finds esoteric meanings that transcend the language of the sacred text; second, he insists on a purposive heaven—that is, a heaven that constantly influences human affairs and can be discovered in the events of history; and third, he repeatedly applies his theory of *yin* and *yang* to the interpretation of *Spring and Autumn Annals*. No notion of heaven as a purposive force can be found in *Gongyang Commentary*, nor is there an attempt in that text to link natural calamities, wherever they are noted in *Spring and Autumn Annals*, with human behavior. In addition, Dong Zhongshu's emphasis upon *yin* and *yang* and his application of the theory of the five processes (*wu xing*), as a means of binding together the affairs of heaven and those of earth, do not appear in the *Gongyang Commentary*.[49]

For our purposes here, the first of these three differences between the thought of Dong Zhongshu and that reflected in *Gongyang Commentary* is most critical, for Dong's ability to fathom the recondite "truths" of *Spring and Autumn Annals* profoundly changed interpretations of that text and set the stage for the apocryphal texts that were to appear in the following two centuries.[50] According to Dong Zhongshu, *Spring and Autumn Annals* is a divinely inspired work that can only be fully fathomed by reading beyond the text: "Those who speak of *Spring and Autumn Annals*," Dong says, "must enter into misleading expressions and follow its tortuous complications, and only then will they fully understand it."[51] Elsewhere, he explains more fully:

> *Spring and Autumn Annals*, as an object of study, describes the past so as to illumine the future. Its phrases, however, embody the inscrutableness of heaven and, therefore, are difficult to understand. To one who is incapable of examining them, it seems as if they contain nothing. To one who is capable of examining them, there is nothing they do not contain.[52]

The degree of actual contact between Dong Zhongshu and Sima Qian is impossible to determine. Sima Qian, as we shall see, quotes Dong Zhongshu's ideas on several occasions and obviously holds his scholarship in the highest regard. In fact, one might reasonably assume, as have many Chinese scholars, that Sima Qian actually studied with Dong Zhongshu.[53] But whatever relationship might have existed between these two great scholars, Dong Zhongshu's teachings on the classics in general and on *Spring and Autumn Annals* in particular obviously influenced Sima Qian. However, before examining this issue, it might be helpful to summarize the tradition of an official canon as it has been traced above and as it existed on the eve of Sima Qian's monumental historical enterprise. The following four points are of greatest importance:

1. A group of Five (or Six) Classics (representing Six Arts) was widely considered to contain the essence of the Confucian tradition. These texts, through the urging of such figures as Xunzi, Lu Jia, Jia Yi, and Dong Zhongshu, had come to occupy a central position in official political and educational institutions.

2. While the classics were identified with Confucius, with the exception of *Spring and Autumn Annals*, they had not been directly ascribed to him either as author or as editor.

3. The one exception to point two, *Spring and Autumn Annals*, had come to be regarded not only as the work of Confucius, but as his most important work. Whatever the significance of *Analects* in the early Han, it is clear that *Spring and Autumn Annals* had much greater status.

4. *Spring and Autumn Annals*, as a consequence of the teachings of such scholars as Mencius and Dong Zhongshu, had been infused with a distinctively political interpretation. Dong Zhongshu even considered this brief history to be an eternal constitution written by the Sage in the most subtle and esoteric language.

Sima Qian, for the most part, accepts this tradition. Furthermore, in his writings the relationship of Confucius to the origin of the Six Arts is finally given a specific, biographical shape. As we have seen in the previous chapter, Sima Qian continually emphasizes the strong connection between Confucius' personal frustration and the transmission of the past. For the Master turns to his sacred work upon the classics only after he fails in the political world. This claim that frustration and failure provide the impetus for the Master's work on the classics is very much in harmony with Sima Qian's theory of literary production and the Han historian's own experience as a shamed and frustrated scholar.

After providing Confucius with the potent motivation of political frustration, Sima Qian proceeds to describe the Master's work on the Six Arts in considerable detail. He first reports that by the time of Confucius "*Ritual* and *Music* had been cast aside, and *Poetry* and *Historical Documents* were defective."[54] Thus the Master's effort is a response to political and cultural decline, and the source of that decline can be traced to a neglect of classical learning. Confucius finally realized, Sima Qian's narrative implies, that his primary political act, an act of enormous cultural importance, would be to rectify an entire tradition.

First, Confucius puts *Historical Documents* in order. The documents included in his new collection begin from Emperor Yao and Shun and come down to the time of Duke Miao of Qin (also known as Mu—r. 659–621 B.C.E.). Sima Qian does not report the precise size of this new collection, but the central role of Confucius as an editor is clearly implied.[55] Confucius' work on *Ritual* is described, alongside his work on *Historical Documents*, as a part of the process of scouring the ancient writings, so that "*Historical Documents* and *Record of Ritual* both came forth from Confucius."[56]

The Master's effort on *Music* and *Poetry*, which Sima Qian presents as interrelated disciplines parallel to the interrelated disciplines of *Ritual* and *Historical Documents*, is described in even greater detail. Confucius discusses *Music* with the music master of Lu, and eventually "*Music* is put in order, the *ya* and *song* each gaining its proper place."[57] Then, from a body of over three thousand poems, Confucius selects approximately three hundred pieces that "could be utilized with regard to ritual and duty." The structure of this new *Classic of Poetry* is presented in outline, and we are told that Confucius "strummed and sang" the chosen poems "in order to seek out the keys appropriate" to the various musical traditions.[58]

As Sima Qian's account continues, Confucius turns to *Changes*. The description in *Records of the Historian* of Confucius' work upon this classic is the subject of some controversy and has sometimes been used to support the later notion that Confucius wrote the "Ten Wings" or "Appendices" to *Changes*, a series of commentaries that provides the older, divination stratum of the classical text with a considerably more philosophical overlay. The controversy centers upon a line in *Records of the Historian* that can be read in two quite separate ways:

1. Confucius, late in life, delighted in *Changes* (yi), "The Sequences" (xu), "The Decisions" (tuan), "The Images" (xiang),

"The Connections" (xi), "The Discussions of the Trigrams" (shuo gua), and "The Words of the Text" (wen yan).[59]

2. Confucius, late in life, delighted in Changes. He arranged "The Decisions," "The Images," "The Connections," "The Discussion of the Trigrams," and "The Words of the Text."

According to the first of these readings, Confucius delighted in Changes and in its appendices, of which nine are mentioned (tuan, xiang, and xi refer to two appendices each). The problematic term xu 序 is taken as a reference to the appendix fully entitled "xu gua" or, in translation, "The Sequence of the Hexagrams." The second reading takes xu as a verb, "to arrange, to put in order," and credits Confucius with editorial work on eight of the ten appendices (xu gua "The Sequence of the Hexagrams" and za gua "Miscellaneous Notes on the Hexagrams" being left out).

Each of the readings presented above has distinguished supporters.[60] Nevertheless, it seems to me that the second interpretation is preferable. Xu, as an abbreviated name of one of the appendices, is out of the traditional order for listing the appendices and leaves us, furthermore, with the somewhat strange notion that "delighting in Changes" does not automatically imply, at least to the mind of Han China, both the older layers of the text and the appendices. Certainly by that time the latter were regarded as an integral part of the text. It is also much easier to see how later interpreters, like Ban Gu, could get from the idea that Confucius arranged the appendices, rather than simply delighted in them, to the idea that he wrote them.[61] At any rate, Sima Qian goes on to say that Confucius "read Changes until the bamboo strip binders broke three times."[62] But it is of considerable interest that Sima Qian claims Confucius "used Poetry, Historical Documents, Ritual, and Music to teach his students," a list reiterating the primary grouping of the Arts that appeared as early as Zuo Commentary and excluded the enigmatic Changes from the earliest Confucian curriculum.[63]

Sima Qian's Confucius is an editor, connoisseur, and transmitter of these five Arts. His description of the labors of Confucius provides information about both the historical context and the specific content of the Sage's great work. However, Sima Qian considers the most important effort of Confucius to be the creation of Spring and Autumn Annals, and that effort is described separately from his work upon the other classics. Confucius, according to Sima Qian, "produced" or "created" (zuo) this text rather than merely arranging or editing it, and Sima Qian clearly believes that Annals is the culmination of the Sage's career:

> Confucius said, "Sad indeed! Sad indeed! The True Gentleman is
> distressed that he will pass away and his name not be praised! My
> doctrines do not go forth. How can I show myself to subsequent
> generations?" Thereupon, he took as basis the historical records
> and produced *Spring and Autumn Annals*. He began with Duke
> Yin (722–712 B.C.E.) and came down to the fourteenth year of Duke
> Ai (481 B.C.E.), in all twelve dukes. . . . Confucius said, "Those in
> later generations who know me will take as basis *Spring and
> Autumn Annals*, and those who blame me will also take as basis
> *Spring and Autumn Annals*."[64]

Thus, in this narrative, *Spring and Autumn Annals* becomes
the Master's attempt to transmit both his name and his doctrine to
later ages. Sima Qian's Confucius also claims here, in a line ex-
tracted from *Mencius*, that those in later generations who praise or
blame him will do so on the basis of this text—the Sage's reputation
ultimately will derive from his work as a historian. Furthermore,
the production of *Spring and Autumn Annals* is, according to Sima
Qian, the last great act of Confucius and immediately precedes his
illness and death.

Apart from the account in the "Hereditary Household of
Confucius" outlined above, there are two other very important
passages in *Records of the Historian* concerning *Spring and Autumn
Annals*. The first, found in the "Self-Narration," is a response to a
question from Sima Qian's fellow official Hu Sui: "In earlier times
why did Confucius write *Spring and Autumn Annals*?" As he answers this question, Sima Qian reveals both his indebtedness to
Dong Zhongshu and the limits of that indebtedness. He begins by
saying that "he heard Master Dong" describe the decline of Zhou
and the noble attempt of Confucius to arrest that decline. But
Confucius' endeavor was thwarted because "the feudal lords abused
him, and the grandees obstructed him." The Master, with that same
frustration Sima Qian has described at such great length in the
"Hereditary Household of Confucius," realized that "his words
would not be used and that his Way would not be carried out." Here,
however, abuse and obstruction are linked directly to the production of *Spring and Autumn Annals*. Still quoting Dong Zhongshu,
Sima Qian says that Confucius "Judged the rights and wrongs of a
period of 242 years and made a standard for the empire." Accord-
ingly, Confucius incorporated his loftiest political principles into
the subtle judgments of a historical text. Moreover, the Master

himself, in this account, announces the superiority of such a method: "If I wished to record them in theoretical words, it would not be as penetrating and obvious as revealing them in actual affairs."

According to this theory, a record of the past, produced with sufficient detail and subtlety, can be a more valuable political guide than an abstract philosophical exposition (i.e., "theoretical words"). The same idea, which Sima Qian quotes approvingly from Dong Zhongshu, does indeed appear in the latter's *Abundant Dew of Spring and Autumn Annals*: "Confucius said, 'I have relied upon actual affairs and added the mind of a true king to them. I think to reveal them in theoretical words is not as profound and clear as in actual affairs.'"[65] Sima Qian goes on, still responding to Hu Sui's question, to place *Spring and Autumn Annals* within the context of the Six Arts and believes, like Xunzi, *Record of Ritual*, and Dong Zhongshu before him, that each of those Arts addresses a particular area of human concern:

> *Changes* elucidates heaven and earth, *yin* and *yang*, the four seasons, and the five processes. Therefore, it is strongest with regard to transformations. *Ritual* regulates human relationships. Therefore, it is strongest with regard to behavior. *Historical Documents* records the affairs of previous kings. Therefore, it is strongest with regard to government. *Poetry* makes a record of mountains, rivers, ravines, and valleys, of birds, beasts, plants, and trees, and of male and female beasts and birds. Therefore, it is strongest with regard to education. *Music* is a means of establishing joy. Therefore, it is strongest with regard to harmony. *Spring and Autumn* discerns right and wrong. Therefore, it is strongest with regard to ruling others. Thus, regulate people with *Ritual*, spread harmony with *Music*, discuss official affairs with *Historical Documents*, express ideas with *Poetry*, discuss transformations with *Changes*, and discuss duty with *Spring and Autumn Annals*.

While Sima Qian's ideal curriculum presented above most closely resembles that of Dong Zhongshu, there are differences. *Changes*, which occupies the fifth position on Dong's list, heads Sima Qian's description, a position it is to retain in the *History of the Han* "Bibliographic Essay."[66] Sima Qian, who was a calendrical scientist responsible for the new calendar promulgated in 104 B.C.E., also expands upon Dong's claim that *Changes* is useful for "calculations" and notes that it can help one understand "the transformations of *yin* and *yang*, the four seasons, and the five processes."

Moreover, whereas Dong Zhongshu recommends *Ritual* for "aesthetic culture," Sima Qian regards it as a guide "to behavior." *Documents*, Dong Zhongshu says, is useful in "official business," while Sima Qian says it is strongest with regard "to government." Whatever the ultimate significance of such differences, however, both writers agree in the essentially political message of *Spring and Autumn Annals*—it is strongest with regard "to ruling." Sima Qian proceeds to expand considerably upon his description of the function of *Spring and Autumn Annals*:

> For dispelling a disorderly generation and turning it back to rectitude, there is nothing better than *Spring and Autumn Annals*. . . . Therefore, those who govern must know *Spring and Autumn Annals*, or before them will be slander, and they will not see it; behind them will be violence, and they will not know. Those who act as ministers must know *Spring and Autumn Annals*, or in protecting and managing official affairs, they will not know what is proper, and in meeting with changes, they will not know their authority. Those who are rulers or fathers and do not comprehend the principles of *Spring and Autumn Annals* must receive a reputation for great evil. Those who are ministers and sons and do not comprehend the principles of *Spring and Autumn Annals* must fall into the punishments for rebellion and regicide and have a reputation for committing capital crimes. In actuality, they all act in accord with what they think good, but they do not know the proper principles. If you cover them with theoretical words (i.e., judgments), they will not dare speak out. Now, if they do not comprehend the meaning of ritual and duty, then rulers will not behave as rulers, fathers will not behave as fathers, ministers will not behave as ministers and sons will not behave as sons. If rulers do not behave as rulers, then there will be offenses; if a minister does not behave as a minister, then there will be punishments; if a father does not behave as a father, then there will be no true doctrine; and if a son does not behave as a son, he will not be filial. These four actions are the greatest faults in the empire. If you present to someone [the fact] that they have one of the greatest faults in the empire, then they accept the judgment and will not dare to speak out. Therefore, *Spring and Autumn Annals* is the grand essence of ritual and duty. Now, ritual restrains what is not yet so, while law acts on what has already become so. The usefulness of law is easily seen; but the restraint of ritual is difficult to know.[67]

Thus, rulers and fathers, ministers and sons, must comprehend *Spring and Autumn Annals* or they will fall into the grossest evils of rebellion, regicide, and general disruption of the proper Confucian order. In fact, Sima Qian seems to believe that the principles in Confucius' text constitute a law code and can be used to judge all kinds of actions. It is of interest, in this regard, to note that Dong Zhongshu actually wrote a lengthy book, now lost, in which he applied *Spring and Autumn Annals* to 232 legal cases.[68]

As I have noted above, Sima Qian makes considerable use of Master Dong's ideas and actual words in his response to Hu Sui. However, before proclaiming the Han historian a slavish follower of his senior contemporary Dong Zhongshu, we must note what is not found here. First of all, none of Dong's distinctive cosmological theories, which assign particular significance to the correspondence of heaven, earth, and man and locate profound meaning in portents and disasters, appears in Sima Qian's comments. Second, there is no claim here or elsewhere in *Records of the Historian* that Confucius was divinely inspired. Insofar as inspiration motivated Sima Qian's Confucius, it was thoroughly literary and came from those same wellsprings of frustration that would inspire such later figures as Zuo Qiuming, Qu Yuan and, of course, Sima Qian himself. Finally, we see no indication that Sima Qian accepted Dong Zhongshu's idea that one had to go well beyond the words of *Spring and Autumn Annals* to find the text's cherished "principles." If this particular passage from the "Self-Narration" gives any indication at all of Sima Qian's reading of *Spring and Autumn Annals*, that reading seems to be relatively concrete and literalistic. Although he does not say so directly, Sima Qian appears to be skeptical of the more "mystical" of Dong Zhongshu's principles, of those aspects of Dong's reading of *Spring and Autumn Annals* where the latter goes beyond the *Gongyang* tradition.[69]

The issue of how Sima Qian reads the Master's great text brings us to his second critical passage concerning *Spring and Autumn Annals*, a passage found in the "Preface to the Chronological Chart of the Twelve Feudal Lords" (chapter 14). This remarkably succinct history of the Western Zhou and Spring and Autumn periods most clearly reveals Sima Qian's notion of the historical significance of *Spring and Autumn Annals* both as the summary of a political tradition and as the initiation of a textual one. He begins the "preface" by tracing the collapse of the utopian Western Zhou order to King Li (r. 878–842 B.C.E.) and the rebellion that led to the Joint-Harmony Regency.[70] After this tragedy, "the strong took advantage of the weak and troops were raised without permission from the Son of Heaven." Feudal strongmen, so-called "hegemons," usurped the power of the Zhou kings, and eventually the four states of Qi, Jin, Qin, and Chu dominated the political world. However, Confucius occupies the central position in this short history, for he appears at the very darkest hour and temporarily dispels the gloom:

> Therefore, Confucius illumined the way of the kings. He sought to serve more than seventy rulers, but none were able to use him. Consequently, he went west to observe the household of Zhou and to discuss the historical records and old traditions. He began in Lu and arranged *Spring and Autumn Annals*. He went back in time to Duke Yin (722–712 B.C.E.) and came on down to the capture of the unicorn in the time of Duke Ai (481 B.C.E.). He made its language economical and did away with unnecessary redundancy. The way of the kings was perfected, and the affairs of man made complete.

Here again, Sima Qian portrays Confucius as one who would restore the way of the kings but, of the political leaders of his day, "none were able to use him." Consequently, the history of the Spring and Autumn period collapses, in Sima Qian's account, into the history of a text, *Spring and Autumn Annals*, which becomes the focus of the last half of his "Preface to the Chronological Chart of the Twelve Feudal Lords." Confucius' great text corrects the errors of a corrupt age, perfects the way of the kings, and points towards the future. The language of *Annals*, Sima Qian notes, is exceedingly terse and suggestive. Much of the history of the Spring and Autumn period, he explains, was too politically sensitive or morally repugnant to be put into writing and was, consequently, transmitted orally. Indeed, from Sima Qian's description, we get the impression that *Spring and Autumn Annals* was a sort of "prompt-book," to borrow a term from later Chinese literary history, and only carried its intended didactic power as the hub of an expansive explanatory discourse:

> The seventy disciples of the Master received teachings that he [i.e., the Master] had transmitted orally, for words that satirize, criticize, praise, conceal, suppress, or ridicule cannot appear in writing. A True Gentleman of Lu, Zuo Qiuming, feared that the various disciples had different premises and that each would depend upon his own ideas and lose the true sense. Therefore, he relied upon the historical records of Confucius, thoroughly discussed its words, and completed *Spring and Autumn Annals of Master Zuo*.[71]

Sima Qian concludes this discussion of the textual history of *Spring and Autumn Annals* by briefly describing several other texts that derive from the exegetical tradition Zuo Qiuming inaugurated, but all of those are in some sense secondary to the work of Zuo Qiuming, to whom Sima Qian grants that loftiest of Confucian epithets "True Gentleman" (*junzi*). Zuo Qiuming's fuller history, according to Sima Qian, provides the necessary, authoritative context to understand Confucius' laconic history. It would be folly, we might surmise from Sima Qian's account, to try to derive any significant meaning from *Spring and Autumn Annals* outside of an interpretive tradition that was transmitted from Confucius through his disciples and is preserved in *Zuo Commentary*.

Sima Qian's description of the early history of *Spring and Autumn Annals* is highly significant. First, it indicates he believed that *Spring and Autumn Annals of Master Zuo* was written very much with Confucius' text in mind—it was an attempt to preserve the "oral" transmissions necessary to understand the terse language of the earlier work. Second, *Zuo Commentary* has a relationship to *Spring and Autumn Annals* that no other text shares. Sima Qian was a historian, so we should not be surprised that he felt much greater interest in the concrete narratives of *Zuo Commentary* than in the subtle exegesis of *Gongyang* and *Guliang* commentaries or in Dong Zhongshu's philosophical speculation and textual divinations. Third, it is perhaps significant that Sima Qian says Confucius did not put his most trenchant comments in his history at all but reserved them for oral transmission. Thus, Sima Qian establishes the most respected possible precedent for evasion and concealment in a written text. He may indeed be telling us something at this point about his own work and the difficult and politically dangerous time in which he lived and wrote.

The fashioning of the Six Arts, and the central role assigned Confucius in this monumental activity, emerges from Sima Qian's narrative with a distinctively historical shape. At a particular moment in his life, the Master turns away from his constant search for political employment and begins to edit, arrange, and write texts that will become standards for all time. Sima Qian's narrative of this activity not only puts Confucius at the center of the tradition, but himself as well, for subsequent generations will think of this critical event *through* the pages of *Records of the Historian*. Whatever the ultimate historicity of Sima Qian's description of Confucius' work, and one or another scholar has questioned virtually every aspect of that description, it becomes, for most Chinese, the definitive account of what Confucius actually did.

As we read Sima Qian's description of that historic moment in Confucius' life when he established an entire classical tradition and wrote a terse annal that, properly understood, is the ultimate political and moral treatise, and simultaneously reflect back on the words of Sima Qian's father, we cannot avoid the suspicion that there is much more to all of this than is immediately apparent. If Sima Qian wants to follow his father's wish to become another Confucius, and much that he says about himself indicates that he harbors just such an ambition, then he is creating the loftiest possible standard for himself and for his history. He must gather, as Confucius did before, the loose strands of a badly frayed tradition and weave them together once again into a comprehensive unity. This unity, if it follows the model of Confucius, must present a coherent political and moral message, reinforcing age-old Confucian verities. It must be so poignant in its message as to throw fear into those evil men who had seemingly lost their awe for the message of the first Confucius.

These are the boundaries within which a second Confucius should work. And if this second Confucius would completely emulate his model, he must employ a highly economical style, creating a terse text that could be fathomed only through brilliant textual divination—it must, just like Confucius' text before it, await the exegesis of a "True Gentleman." But, as we shall see, Sima Qian's inclinations often run contrary to the task implied by the model of Confucius. He does indeed ingest and digest the texts of the past with astounding energy. For generations of Chinese, *Records of the Historian* is a mirror used to reflect all that precedes it. The problem is that, quite unlike the Confucius implicit in *Spring and Autumn Annals*, Sima Qian is a teller of tales. He is at his most powerful in those portions of *Records of the Historian* where his passion for narrative is most freely indulged. In this respect, his work shows a much greater affinity for *Zuo Commentary* than for *Spring and Autumn Annals*. It is perhaps this affinity with the more expansive *Zuo Commentary*, and Sima Qian's belief that history should be written in lively detail, that leads him to legitimatize *Zuo Commentary* by claiming, for the first time in the Chinese written record, that it preserves the necessary and orthodox elucidation of *Spring and Autumn Annals*. From such a perspective, the "real" *Spring and Autumn Annals* is not just the terse text of the Master but also the elucidation of a later "True Gentleman," Zuo Qiuming.

Most importantly, Sima Qian regards Confucius as a failure in the immediate political world. Confucius' frustration becomes a series of texts, "Confucian Classics," that will provide a political standard for all generations to come. Chief among those classics, the most political of them all, is a historical text, *Spring and Autumn Annals*, which contains the essence of the Master's doctrine. A highly moralistic and pedantic content, derived largely from a rich exegetical tradition, turns *Spring and Autumn Annals* from "mere" history into a classic. But, as we shall see, although Sima Qian obviously regards this tradition as his precursor, the stories in his history sweep forward with an energy quite different from that of the Confucian moralist. That energy sometimes derives from a very personal source, bursting out from those wellsprings of frustration that Sima Qian believed created all great art, and could not be easily contained along neat "classical" lines. Ultimately, this enormous creative energy subverts the control and restraint required of the second Confucius!

4

Dying Fathers and Living Memories

Confucius loved much—he loved propriety. Zizhang (Sima Qian) loved much—he loved the curious.

—Yang Xiong, *Model Sayings* (*Fa yan*)[1]

As discussed in the previous chapter, when Sima Qian's Confucius wrote *Spring and Autumn Annals*, "he made its language economical and did away with unnecessary redundancy."[2] The Chinese word that I have translated as "economical," *yue* 約, actually means "to bind up, to restrain, to control."[3] Confucius uses the same word when he speaks of the power of ritual "to restrain."[4] Thus, history written in the model of the Master is identified with those forces, ritual chief among them, that contain and restrain. The problem with such an approach to writing history is that excessive economy can result in too many gaps, too much that must be supplied by "textual divination" and "reading between the lines." In his description of *Spring and Autumn Annals* found in the "Preface to the Chronological Table of the Twelve Feudal Lords," Sima Qian acknowledges this problem and claims that the Master's history depends upon oral explication. But the spoken word is unstable, so the "True Gentleman," Zuo Qiuming, wrote *Spring and Autumn Annals of Master Zuo* to fill in the gaps and stabilize later interpretations of the great work of Confucius.

In view of Sima Qian's admiration for *Spring and Autumn Annals* and his desire to become a second Confucius, it is startling to compare *Records of the Historian* to the Master's historical text. Perhaps the best way to approach this issue is through the eyes of one of ancient China's most critical and brilliant readers, the Tang historian Liu Zhiji (661–721). In the first chapter of his *Study of History* (*Shi tong*), an impressive critique of all previous Chinese

71

historiography, Liu identifies six schools of historical writing. The first of these schools is the "School of *Spring and Autumn Annals*" (*chun qiu jia*). Initially, he considered placing Sima Qian's *Records of the Historian* in this school, for the backbone of this text is the "Basic Annals" section, a section that follows the chronological arrangement of *Spring and Autumn Annals*. But ultimately Liu decides that such a classification is inappropriate, for Sima Qian does not use the cherished "praise and blame" style to evaluate historical events, and so "How could his work be compared to *Spring and Autumn Annals*?"[5] In other words, Liu discerns in Sima Qian's text no consistent application of a standard of right and wrong such as he finds for Confucius' work. Consequently, the distinguished author of *A Study of History* establishes a separate "School of *Records of the Historian*," which he lists as the fifth of his six schools. As we might expect, he is highly critical of the work which stands as the head of this school:

> When we inquire into *Records of the Historian*, [we find] the boundaries expansive and the time-frame vast. It is divided into "Annals" and "Traditions" and is spread across "Treatises" and "Charts." Each time it discusses a single government of a clan or a state, much that is similar is far apart. When it tells of a single era of rulers and ministers, interrelated figures are separated. This is a failing of its structure. It assembles what has been recorded, gathers up many old records and, at times, selects miscellaneous reports. Those who read it are made to feel that events are few but there are different accounts of those events, and that words are many and with considerable repetition. This is an annoying aspect of its composition.[6]

Thus, the second Confucius, who describes his forerunner as a master of verbal economy, is criticized in turn for verbosity and "annoying" repetitions. According to Liu Zhiji, *Records of the Historian* errs precisely with regard to those qualities that Sima Qian himself so admired in *Spring and Autumn Annals*! Liu returns to these problems again and again in his study, and he occasionally holds up *Zuo Commentary* as an example of an expansive history that does not contain the tedious redundancy and confusing organization of *Records of the Historian*.[7]

Certainly any reader of *Records of the Historian*, however great an admirer of Sima Qian, must admit that the structure of the text does result in considerable redundancy. Single events are often described in as many as five separate places, and the reader with a desire to reconstruct a complete picture of any one event frequently must turn back and forth between different, sometimes conflicting, accounts. To Sima Qian an event often seems to have no stable essence but exists only in a matrix of varied contexts and different points of view. Thus, an event can be one thing as an element of a biography, but something quite different as an episode in the political life of a state.[8] Anyone fresh from the "uninterrupted flow" (Průšek's *ununterbrochener Fluss*) that characterizes Western narratives—that is, anyone who wants a single, clean narrative line—is bound to find this feature of *Records of the Historian* annoying.[9]

Liu Zhiji attributes the style of *Records of the Historian* to the fact that Sima Qian "gathers up many old records and . . . selects miscellaneous reports." Thus, the organization of Sima Qian's history, which troubled Liu Zhiji and so often troubles the Western reader as well, might result not only from a more contextual notion of an event but also from the more immediate problem of a historian confronting an unprecedented collection of sources. In the words of Grant Hardy, "Ssu-ma Ch'ien's composition of separate, contrasting accounts reflects the ambiguity of his evidence in a way that a neat, unifed narrative would not."[10]

We do not know precisely what historical sources existed during the time of Confucius, undoubtedly much more information was available than is reflected in an elliptical work like *Spring and Autumn Annals*. However, the challenge confronting Sima Qian was certainly of a different order than that confronting the Sage, or, for that matter, the author of *Zuo Commentary*. Sima Qian not only undertook the task of writing the first comprehensive history of the Chinese past, but as a result of the breakdown of central order in the mid-Zhou and the subsequent proliferation of written records, he also was forced to consider and balance much more textual material than historians who preceded him. In an impressive study of Sima Qian's sources, Jin Dejian lists eighty-one different texts mentioned by name in *Records of the Historian*, while another scholar has raised this number to eighty-eight.[11] Even though such numbers are impressive, we are safe to assume that Sima Qian's sources went well beyond those that can be clearly discerned today.

In addition to the problems inherent in the structure of *Records of the Historian*, and the difficulty of dealing with a proliferation of historical sources, Sima Qian's perception of himself as standing in a powerful lineage of frustrated authors assuredly influenced his writing of the past, as well as his writing of himself. As noted previously, time and time again one encounters on the pages of

Records of the Historian a striking resonance between Sima Qian's self-portrayal, as found in his letter to Ren An and in his "Self-Narration," and his portrayal of the prominent figures of the past.

All three of these issues, the structure of *Records of the Historian*, the sources of Sima Qian's narrative, and Sima Qian's own peculiar vision, are encountered in the "Traditions of Wu Zixu" (chapter 66), one of the Han historian's most frequently studied chapters.[12] The significance of this particular chapter for the present study is enhanced by the fact that it is one of the very few "Traditions" chapters dealing with a figure from the Spring and Autumn period. Thus, we can use the narrative of Wu Zixu to examine the problems noted above and also to scrutinize Sima Qian's use of *Zuo Commentary*, the text he himself considered central to understanding *Spring and Autumn Annals*.

Although Wu Zixu, the hero of this "Traditions" chapter, was a contemporary of Confucius, he is in many ways the antithesis of the Master. First of all, he was a man of action who had ample opportunity over many years to serve in the most important governmental positions. Second, unlike Confucius, whose political life was largely characterized by adherence to lofty goals, Wu Zixu's career was organized primarily around personal revenge, self-preservation, and raw power. Finally, his life hardly mirrors Confucian virtues of restraint and moderation—in fact, excess was his undoing. When Wu Zixu's official life floundered, he did not turn to editing and writing, the proper outlet for frustrated scholars like Confucius, but to an escalating confrontation that finally ended with suicide and mutilation.

Despite these striking differences between Confucius and Wu Zixu, Sima Qian held the latter in high esteem. Wu Zixu is praised throughout *Records of the Historian*, and in other early Chinese sources too, as a model minister who dared to speak the truth. Sima Qian describes him as one who "died because he remonstrated" and commends him for being "loyal to his ruler." Indeed, Wu Zixu is listed alongside the legendary Shang minister Bigan as "a man who paid for integrity with his life," and in his final evaluation of this figure, an evaluation to be considered in greater detail later, Sima Qian proclaims Wu Zixu "one who achieved merit and fame."[13]

Although one can find passing references to Wu Zixu in virtually all late Zhou texts, three pre-Han sources are particularly rich in such information: *Zuo Commentary* (hereafter, simply *Zuo*), *Discourses of the States* (hereafter, *Discourses*), and *Spring and Autumn Annals of Master Lü* (hereafter, *Master Lü*). As I have noted earlier, Sima Qian knew and made abundant use of all three of these sources, and he particularly admired *Zuo*, which he regarded as the authoritative companion to *Spring and Autumn Annals*.[14] Since *Zuo*, as we have it today, is a general history structured chronologically around *Annals*, information concerning any particular individual must be gleaned from a whole series of episodes occurring during that individual's lifetime. In the case of Wu Zixu, there are eight critical *Zuo* episodes, a number that can be increased somewhat by including several other episodes that provide useful information on the historical context of Wu Zixu's life. However, I list below only those *Zuo* episodes that mention Wu directly:

1. *Zuo*, Zhao 20 (522 B.C.E.), Yang Bojun edition, pp. 1407–9. Fei Wuji, a minister of Chu, tells the king of Chu that the heir-apparent, Jian, and his grand preceptor, Wu She, are going to revolt. Wu She is arrested and Jian flees to the state of Song. Fei Wuji then informs the king that Wu She has two sons who will seek to avenge their father unless they too are imprisoned. The king sends an emissary to summon the sons and promises that if they come, he will release their father, but that if they do not come, their father will be executed. The eldest brother, Shang, tells the younger brother, Yun (Wu Zixu), that he will return to be with his father even though he knows both of them will be put to death, for such are the demands of filial piety! He instructs Yun to flee so he, at least, may live and gain revenge against the king. Shang returns, and, just as he foresaw, the king executes both him and his father. Yun flees to the state of Wu and immediately urges Wu to attack Chu. However, Prince Guang of Wu, who is a powerful advisor to the king of Wu, understands that Yun is merely trying to gain revenge for his own family and is not necessarily promoting the interests of his newly adopted state. Yun suspects that Prince Guang has political ambitions and introduces a retainer by the name of Zhuan Shezhu, whom he knows will one day prove useful to Guang. Yun then retires from politics and becomes a farmer.

2. *Zuo*, Zhao 30 (512 B.C.E.), p. 1509. Prince Guang uses the retainer Zhuan Shezhu to assassinate the king of Wu and seizes the throne under the name "King Helu" (see Zhao 27, pp. 1482–84). He tells Wu Zixu that he will now follow his earlier counsel and invade Chu, thus giving Wu Zixu an opportunity to return to political life and put his anti-Chu plans into action. The plot against Chu begins to work, for we are told that Chu, as a result of Wu Zixu's policies, "began to be distressed."

3. *Zuo*, Zhao 31 (511 B.C.E.), p. 1512. The state of Wu utilizes

Wu Zixu's anti-Chu military plans and harasses such walled Chu cities as Qian, Liu, and Xuan.

    4. *Zuo,* Ding 4 (506 B.C.E.), p. 1542. With the encouragement of Wu Zixu, now serving as official receptionist (*xingren*), and the grand counselor Pi, and as a result of the ascension of a new and weaker king in Chu (King Zhao), "there is no year when there are no Wu troops in Chu." In this particular year, Wu Zixu wins a series of spectacular military victories and eventually enters the Chu capital of Ying, forcing the king of Chu to flee. At this point in the narrative, a flashback informs the reader that Wu Zixu, before fleeing Chu, was friends with a certain Shen Baoxu. When the former originally fled Chu to escape the punishment that had befallen his father and brother, he told Shen Baoxu, "I must overturn Chu." Shen Baoxu replied, "Do your best at this. If you can overturn it, I must be able to restore it." This same Shen Baoxu, in Chu's hour of desperation, goes to Qin to seek help for Chu against the Wu invasion. Qin provides the requested assistance, and, as a result, Chu begins an offensive that will drive the Wu troops from its state (see Ding 5, p. 1551).

    5. *Zuo,* Ding 14 (496 B.C.E.), pp. 1595–96. The state of Yue inflicts a series of defeats on Wu, and Wu Zixu's patron, King Helu, dies from a wound received in one of these battles. His son and successor, King Fuchai, orders a servant to stand in his courtyard and say to him each time he enters or leaves, "Fuchai, have you forgotten that the king of Yue killed your father?" This is, of course, a constant reminder that he must gain revenge.

    6. *Zuo,* Ai 1 (494 B.C.E.), pp. 1605–7. Wu defeats Yue, and Yue relies upon the Wu minister Pi, whom they have generously bribed, to seek peace. Wu Zixu objects strenuously to making peace with Yue and delivers a long speech to King Fuchai. In this speech, he tells the story of Shao Kang, a successor to the Xia dynasty throne who was able to gain revenge and destroy the state of Guo, which had killed his father and put the rebel Jiao on the throne.[15] If Shao Kang was able to make such a comeback, reasons Wu Zixu, so can Yue. He goes on to note the attempts by King Goujian of Yue to build support among the people in his state, support which will make Yue an even more formidable enemy in the future. Wu Zixu also argues that the geographical proximity of Wu and Yue guarantees that the two will remain rivals, and he says that if Wu continues to strengthen its enemies, Wu will certainly regret this action. King Fuchai refuses to follow Wu Zixu's advice, so Wu Zixu angrily predicts that after twenty years, "Wu will be a pond," and he retires

from public life. The state of Wu does, in fact, make peace with Yue. Wu Zixu's anti-Yue policy has failed.

7. *Zuo*, Ai 11 (484 B.C.E.), pp. 1664–65. The state of Wu is about to attack Qi. Yue has sent gifts to Wu and everyone in Wu is happy about this except Wu Zixu, who inexplicably is active in court life once again. Wu Zixu rebukes the king of Wu, pointing out that Yue is the "illness in Wu's gut" and that Qi is really no threat to Wu at all. Again, his advice is rejected. Wu Zixu is then sent as an emissary to Qi, where he entrusts his son for safekeeping to an acquaintance. When Wu Zixu returns from Qi, the king hears from Pi that Wu Zixu has left his son there. Assuming that Wu Zixu has somehow been disloyal, the king sends him a sword with which to commit suicide. Just before Wu Zixu kills himself, he says, "Plant *jia* trees on my grave, *jia* can be used as lumber. Wu, I expect, will perish. In three years it will start to weaken! For the replete to be destroyed is the way of heaven."[16]

8. *Zuo*, Ai 22 (473 B.C.E.), p. 1719. In fulfillment of Wu Zixu's predictions, Yue does indeed destroy Wu. King Fuchai, unwilling to serve his conqueror, hangs himself.

Thus, *Zuo* presents Wu Zixu as a Chu expatriate who became a powerful political figure in the state of Wu, and who argues initially for an anti-Chu policy and subsequently for an anti-Yue policy. His hate for Chu is, of course, motivated by a wish to avenge the deaths of his father and older brother. The anti-Chu stage of his political career culminates with Wu's conquest of the Chu capital of Ying, but in *Zuo* nothing is said of his personal involvement in the conquest nor of his reaction to the defeat of his enemies. We are told only that Wu Zixu's former friend, Shen Baoxu, plays a key role in reviving Chu power. With Yue's defeat of Wu, and the death of King Helu, Wu Zixu urges military action against Yue. Such an action could also be interpreted as motivated by a desire for revenge, this time for his patron, King Helu. Of course, Helu's own son Fuchai should carry the burden of revenge. But Fuchai soon abandons his initial resolve, makes peace with Yue, and turns his attention to attacking the state of Qi to the north. Fuchai ignores Wu Zixu's advice, advice history will prove to be wise, and finally orders Wu Zixu to commit suicide. Wu Zixu predicts Wu's fall before he dies, and those predictions come true with the destruction of Wu in 473 B.C.E. and the suicide of King Fuchai.

If we regard these few episodes, assembled from nearly fifty years of *Zuo* entries, as a fragmentary biography, then the tantalizing gaps in the story of Wu Zixu invite further development. The trend, as we shall see from the accounts found in later texts, is toward a more coherent "romance" of Wu Zixu, a process that will go on well beyond Sima Qian and lead through such works as the *Book of the Culmination of Yue* (*Yue jue shu*) and the *Spring and Autumn Annals of Wu and Yue* (*Wu Yue chun qiu*) to a now famous Tang dynasty "transformation text" (*bianwen*).[17]

As noted above, *Discourses* provides a second early source of material on Wu Zixu. By considering the contribution of *Discourses* to the Wu Zixu legend after having already examined *Zuo*, I do not necessarily imply that this is the correct chronological sequence of these two sources. While there is strong evidence that *Discourses* and *Zuo* are not by the same author, as both Sima Qian and Ban Gu seem to have believed, the precise temporal relationship between these two texts remains a difficult and controversial question. I discuss the *Zuo* accounts before those of *Discourses* only because Sima Qian regards *Zuo* as the definitive record of the early oral interpretation of *Spring and Autumn Annals*, and my purpose here is to consider the way in which Sima Qian used and shaped his sources, particularly those he most esteemed.[18] Still, that Sima Qian knew *Discourses* and frequently used it in his history is certain.[19]

"The Discourses of Wu," the section of *Discourses* containing information on Wu Zixu, covers only the twenty-two years from King Fuchai's attack on Yue in 494 B.C.E. to Yue's final conquest of Wu in 473 B.C.E. Consequently, Wu Zixu's years of greatest political success, his years serving King Helu, are not covered in this text. Instead, the narrative begins with Wu Zixu's attempt to dissuade King Fuchai from concluding an alliance with Yue. True to the general style of *Discourses*, the episodes concerning Wu Zixu consist largely of speeches. These either add to or differ from the *Zuo* passages on Wu Zixu in the following ways:

1. Wu Zixu's first speech to King Fuchai, corresponding to *Zuo* episode six above, does not allude to Shao Kang nor to any other historical precedents. Instead, he simply warns Fuchai not to trust Yue's policy of appeasement. Yue's plan, as Wu Zixu describes it, is to encourage Wu to grow complacent while they, Yue, use the time to build additional military strength.[20]

2. Wu Zixu's second speech, corresponding to the speech in *Zuo* episode seven above, is considerably longer in *Discourses* and recounts the sad story of Duke Ling of Chu (r. 539–527 B.C.E.), whose military ambitions exhausted his people and finally precipitated a revolt. Duke Ling is forsaken by all, as Wu Zixu tells the

story, and in lonely despair hangs himself. Wu Zixu goes on to say that the people of Wu, like those of Chu under Duke Ling, are exhausted and that "the people of Yue certainly will come and attack us."[21]

3. After the state of Wu's defeat of Qi, King Fuchai reproaches Wu Zixu. However, there is no mention of Wu's entrusting his son to a friend (as in *Zuo* episode seven above) and Fuchai neither sends a sword nor orders Wu Zixu's suicide.[22]

4. Wu Zixu responds to King Fuchai's reproach with a speech that has no *Zuo* equivalent. He argues that Fuchai's success in Qi has actually brought the state of Wu closer to disaster. He concludes the speech by announcing his intention to commit suicide, for he cannot bear "to see the king made a captive of Yue." Just before dying, Wu Zixu announces, quite in contrast to his final statement in *Zuo*, "Hang my eyes from the East Gate so that I might see Yue enter and Wu fall!" The king is angry at this and says, "I will not let the minister be able to see anything;" then, wrapping Wu Zixu's corpse in a leather bag, he throws it into a river.[23]

5. After Yue's final defeat of Wu, a defeat Wu Zixu predicted, King Fuchai hangs himself. But before he dies, he announces, "If the dead are without consciousness, then it is over! If they have consciousness, with what face will I look upon Yun (Wu Zixu)!"[24]

Thus, *Discourses* adds to our story of Wu Zixu in at least two significant ways: first, the account of Duke Ling foreshadows the eventual death of the powerless Fuchai; and second, the deaths of the two antagonists, Wu Zixu and Fuchai, are much more dramatic. Wu Zixu says nothing in *Discourses* about planting *jia* trees on his grave. Instead, he asks that his eyes be dug out and suspended on the east gate of the Wu capital, so that he may "see" the dire event he has predicted. Fuchai makes sure that Wu Zixu will see nothing by sealing his corpse in a bag and throwing it into a river. Fuchai, on the other hand, dies with the worry that he will see Wu Zixu in the underworld. These two final scenes, as they appear in *Discourses*, constitute a complementary pair and introduce a new and important theme into our story. One antagonist, Wu Zixu, wants to see so as to be vindicated, and the other, Fuchai, does not want to see so as to avoid shame. However, the first will not see; his dead eyes are tightly wrapped with his body in a leather bag, which is then floated in a river. The second, who does not want to see, may or may not see, depending upon whether the dead have consciousness. The issue of seeing versus not seeing, first encountered in *Discourses* as part of the textual history of the Wu Zixu story, will be inherited and developed in Sima Qian's account.

The third important pre-Han source for information concerning Wu Zixu is *Master Lü*. This work is unique among pre-Han texts both because it can be dated with precision and also because it has been transmitted to the present time with very little textual corruption. *Master Lü* was compiled under the patronage of Lü Buwei, who served King Zheng of Qin (later known as the First Qin Emperor) from 247 to 237 B.C.E.. A "postface" appearing at the end of the "Twelve Chronologies," the first major division of the text, can be dated to 241 B.C.E.[25] Liang Qichao's (1873–1929) estimate of the text's authenticity, although perhaps slightly exaggerated, is essentially accurate: "This book, through the course of two thousand years, has had no deletions nor corruptions. Moreover, it has the excellent commentary of Gao You. Truly it is the most perfect and easily read work among the ancient books."[26]

Master Lü, as we have seen in the previous chapter, was a text Sima Qian admired and recognized as derived from Confucius' *Spring and Autumn Annals*. Despite the fact that Sima Qian categorizes the work with other historical sources, *Master Lü* is more a work of philosophy than of history and has been traditionally classified by Chinese bibliographers as belonging to the "Eclectic School" (*zajia*).[27] However, the text does include numerous historical episodes, usually used to illustrate particular philosophical arguments, and four of those episodes concern Wu Zixu.

The Wu Zixu episodes found in *Master Lü*, more clearly than anything we have seen thus far, bear the stamp of a living story tradition, a tradition that Henri Maspero describes as a *"roman."* Obviously, this engaging figure had caught the popular imagination and was becoming the stuff of the ever expanding legend that David Johnson has documented so thoroughly. Evidence of this trend can be seen, I believe, in each of the four passages from *Master Lü* summarized below:

1. After Wu Zixu leaves Chu (no explanation of his departure appears here), he wanders from state to state trying to determine which state to serve. He ultimately decides to serve Wu but must travel back through his native state of Chu, where he is a wanted man. He meets a fisherman in Chu who ferries him across the Yangtze. Wu Zixu wants to repay the fisherman for his help by giving him a treasured sword, but the fisherman refuses the gift and says that if he had wanted to obtain rewards, he could have acquired much more than the value of the sword simply by turning Wu Zixu

over to the Chu authorities. Thereafter, every time Wu Zixu eats, he offers a sacrifice and a prayer on behalf of the benevolent fisherman.[28]

2. Wu Zixu, trying to gain a patron in the state of Wu, is introduced to Prince Guang (see *Zuo* episode one above). However, Guang finds Wu Zixu so ugly that he refuses to listen to him. Wu Zixu agrees to speak to Guang from behind a curtain, and Guang is so impressed by Wu Zixu's wisdom that he accepts his service. Later, with Wu Zixu's assistance, Guang becomes king of Wu and wins a great military victory over Chu. Wu Zixu, having re-entered Chu with the victorious army, "personally shot an arrow at the king's palace and whipped the tomb of King Ping of Chu with three hundred strokes."[29]

3. The king of Wu plans to give aid to the state of Yue. Wu Zixu objects and argues that the two countries are contiguous and are certain to be enemies: "If it is not Wu that destroys Yue, then Yue will certainly destroy Wu." Fuchai, The king of Wu, does not accept Wu Zixu's advice and sends aid.[30]

4. King Fuchai is about to attack Qi. Wu Zixu argues that Yue is the real threat. Qi is far away, and its language and customs differ from those of Wu, while Yue shares a border with Wu, and the languages and customs of the two states are similar. To go to war with Qi instead of Yue, says Wu Zixu, is like "fearing the tiger but stabbing at the cub." Fuchai refuses to heed Wu Zixu's advice and attacks Qi. He wins a great victory and, upon returning, is going to punish Wu Zixu. Wu Zixu commits suicide; but just before he dies, he says, "Would that I could have a single eye in order to see the people of Yue enter Wu." Fuchai consequently gouges out the eyes of Wu Zixu's corpse, hangs them from the east gate, and says, "How will you see the people of Yue enter my state!" Fuchai then throws Wu Zixu's remains into a river. Yue does, in fact, conquer Wu, and Fuchai is captured. Just before Fuchai dies (and we are not told in this account whether it is a suicide or an execution) he says, "If the dead have consciousness, how will I have the face to look upon Zixu in the world below!" To avoid this possibility, Fuchai "pulled a hood over his face and died."[31]

These episodes from *Master Lü* significantly add to the story of Wu Zixu as found in *Zuo* and *Discourses*. Wu Zixu's search for a suitable lord and his ultimate introduction to Guang are the subjects of two episodes, and both of these contain familiar folklore elements. Episode one tells of an encounter with a fisherman, who ferries Wu Zixu to safety and refuses any reward. Such encounters with virtuous or wise fisherman are frequent in ancient Chinese texts, and the protection of such a figure bequeaths a kind of legitimacy upon Wu Zixu and his mission.[32] Episode two portrays Wu Zixu as ugly but wise, a theme common in folklore tales but not pursued in later accounts of Wu Zixu.[33]

Perhaps the most significant addition provided by the episodes above, and one that becomes critical in Sima Qian's account, is the more detailed explanation of how Wu Zixu avenged King Ping's execution of his father and older brother. The whole point of Wu Zixu's flight from Chu, it will be remembered, was to stay alive and gain revenge against King Ping. However, in neither *Zuo* nor *Discourses* is there any indication of how he obtained his reprisal apart from the implication that he participated, in some way, in the conquest of the Chu capital. Here we are told that Wu Zixu, after entering the capital, first shot an arrow at the king's palace, perhaps symbolic of his wish to kill the former king who once lived there, and then whipped King Ping's tomb with three hundred strokes, a number sufficient to kill a living man and adequate, one might assume, to vex the spirit of a dead one.

The death of Wu Zixu, as narrated in *Master Lü*, and summarized in episode four above, is quite unlike anything we have seen before.[34] It is Fuchai who angrily gouges out Wu Zixu's eyes and hangs them on the east gate to prove to Wu Zixu that his prediction will not come true. In *Discourses*, Wu Zixu himself wants his eyes gouged out and the whole point of Fuchai's sealing his corpse in a leather bag is to frustrate Wu Zixu's wish. The irony of the account in episode four above is that Fuchai gives Wu Zixu's eyes a chance to see. And because they see what Fuchai was sure they would not see, he himself must blind his own eyes so that he will not see what he fears he might see—Wu Zixu in the hereafter!

Our survey of information on Wu Zixu could be prolonged. Texts other than those considered above also contain references to this romantic figure.[35] But our purpose here is not to trace the rise of a Wu Zixu legend so much as to consider the way Sima Qian constructed his own account of Wu Zixu from the variety of sometimes contradictory sources before him. It is particularly important, as I have noted before, to consider Sima Qian's use of *Zuo* as a "paradigmatic history" and the definitive interpretation of Confucius' sacred *Spring and Autumn Annals*.

When we turn to *Records of the Historian*, we discover that information on Wu Zixu appears in at least five different chapters, with considerable repetition in these separate accounts. Thus, this particular case clearly illustrates the "weakness" Liu Zhiji found in

Sima Qian's work: "Those who read it are made to feel that events are few but that there are different accounts of those events."[36] Sima Qian's fullest and most important account, for our purposes here, is the "Traditions of Wu Zixu" (chapter 66). Unlike the other sections of *Records of the Historian* that concern this historical figure, it can be read as a single narrative in which the primary focus remains firmly fixed upon Wu Zixu throughout. However, we begin our consideration of Wu Zixu in *Records of the Historian* with those sections that mention him as a secondary topic and will then turn to the richer account found in "Traditions" (chapter 66).

The first three of the secondary accounts of Wu Zixu appear in the "Hereditary Household" chapters and consequently focus upon events of direct significance to particular feudal states. Since almost all of Wu Zixu's political career was spent in Wu, and since his involvement there was of critical importance to the government, the "Hereditary Household of Wu Taibo" (chapter 31) contains a considerable amount of information that usually parallels, but occasionally goes beyond, the "Traditions" chapter.[37] The "Hereditary Household of Chu" contains the stories of the execution of Wu Zixu's father and brother in the state of Chu, of Wu Zixu's subsequent flight from the state, and of his participation in the Wu conquest of the Chu capital in 506 B.C.E.[38] The "Hereditary Household of King Goujian of Yue" recounts Wu Zixu's unsuccessful attempts to persuade King Fuchai of Wu to attack Yue and also tells of Wu Zixu's demise.[39] Finally, Wu Zixu appears briefly in the "Traditions of the Assassins," where he introduces Zhuan Zhu to Prince Guang and thereby creates the circumstances where Prince Guang can use this knight-errant to kill King Liao and succeed to the throne as King Helu.[40]

The "Traditions of Wu Zixu," as Sima Qian constructs it, deals with at least two issues of profound and personal interest to the Han historian: first, what is the responsibility of a son to his father, and how is that responsibility to be balanced against cultural demands for moderation and control; and second, how do the failed and the rejected find comfort at the moment of death in a future from which they will be absent. The theme of responsibility to one's father is introduced in the very first passage of the "Traditions of Wu Zixu." The textual antecedent for this story is apparently *Zuo* episode one above. However, before examining Sima Qian's adaptation of this particular episode, it is useful to digress briefly and consider the way in which Sima Qian has generally utilized *Zuo Commentary*, his prestigious antecedent.

Sima Qian's reliance upon *Zuo* is especially obvious in the

"Hereditary Household" and "Basic Annals" sections of his history, for large segments of these sections deal specifically with the period of time *Zuo* covers, the Spring and Autumn period. By way of contrast, only the first five of the "Traditions" chapters concern figures from this period, and only the "Traditions of Wu Zixu," the chapter under consideration here, relies substantially upon *Zuo*.[41] In a recent study of Sima Qian's use of *Zuo* narratives, Gu Lisan notes that the general tendency in *Records of the Historian* is to abbreviate the earlier source. Specifically, Sima Qian (1) deletes or simplifies the *Zuo*'s more ornate language, (2) removes information that is not relevant to the central historical narrative, particularly long *Zuo* passages dealing with such topics as ritual and warfare, and (3) reduces information concerning states not of major importance during the Spring and Autumn period (particularly, states not considered significant enough to warrant a separate "Hereditary Households" chapter). Sima Qian expands on a *Zuo* narrative only in a few cases and usually only when full understanding of the historical "facts" requires expansion.[42]

Gu Lisan believes that the differences in these two ancient histories can be understood if one realizes that *Zuo* is primarily concerned with explicating a classic, and that the purpose of that classic, *Spring and Autumn Annals*, is to "propagate the teaching of ritual." *Records of the Historian*, by way of contrast, "takes historical facts as its central focus."[43] Such an argument is problematic with regard both to *Zuo* and to *Records of the Historian*. As noted earlier, some question exists as to whether *Zuo* originally was written as a commentary, and, furthermore, *Records of the Historian* assuredly is shaped by forces other than "historical facts."[44] Nevertheless, Gu Lisan is correct in perceiving a fundamental difference in the perspective of the two texts, a subject to which we will return.

Gu Lisan's study is important here because it highlights the unusual nature of the first episode of the "Traditions of Wu Zixu," where Sima Qian's account is rather more expansive than that found in *Zuo*. Moreover, this particular expansion cannot be explained by a need "to clarify historical facts." Indeed, Gu Lisan himself recognizes the unusual status of this story as it is adapted in *Records of the Historian* and suggests, quite correctly I believe, that Sima Qian's treatment of Wu Zixu is shaped by the Gentleman Grand Astrologer's own peculiar situation.[45]

To understand how Sima Qian reshaped this particular *Zuo* story, we turn to the account in question.[46] In 521 B.C.E., King Ping of Chu appointed a certain Wu She to act as tutor to the prince regent. In a court struggle over the succession, the heir-apparent, named Jian, is forced to flee the state. Wu She, the tutor, is then slandered by a rival named Wu Ji and imprisoned by the king. Wu She has two sons who temporarily reside in the state of Wu. The *Zuo* account continues our story as follows:

> Wu Ji said, "She's sons are talented. If they are in Wu, they assuredly will trouble the state of Ch'u. Why not summon them on the pretext of pardoning their father? They are humane and certainly will come. If we do not do this, they will bring trouble."
>
> The king sent someone to summon them, saying, "If you come, I will pardon your father."
>
> Shang, the Lord of Tang [the older of the brothers], said to his younger brother [Wu Yun or Wu Zixu], "You go to Wu. I will return and die. My wisdom is not equal to yours. I can die, and you can avenge us. After hearing the order that he will pardon father, I must go. But when a parent is slaughtered, one must avenge him. To run toward death in order to gain pardon for a father is filial. To weigh results in order to act is humaneness. To choose duty and go forth is wisdom. To know one will die and not flee is courage. Father cannot be abandoned, but our name cannot be cast aside. Do your best! For each one to follow his separate way is best."[47]
>
> Wu Shang returned. When Wu She heard Yun was not coming, he said, "The ruler and nobles of Chu, I expect, will take their meals late!"[48]
>
> The people of Chu killed them both.[49]

Sima Qian's version of this same story, as it appears in the "Traditions of Wu Zixu," is as follows:

> Wu Ji said to King Ping, "Wu She has two sons who are both virtuous. If we do not execute them, they will cause trouble for Chu. We can take their father as a hostage and summon them. If we don't do this, they will create a disaster for Chu."
>
> The king sent an emissary to say to Wu She, "If we can cause your two sons to come, then you will live. If we cannot, then you will die."
>
> Wu She said, "Shang, as a person, is humane! If you summon him, he assuredly will come. Yun, as a person, is stubborn and can bear shame. He is capable of completing a great affair. When he sees that

if he comes we will all be seized together, then he certainly will not come."

But the king did not listen and sent a person to summon the two sons, saying, "If you come, I will allow your father to live. If you do not come, I will kill She."

Wu Shang wanted to go, but Yun said, "Chu has summoned us, we two brothers, not because they wish our father to live, but because they fear that if we escape, we will bring calamity later. Therefore, they have taken our father as hostage and have deceitfully summoned us. When the two of us arrive, father and sons will die together. How will that benefit our father's death? By going we will only insure that our enemies will not be avenged. It would be better to flee to another state and utilize its power in order to wipe away our father's shame. To perish together is of no use!"

Wu Shang said, "I know that by going I will not, in the end, save father's life. But I would hate the idea that my father had summoned me in order to seek his own life and I had not gone. If later on we do not wipe away the shame, in the end we will be ridiculed by the people of the empire!" Then he said to Yun, "You can indeed depart. You can avenge the enemies of your father and his son. I will return and die."

. . . When Wu Shang reached Chu, Chu killed She and Shang together.[50]

In the *Zuo* version cited above, the father says nothing. The older brother, having received the summons, lectures his younger brother on the proper course of action. The younger brother, in accord with the Confucian principle of "fraternal respect" (*ti*), silently complies. In Sima Qian's version, the father anticipates the reactions of his sons: he knows that Shang will come to his side and that Yun will not. The narrator here presents both the father and his sons as distinct personalities. In fact, as Sima Qian tells the story, the younger brother, Wu Zixu (Yun), does most of the talking and proposes flight. This not only varies from the *Zuo* version but also from a second account presented in *Records of the Historian* itself. That account, found in the "Hereditary Household of Chu," is a splendid example of a "different version" within *Records of the Historian*, the very feature of Sima Qian's text that Liu Zhiji found so distressing. It reads as follows:

Wu Ji said, "Wu She has two sons. If we do not kill them, they will make a calamity for our state. Why not summon them on the pretext of pardoning their father? They certainly will come."

Thereupon the king sent an emissary to tell Wu She that if he could make his two sons come, he would live. If he could not make them come, he would die. She said, "Shang will come. Xu will not come."

The king said, "Why?"

She said, "Shang, as a person, is upright and will die for honor; he is kind, filial and humane. When he hears that being summoned will gain his father's pardon, he will certainly come, and will not be concerned that he will die. Xu, as a person, is wise and fond of schemes; he is courageous and is arrogant about his achievements. If he knows that by coming he must die, he certainly will not come. Thus, the one who will make trouble for the state of Chu certainly is this son."

Thereupon, the king sent someone to summon him, saying, "If you come, I will pardon your father."

Wu Shang told Wu Zixu, "To hear father will be pardoned and neither of us hasten there is unfilial. For father to be slain and neither of us gain revenge is to be without schemes. To measure abilities and assume tasks is wise. You should act! I should return and die!"

Wu Shang, thereupon, went back. . . . The people of Ch'u consequently killed Wu She and Shang.[51]

It is tempting to consider this second account as only an abbreviated version of the basic text found in the "Traditions," but the speech of Wu She describing his sons and predicting their reactions is more expansive than in Sima Qian's other account. I cannot avoid the impression that Sima Qian is either using variant accounts of the story, accounts no longer extant, or that in this case, and perhaps elsewhere too, he creates the dialogues and speeches so essential to his narrative style without any compulsion to examine how he might have created the same dialogues or speeches elsewhere.[52]

As noted above, the speech of the father, which Sima Qian gives in two versions, has no analogue in *Zuo*, where Wu She remains silent. Words spoken by a father facing death, as we have already seen, hold a special interest for Sima Qian. And in this case, the father gives a highly perceptive appraisal of his sons—he accurately assesses their personalities and predicts how each will react to a summons. Wu Zixu's speech, delivered after he and his brother have been called to their father's side, appears neither in the *Zuo* nor in the "Hereditary Household of Chu" versions. Wu Zixu, of course, is the protagonist of the "Traditions," so it is quite natural to establish his presence from the outset as the dominant character of the narrative. But, in addition to this consideration, his strong presence and compelling speech create a tension absent from the other two versions. Far from being a passive listener to an older brother's wise words, Wu Zixu suggests that both of them flee. His brother's response thus becomes a compromise between two opposing desires and fulfills the prediction of their father. The hinge of the decision in Sima Qian's account is not, like in *Zuo*, so much each brother's respective virtues, and an older brother's wise perception of those virtues, as it is is an attempt to resolve a dilemma: a filial son obeys his father, he must answer the summons and die; but a filial son avenges his father, he must reject the summons and live on to act! The sons can be filial and meet both requirements, but only *as a team* and not as individuals. Shang fulfills his half of the obligation forthwith, and, in fulfilling that obligation, is executed, achieving his appropriate "honor" and disappearing from the remainder of the narrative.

Sima Qian's story turns to the son who "can bear shame," who defers honor until he can complete his portion of the filial obligation. Wu Zixu lives beyond the death that, from at least one point of view, he should have suffered. Constantly looking toward the future for vindication, he is described as a master of "plots." Moreover, his plots construct *the plot*, for there can be no story without his presence. The reader of the "Traditions of Wu Zixu" also looks to the future and reads on toward the remaining son's inevitable attempt at revenge and the resolution revenge will bring. Thus, the second theme, the theme of looking to and finding fulfillment in the future, enters the narrative and intertwines with the theme of filial responsibility. Wu Zixu, a temporary refugee from death, must justify his existence by projecting into the future. His plot must have the right outcome or he can enjoy no comfort. At this point Sima Qian's personal involvement in his narrative becomes even more apparent. He, too, is a refugee of death who must defer honor into the future, but his vindication, as a man of the written word, will be gained in a less dramatic and less violent fashion.

The next portion of the "Traditions" account of Wu Zixu alternates between following *Zuo* and *Master Lü*. First, Sima Qian includes the episode of the fisherman, a story that is found only in *Master Lü* and confers moral legitimacy upon the hero, but he does not go so far as to say, after *Master Lü*, that Wu Zixu never ate again without offering a prayer and a sacrifice to the benevolent fisherman. With the help of the fisherman, Wu Zixu reaches Wu. Sima

Qian appears to follow *Zuo* as he describes Wu Zixu's immediate attempt to convince the king of Wu to attack Chu. Prince Guang dissuades the king from such a course by noting that Wu Zixu "desires thereby to gain revenge against his own enemy." By following this version, and not the strange *Master Lü* story of Wu Zixu's extreme ugliness, Sima Qian keeps the reader's focus on the central issue—revenge. Nevertheless, Wu Zixu appears, at this stage of the narrative, to be frustrated politically. He withdraws "to plow in the countryside," and, in addition, King Ping of Chu, the murderer of his father and brother, dies a natural death, a fact not mentioned in "Traditions" but duly noted in the "Hereditary Household of Chu." However, as we have seen, Wu Zixu is a creator of plots who has an astonishing ability to plan for the future. He already had foreseen Prince Guang's political ambitions and, before going into retirement, introduces a courageous man named Zhuan Zhu into Guang's service. Indeed, it is Zhuan Zhu, more fully immortalized in the "Traditions of the Assassins" (chapter 86), who slays King Liao of Wu and helps Prince Guang to seize the throne as King Helu. This tumultuous event, which our hero foresees and which takes place while he is quietly plowing fields in retirement, sets the stage for Wu Zixu's return to power. King Helu not only brings Wu Zixu back to court, but in Sima Qian's account, as well as in that of *Zuo*, he immediately begins to use Wu Zixu's advice and adopts an anti-Chu policy.

After several conflict-filled years, which *Records of the Historian* covers in a few hundred characters, the armies of Wu enter the Chu capital of Ying and force King Zhao to flee. As noted earlier, the *Zuo* account of this episode, although implying Wu Zixu's involvement in the critical battle, neither highlights that involvement nor explains how he gained personal revenge against the state that had killed his father and brother. *Zuo* does, however, introduce Shen Baoxu, a former friend of Wu Zixu, and links the eventual recovery of Chu to Shen's valiant action:

> Formerly, Wu Yun was friends with Shen Baoxu. When he fled, he told Shen Baoxu, "I must overturn the state of Chu."
>
> Shen Baoxu said, "Do your best. If you overturn it, then I must be able to restore it!"
>
> When King Zhao was in Sui [where he had fled], Shen Baoxu went to Qin and begged for troops, saying, "Wu's [like] a great pig or a long snake. They will repeatedly eat away at the states above them. And their cruelty has begun with Chu."[53]

Initially Qin refuses to provide aid to Chu, but after Shen Baoxu cries day and night for seven days, "not even drinking a spoonful of water," Qin is moved by his devotion and sends troops. Thus, in the *Zuo* account, the theme of revenge is subordinated to the compelling tale of Shen Baoxu's loyalty to his state and the suasive power of that loyalty. This, I believe, is one example of how the *Zuo*'s overriding moral concerns shape its narratives and influence plot "choices."

As we have seen, a *Master Lü* tale states that Wu Zixu gained revenge by shooting an arrow at the palace of the king of Chu and whipping the tomb of the former King Ping. This act of personal revenge, not narrated in *Zuo*, now appears as a critical episode in *Records of the Historian* and is cleverly integrated with the *Zuo* story of Shen Baoxu. But in the "Traditions," Wu Zixu's action is much more shocking than in any earlier source:

> Before all this started, Wu Yun was friends with Shen Baoxu. When Yun fled, he told Shen Baoxu, "I must overturn Chu."
>
> Baoxu said, "I must preserve it."
>
> At the time Wu's troops entered Ying, Wu Zixu sought for King Zhao, but he could not find him. So he dug up the tomb of King Ping of Chu, took out his corpse and beat it with three hundred strokes.
>
> Shen Baoxu had fled into the mountains. He sent someone to say [to Wu Zixu]: "How could your revenge against an enemy be so extreme! I have heard that when people are numerous, they can overcome heaven. But heaven, once determined, also can break a man. Now, you formerly were a subject of King Ping. You faced the north and served him. Now you go so far as to insult a dead man! How could this not be the epitome of unrighteousness?"
>
> Wu Zixu said, "Apologize to Shen Baoxu, saying, 'The day is late, and my road long. And so I act perversely!' "
>
> Thereupon, Shen Baoxu fled to Qin and, reporting the emergency, requested assistance from Qin. Qin would not agree. Baoxu stood in the court of Qin crying day and night. This went on for seven days and nights without ceasing. Duke Ai of Qin pitied him and said, "Though Chu is without principles, if it has ministers like this, can we not preserve it?" He then sent five hundred chariots to save Chu.[54]

Shen Baoxu's credibility as a loyal, upright minister is explicitly established in this passage. Moreover, he is shocked at his former friend's extreme behavior. Plainly, by exhuming the body of a man ten years dead and beating it, Wu Zixu has gone too far. Sima Qian not only reports this macabre event here but in the "Hereditary Household of Wu Taibo" as well.[55] Commentators, who are chiefly concerned with "historical accuracy" and not with literary effect, have noted that earlier accounts only refer to beating the tomb, and they consequently question the historicity of Sima Qian's version.[56]

Our purpose here is not to reconstruct a past. From a literary point of view, the desecration of King Ping's corpse is the center of the chapter and marks a turning point in the plot. Wu Zixu's success culminates with this event and his decline begins, a decline that is to end with still another macabre episode. While Sima Qian generally portrays Wu Zixu sympathetically, he reveals him here as a man who has gone too far.[57] Driven by an extreme passion for vengeance, Wu Zixu loses his foresight and is blind to the consequences of his immoderate behavior. It is Shen Baoxu, rather than Wu Zixu, who sees and hints that heaven will now destroy his former friend. Too fanatical in pursuing revenge, Wu Zixu becomes the antithesis of the dominant figure of the second half of the "Traditions of Wu Zixu," King Fuchai, who will not go far enough in avenging his father.[58]

Wu's military supremacy over Chu is short-lived. It almost seems in the "Traditions" account that once Wu Zixu, who provokes Wu's anti-Chu policy, has gained his private revenge, the state of Wu's interests turn in other directions. Wu's chief political problem comes from neighboring Yue, which Wu attacks in 496 B.C.E. King Goujian of Yue not only defeats Wu in this battle, but King Helu, Wu Zixu's patron, is also wounded and eventually dies. On his deathbed, King Helu summons heir-apparent Fuchai and says, "Will you forget that Goujian killed your father?" Fuchai responds, "I dare not forget."[59] This episode, as we have seen, is found in *Zuo*, where it further states that Fuchai had a servant remind him at each coming and going of his promise to avenge his father.

King Fuchai initially follows his promise to his father. Two years after Helu's death, he defeats Yue at Fujiu.[60] Yue, however, immediately adopts a conciliatory policy towards Wu. By manipulating Bo Pi, the grand councilor of Wu, Yue manages to pacify Wu and buy time in which to enhance its own military strength. Blinded by Yue's deceitful pursuit of peace, Fuchai gradually turns away from Yue to pursue military ambitions to the north.

Most of the remainder of the "Traditions" account concerns

Wu Zixu's futile attempts to convince King Fuchai that Yue, not the states to the north, is his real enemy. Sima Qian reports three instances where Wu Zixu protests King Fuchai's policies. The first is a short passage in which Wu Zixu simply warns that "The king of Yue, as a person, is able to bear difficulty . . . if you do not destroy him, later you will certainly regret it."[61] Interestingly, this first speech appears at considerable length in the "Hereditary Household of Wu Taibo," and the version Sima Qian presents there is obviously based upon *Zuo* (episode six above). This important speech also deals with the topic of a son's revenge for the unjust death of his father, and it seems curious, at first glance, that Sima Qian chooses to report it in greater detail elsewhere than in the "Traditions" chapter. However, in the "Traditions," Sima Qian is concerned largely with Wu Zixu's growing frustration and not with the precise political details of his arguments.[62]

Wu Zixu's second speech is provoked by Wu's expedition against Qi in the north. The speech is very loosely based upon *Zuo* (episode seven) and takes as its central motif that "Yue is a sickness in our gut."[63] Most of the speech is a warning that Goujian, while assuming the pose of a man of peace, is really building support in his own state which will eventually be turned against Wu.

Fuchai continues his anti-Qi policy and provokes Wu Zixu's third rebuke. This speech has no close analogue in either *Zuo* or *Discourses* but appears to be loosely abbreviated from a speech in *Master Lü* (episode four above). Wu Zixu describes Qi as "rocky fields that are of no use." But rather than going on, as in *Master Lü*, to argue that the similarity of Wu and Yue with regard to language and customs makes them natural enemies, Wu Zixu quotes the "Announcement of Pan Geng" to the effect that a ruler should leave no remnants of enemies or they will come back to plague him.[64] This, Wu Zixu, a remnant of a Chu "enemy," should know from personal experience.

All three of these speeches could have been expanded considerably by reference to earlier sources, and one of them, as we have seen, appears in a vastly longer version elsewhere in *Records of the Historian*. But Wu Zixu, in neither *Zuo*, *Discourses*, nor *Master Lü*, gives more than two speeches before the fateful day of his death. The "Traditions," as noted here, contains three speeches, all of them brief. Sima Qian's emphasis is not so much on the persuasive rhetoric of Wu Zixu's oratory, which can be seen more explicitly in earlier sources, but rather on Wu Zixu's building frustration in the face of Fuchai's "stupid" foreign policy and lack of filial regard for his dead father. Finally, Wu Zixu loses hope, entrusts his son to a friend in Qi, and says, "I have remonstrated with the king several times, but it was no use. Now I see that Wu will fall!"[65]

In this instance, however, Wu Zixu will not live to see the outcome he predicts. His death, as we have already seen, is reported quite differently in the three antecedent texts discussed above. To review, in the *Zuo* account, King Fuchai orders him to commit suicide, and Wu Zixu, before complying, asks that *jia* trees be planted on his grave. As commentators explain, *jia* wood is good for coffins and surely a defeated Wu will need coffins! In *Discourses*, Wu Zixu's suicide is not ordered, he simply "cannot bear to see King Fuchai taken captive." Then, strangely, he asks that his eyes be suspended on the gate so he can see the troops of Yue enter. Thus, in the *Discourses* account, it seems that Wu Zixu both wants and does not want to see! *Master Lü* says Wu Zixu was ordered to commit suicide and dies wishing he could see into the future when his prediction would be fulfilled. Furthermore, it is King Fuchai, in an act of spite, who puts Wu Zixu's eyes on the gate where he is confident they will not see Yue soldiers enter his state. Obviously, the death of Wu Zixu had become one of the most flexible parts of the Wu Zixu romance.

In Sima Qian's version, the villainous grand councilor Bo Pi first delivers a speech to King Fuchai persuading him that Wu Zixu is a disloyal obstructionist. Then,

> The king of Wu [Fuchai] . . . sent a messenger to present Wu Zixu with a *shulü* sword and say, "You may use this to die!"[66]

> Wu Zixu looked towards heaven and sighed, "Alas! The slandering minister Pi brings disorder! And thus, you, king, have turned against me and will have me executed. I made your father leader of the feudal lords. When you had not yet succeeded to the throne, and the various princes struggled with one another to succeed, I fought nearly to the point of my death before the former king, and still you almost did not succeed. After you had managed to gain the throne, you wished to divide the state of Wu and give part to me. I, however, did not dare to expect such a thing. Nevertheless, you now listen to a slandering minister's words and kill an elder!"

> Then he told a retainer, "You must plant catawba on my tomb. They can be made into vessels.[67] And gouge out my eyes and hang them on the East Gate so that I can see the bandits of Yue annihilate Wu." Thereupon, he cut his throat and died.

> When the king of Wu heard this, he was furious. He took Wu

Zixu's corpse, loaded it into a leather bag and floated it in a river.[68]

King Fuchai, as Wu Zixu's final speech reminds us, has forgotten Wu Zixu's loyal service to his father, King Helu. This, in itself, is an unfilial act. Furthermore, far from gaining the revenge he promised his dying father, Fuchai has actually created the circumstances for Yue to destroy the state that his father, with Wu Zixu's help, brought to such great power. If Wu Zixu overemphasizes filial duty, and goes to the absurd extreme of beating a corpse to gain revenge, plainly Fuchai does not go far enough. As I have argued previously, Sima Qian, as he writes the text of his own life, is concerned with the words of a dying father and the duty such words impose upon a son. This same topic appears as a major theme of the "Traditions of Wu Zixu," where Sima Qian presents two extremes and then seeks a middle ground between fanatical adherence to a father's request (i.e., Wu Zixu) and unfilial neglect (i.e., Fuchai). Perhaps Sima Qian also locates a middle ground in his own life between a fanatical adherence to his father's wish, which would imply subordinating himself entirely to the Confucian ideal, and the unfilial neglect that would result either from not writing a history at all or from committing suicide before such a work is complete.

The contrast between Wu Zixu and Fuchai, and Sima Qian's own emotional entanglement within the lines he writes, does not end here. One of Wu Zixu's characteristics, stated somewhat simplistically, is that he cannot allow death to interfere with his plots. His story begins with him as the brother who lives beyond the death some would say he should have suffered at his condemned father's side. Consequently, there is a strange and bizarre consistency in his pursuit of revenge beyond the death of King Ping as well as in his desire to extend his vision beyond his own death so that he can have the satisfaction of "seeing" that he was right and Fuchai wrong. As Sima Qian's tale continues, and Wu Zixu's rival King Fuchai dies, the theme of "seeing" into the future appears once again. As Wu Zixu predicted, but is not allowed to see—his eyes being cruelly sealed with his body in a leather bag at the bottom of a river—Yue destroys Wu.

The death of Fuchai is one of those events Sima Qian reports several times, each time slightly differently. In the "Traditions of Wu Zixu," he says only, "King Goujian of Yue destroyed Wu and killed King Fuchai." So far as I know, there is no earlier textual basis for the implication here that King Fuchai was killed as a part of the destruction of Wu. The "Traditions" account advances very quickly towards a conclusion once the central character is dead, and King Fuchai is therefore disposed of with very little detail.[69] The "Hereditary Household of Wu Taibo," contains a somewhat longer report of Fuchai's death:

> When Yue defeated Wu, King Goujian wanted to move King Fuchai to Yongdong and, giving him one hundred households, have him reside there. But the king of Wu said, "I am old! I cannot serve you, king. I regret that I did not use Zixu's words and that I have caused myself to fall into this." Consequently, he slit his throat and died.[70]

Sima Qian's third report of Fuchai's death, found in the "Hereditary Household of King Goujian of Yue" is the most detailed, and says:

> Goujian sent someone to say to the king of Wu, "I will establish you at Yongdong and allow you to rule over one-hundred families."
>
> The king of Wu declined, saying, "I am old! And I am not able to serve you, king."
>
> Consequently, as he killed himself, he covered his own face and said, "I have no face to see Wu Zixu."[71]

This account resembles the death scene in *Discourses* and is also reminiscent of the account in *Master Lü*, although the latter text reports the death in considerably greater detail. Fuchai, according to Sima Qian's fullest account, dies, like his foil Wu Zixu, concerned about "seeing." But while Wu Zixu wants to see, Fuchai wants his own vision to cease, just as he tried to ensure that Wu Zixu's vision would cease.

Wu Zixu is a master of plots. It is only natural that he should look to the future, to the time when either his plans bear fruit or his predictions come true. He is active and is motivated in large measure by the compelling emotion of revenge. Twice frustrated by the intercession of death—once by the death of King Ping and once by his own death—his continued activity, or wish for activity, becomes absurd. But if Wu Zixu is dynamic, Fuchai is static. Throughout the narrative, Fuchai avoids the action that his father has thrust upon him. Like so many "blind" kings in *Records of the Historian*, he cannot see the consequences of his policies, and he dies, appropriately enough, wanting to remain blind.

Still, whatever disapproval for Wu Zixu's extreme behavior we might find within the lines of *Records of the Historian*, there is no doubt but that Sima Qian, as a "lover of the curious," generally admires Wu Zixu. Few of his judgments are filled with more praise than the one that concludes this particular chapter:

> The Gentleman Grand Astrologer says, "The poison of resentment in man is extreme indeed! A king cannot provoke it in a minister, much less in a peer! If previously Wu Zixu had been made to follow Wu She in death, how would he differ from an ant? But he rejected a small principle to wipe away a great shame, and his name is passed on to later generations. Now, whether hard-pressed on the Yangtze River or begging food along the road, how could his mind, even for a moment, forget Ying [the capital of Chu]? Therefore, he silently endured and obtained merit and fame. If not a man of virtue, how could he have reached to this?"[72]

As I have noted above, Sima Qian clearly identifies with Wu Zixu at several points in his narrative, and that sense of identification is reiterated in this final judgment, for Sima Qian too has rejected a "small" principle and chosen to stay alive to complete his work. But do the final sentences of Sima Qian's judgment, quoted above, indeed reflect Wu Zixu's behavior? Did he quietly endure? Sima Qian's judgment is hardly congruent with the story he himself has presented. The "Traditions of Wu Zixu" may be about a man who can temporarily bear shame, one topic highlighted in Sima Qian's final comments, but it is not about a man who silently endures, nor does it appear to be about a man who is primarily motivated by a desire "to leave a name." Wu Zixu simply wants revenge, and he pursues that goal with a perverse disregard for the natural limitations of such revenge. Satisfying his revenge or knowing that his prediction is right must be realized as concretely as possible—by beating a corpse or by hanging his eyes on a gate; Wu Zixu wants to *experience* the outcome and not just draw strength from contemplation of the future.

With regard to this issue, Wu Zixu and Sima Qian are hardly similar. Sima Qian, standing in the tradition of writers of pent-up frustration, draws consolation from the hope that his record will one day "penetrate the villages and cities."[73] In other words, he draws consolation from contemplating his future readers and anticipating their praise. The written word will live beyond his own demise and will keep his memory and the memory of others alive. Sima Qian, as he wrote and pondered his future fame, "silently endured." Thus, his judgment at the conclusion of the "Traditions of Wu Zixu" is much more a description of his own situation than that of Wu Zixu.

In the judgment, as in the Wu Zixu story itself, the themes and conflicts of Sima Qian's own life, as he himself has presented that life, repeatedly surface and shape his history. He cannot simply transmit, not only because the texts before him are so vast and demand interpretation, but also because of the immense *personal* interest he finds in those texts. At the intersection of his great learning and his passionate involvement in his tales, there emerges a highly complex and ambiguous thematic pattern. Liu Zhiji, I believe, is quite correct in failing to see a consistent "praise and blame" perspective in Sima Qian's works. *Records of the Historian*, however much Confucian admirers have tried to search out consistent threads of morality, is a disquieting work that refuses to fit neatly into any didactic mould. And on this point Sima Qian's text stands, in direct contrast to *Zuo*, a book with a consistent and quite simple moral perspective.[74]

Ban Gu, one of Sima Qian's earliest critics, may not have been correct in ascribing Sima Qian's deviance to Taoist loyalties, but he is not misreading his predecessor when he says that Sima Qian "strays somewhat from [the doctrine] of the Sage."[75] Yang Xiong (53 B.C.E.–18 C.E.), a still earlier reader and one of the finest minds among Sima Qian's critics, is even more perceptive:

> Loving much and not enduring, such was Zizhang (Sima Qian). Confucius loved much—he loved propriety. Zizhang loved much—he loved the curious.
>
> Someone said, "Huainan and the Gentleman Grand Historian knew so much! How could they be so eclectic?" [Yang Xiong] says, "Certainly they were eclectic! It is a human weakness to make abundant knowledge into eclecticism. Only the Sage did not become eclectic. If his writings did not comply with the classics, then he did not write. If his words did not accord with the classics, then he did not speak."[76]

Yang Xiong describes Sima Qian, like Confucius, as one who "loved much." But Sima Qian's love was for "the curious," and Yang implies that this led him into an eclecticism that "did not comply with the classics." This is a serious charge to level at one who wished to be a second Confucius. However, Yang's charge, I believe, is justified by the complex and morally ambiguous stories that Sima Qian wove, stories that often reflect more the shape of his own life and his peculiar curiosity than the consistent moral vision required of either a "True Gentleman," like Zuo Qiuming, or a "Sage," like Confucius.

5

(Wo)men with(out) Names

The Master said, "The True Gentleman hates that he might perish from the earth and his name not be praised."

—*Analects* 15:4b (15.19)

The Master said, "I do not worry about whether others know and appreciate me, I worry about whether I know and appreciate others."

—*Analects* 1:5a (1.16)

Spring and Autumn Annals, which Sima Qian describes as "the greatest manifestation of the Kingly Way," ends with the death of Confucius in 479 B.C.E., while *Zuo Commentary*, the authoritative interpretation of Confucius' classic, continues on to 468. Far from ushering in a time of rectitude and peace, these works verge on the strife-ridden Warring States period, an epoch that continues until the Qin unification of 221 B.C.E. Sima Qian describes this era in the following words:

> Effort was placed upon strengthening armies and upon absorbing enemies. Plots and deceits were employed, and the theories of the Vertical and the Horizontal, and the Long and the Short arose.[1] False titles appeared in swarms, and oaths and alliances were not sincere. Although states sent hostages and broke tallies, they still could not be restrained.[2]

As I have noted previously, the Warring States period was also a time when texts proliferated and became more diverse in content. The political disarray and competition between states created an atmosphere in which contending schools vied for patronage; and

99

skillful writing, as well as clever speech, could attract the attention of rulers.[3] Still, when Sima Qian turned his attention to composing a history of this period, he complained of a lack of reliable historical texts upon which to base his account. He explains the problem as follows:

> After the Qin achieved their desire throughout the empire, they burned copies of *Poetry* and *Historical Documents*. They were especially harsh in their treatment of the historical records of the feudal lords because those records contained information critical of Qin. The reason *Poetry* and *Historical Documents* appeared again was that many copies were hidden in peoples' homes. But the historical records were stored only in the Zhou household and, because of this, they were destroyed. What a pity! What a pity! We only have the records of Qin, and they, moreover, do not record dates, and have accounts that are sketchy and extremely incomplete.[4]

Thus, Sima Qian not only lacked a comprehensive and authoritative history for this period, such as *Zuo Commentary* provides for the Spring and Autumn period, he even lacked, so he tells us here, the basic annals necessary to piece together a complete picture of these critical centuries. Despite such problems, Sima Qian's history of the Warring States period occupies a significant portion of his work. Indeed, one modern scholar has estimated that thirty-eight percent of *Records of the Historian* concerns this period of slightly less than 250 years, a figure that reflects the general thickening of Sima Qian's text as he approaches his own age.[5] So how did Sima Qian, despite his complaint about usable sources, manage to fill out his history of the Warring States period? Ban Gu answers this question, near the end of his biography of Sima Qian, when he lists the most important sources of his predecessor's vast history:

> Sima Qian relied upon *Master Zuo* and *Discourses of the States*; he made selections from *Genealogical Origins* (*Shi ben*) and *Intrigues of the Warring States* (*Zhanguo ce*); and he transmitted the *Spring and Autumn Annals of Chu and Han* (*Chu Han chun qiu*).[6]

As noted in the previous chapter, the first two texts mentioned here form the foundation for much of Sima Qian's work on the Spring and Autumn period. *Genealogical Origins*, a work now lost, apparently contained a record of the lineages of emperors, kings, and feudal lords "from the Yellow Emperor down to the time of the

Spring and Autumn" and was an important source for Sima Qian's history of this earliest period.[7] The last of the works Ban Gu lists, the *Spring and Autumn Annals of Chu and Han*, concerned the struggle at the end of the Qin between Liu Bang (eventually Han Gaozu, "The High Progenitor of the Han") and Xiang Yu for control of China and will be discussed in the next chapter.[8] What remains, among Ban Gu's list of Sima Qian's basic sources, is only *Intrigues of the Warring States* (hereafter, *Intrigues*), an account of events that took place during the Warring States years (403–221).

By listing *Intrigues* as one of Sima Qian's sources, Ban Gu is guilty of an anachronism, for no such text existed in Sima Qian's time. *Intrigues* was first edited and given its modern title by Liu Xiang (77–6 B.C.E.), almost one hundred years after Sima Qian's death. Ban Gu, a learned historian and bibliographer, certainly was aware of this fact and presumably meant that Sima Qian had used the same sources *later* compiled into *Intrigues*.[9] The precise nature of these sources has been the subject of considerable controversy. For example, Luo Genze, one of modern China's foremost literary scholars, has argued in several articles that Liu Xiang did little more than edit and transmit a unified work originally written by Kuai Tong, a skilled rhetorician of the early Han who is mentioned in *Records of the Historian*.[10] However, a masterful recent study of *Intrigues* by Zheng Liangshu allows us to put aside Luo Genze's theories and state with confidence that Liu Xiang did indeed edit this text from a variety of disparate sources: "The forerunners of *Intrigues*," concludes Zheng Liangshu, "were several different sources. These can be divided into works by different authors that were written at various periods of time and show quite different points of view."[11]

Zheng argues that much of Liu Xiang's source material comes from the School of Diplomatists (*zongheng jia*) so active in political life during the Warring States period.[12] In fact, both he and James Crump, the foremost Western expert on *Intrigues*, believe that many of the sections of this fascinating work were originally composed as "model" arguments to be used as examples in instructing aspiring rhetoricians.[13] As such, many of the passages in *Intrigues* are of dubious historical value, and even a casual reader cannot avoid the impression that, to use Zheng's words, "sometimes it distorts historical facts; and sometimes it even goes so far as to fabricate historical facts."[14] Crump is still more emphatic on this issue: "*Chan-kuo Ts'e* (*Zhanguo ce*) is not history."[15] Indeed, for centuries there has been an argument among China's most famous bibliographers as to whether *Intrigues* merits listing in the "History Section" of bibliographies or belongs elsewhere. For example, the great Song bibliographer, Chao Gongwu (d. 1171 c.e.) doubted the value of *Intrigues* as a historical source and placed it among the texts of "the Masters," noting that it "was written by those who studied with the Diplomatists."[16]

Historical accuracy is not the only question that has been raised concerning Sima Qian's primary source for his history of the Warring States period. *Intrigues* largely ignores the Confucian virtues of humaneness and duty and repeatedly emphasizes policies and practices that are "profitable," however questionable their morality.[17] Indeed, Zeng Gu (ca. 1020–ca. 1090), the Northern Song editor of *Intrigues* who was responsible for putting this work into its present thirty-three sections, could only justify the preservation of *Intrigues* as a powerful negative example:

> Now some may object that heretical theories harm what is proper and must be acted against and ended. Therefore, must we not destroy this book? The reply should be that if a ruler wishes to suppress pernicious doctrine he will first cause it to be made clear to all the empire so that men of his time may understand why it cannot be used—then suppression will be properly achieved.[18]

Despite the historical and ethical questions that have been raised concerning *Intrigues*, Ban Gu claims that Sima Qian used this text extensively; and a close comparison of *Intrigues* and the relevant portions of *Records of the Historian* supports Ban Gu's contention. Indeed, Zheng Liangshu calculates that forty-four percent of Sima Qian's accounts of the Warring States period are drawn directly from "*Intrigues*." This, as he explains, is obviously a very conservative figure, for we know that much of the original *Intrigues* has been lost and that Sima Qian utilized some of those now lost passages.[19] Sima Qian's dependence on "*Intrigues*" for his history of the Warring States period at least equals his dependence upon the much more highly regarded *Zuo Commentary* for the Spring and Autumn period.[20] This "contamination" of Sima Qian's history by the highly questionable "*Intrigues*" has not gone unnoticed. Indeed, one of the first appraisals in the Chinese tradition of *Records of the Historian* raises this very point. In 32 b.c.e., King Yu, one of the five sons of the Han Emperor Xuan (r. 74–50 b.c.e.) and the ruler of the small kingdom of Dongping, came to court seeking copies of the works of the "Masters" and the "Book of the Gentleman Grand

Astrologer," the title under which *Records of the Historian* was originally known.[21] Wang Feng, who was the newly appointed marshal of state, replied:[22]

> I have heard that when a feudal lord comes to court, he examines his literary culture, puts in order his laws and regulations and does not speak what is not in accord with ritual. Today, you, the king of Dongping, fortunately, have managed to come to court; but you do not consider establishing your principles and showing care about your regulations so as to prevent danger and loss. Instead, you seek various books. This is not the proper principle of coming to court. The books of the Masters sometimes go contrary to the teachings of the classics and are not in accord with the Sage. Sometimes they speak of ghosts and spirits and put faith in the supernatural and bizarre. The *Book of the Gentleman Grand Astrologer* contains the machinations of Diplomatists and schemers from the Warring States period, strange intrigues of plotting ministers from the first years of the rise of Han, disasters and unusual occurrences of the "Heavenly Offices,"[23] and strategic points of earth's terrain. These all are not suitable to be found among the feudal lords and kings.[24]

Thus, the pious Wang Feng criticizes Sima Qian's work for containing the "crafty plots of rhetoricians from the Warring States period." The full context of this comment, as one can clearly see in the passage above, indicates that Wang may have been more concerned about information in *Records of the Historian* useful to potentially rebellious leaders of petty kingdoms than about the question of historical accuracy, but he plainly is concerned about those portions of *Records of the Historian*, among others, that derive from "*Intrigues.*"

As a result of Sima Qian including so much of "*Intrigues*" in *Records of the Historian*, criticism directed at *Intrigues* also directly implicates Sima Qian's account of the Warring States period. Only the most fanatical defender of Sima Qian's standards as a historian would maintain that the Han historian has used careful judgment in determining which of those "crafty plots," mostly drawn from "*Intrigues*," are verifiable and deserve inclusion in a sober historical account. To cite a single famous example, Sima Qian copies from "*Intrigues*" into his own history virtually the entire story of Su Qin (fl. ca. 320 B.C.E.), the brilliant strategist who supposedly strove to maintain a strong anti-Qin alliance, despite the serious and obvious historical problems inherent in this story.[25] Perhaps Sima Qian's rather uncritical use of "*Intrigues*," as much as anything else, led

Wang Shizhen (1526–90), one of China's greatest literary critics, to describe his writings about the Warring States period as "bold but reckless."[26]

From another perspective, such criticism of *Intrigues* and concern over its influence upon *Records of the Historian* may miss the point. As James Crump has noted, Chinese scholars perhaps have paid too much attention to the questionable historical accuracy of this text and too little attention to its brilliant literary qualities. The same could be said of *Records of the Historian*, despite the fact that generations of readers have turned to Sima Qian as much for his "good stories" as for his depiction of the past. However, in the case of *Records of the Historian*, as opposed to *Intrigues*, the whole issue of historical accuracy is compounded by Sima Qian's claim that he is a historian of the loftiest critical standards. In his "preface" to the table of the meritorious ministers of the early Han dynasty, he says:

> Therefore, I have shown care [in recording] their ends and beginnings and have presented this text in the form of a table. There are some cases where the details cannot be completely known. I have recorded what is clear; and what is doubtful, I have left out.[27]

It is obvious in this passage, and elsewhere in *Records of the Historian*, that Confucius' standard for all speech rings loudly in Sima Qian's ears: "If you hear much and leave out the doubtful, and speak with great caution about the remainder, then you will have few errors."[28] Caution in what one passes on—putting aside all that is doubtful—characterizes the good Confucian, and surely *Spring and Autumn Annals*, the one historical text ascribed to Confucius, contains no dangerous literary flights but, instead, presents an economical list of events.

Sima Qian, as I have noted earlier, was not always contained by Confucian principles of restraint and moderation. When all is said and done, he is as much an exuberant literary anthologist as a sober historian. In his use of "*Intrigues*," as in his use of other sources, Confucian critical standards often yield to the power of the story itself as Sima Qian's measure of value. One is reminded here of Harold Bloom's judgment of another vast, albeit quite different, collection: "The Hebrew Bible, from its origins onwards, is anything but a theological library; it is the product of aesthetic choices."[29] Sima Qian's choices are also, to some degree, aesthetic. Moreover, his aesthetic criteria are obviously influenced by the realization in narrative of those themes he considers of critical and personal interest. It is here that "*Intrigues*," as a text, and the Warring States, as a period of history, gain their peculiar power—they make available to Sima Qian an unusually rich assortment of characters and stories that allow him to contemplate those themes for which he appears to have such an abiding interest. The tumultuous and dramatic Warring States period, as mirrored so brilliantly in *Intrigues*, is a time of fanatical loyalties, of both the appreciation and also the undeserved rejection of the talented, and of violent death.

Instead of utilizing examples from *Records of the Historian* where Sima Qian's text repeats virtually verbatim accounts found in today's *Intrigues*, famous stories like those of Yu Rang, Jing Ke, or even the brilliant diplomat Su Qin, we turn to two fascinating cases where he apparently swerves from his source in order to confront, in a more direct and powerful way, his own peculiar interests.[30] The first of these examples comes from one of the most literarily significant chapters in *Records of the Historian*, "Traditions of the Assassins" (chapter 86). The very inclusion of such a chapter in *Records of the Historian* is something of an un-Confucian act. After all, the several men immortalized there, "whose names are passed down to later generations" and whom Sima Qian credits for "not disregarding the dictates of their conscience," were men of violence who threatened or killed political authorities.[31]

One of the most carefully crafted of these tales of assassins is the story of Nie Zheng (ca. 375 B.C.E.).[32] As this story begins, Nie Zheng is presented as a man who has fled an enemy and is living in obscurity as a dog butcher. Of course, his true merit cannot long remain hidden even in such a lowly environment. A certain Yan Zhongzi, who has had a dispute with Xia Lei, the grand minister of Han, and wishes to hire a brave man to help him gain revenge, hears of Nie Zheng and seeks him out. Yan Zhongzi offers gifts to Nie Zheng's mother to encourage her son's service, but Nie Zheng refuses Yang Zhongzi's patronage precisely because his mother is still alive and requires her only son's support. Later, however, Nie Zheng's mother dies, freeing him from filial obligations, and he remembers that Yan Zhongzi previously "recognized and appreciated" his talent even though he, Nie Zheng, was "a common man of markets and wells." Nie Zheng visits Yan Zhongzi and offers his service in gaining revenge upon Xia Lei, Yan Zhongzi's enemy. Yan Zhongzi accepts Nie Zheng's service and wishes to provide him with assistants for his dangerous mission, but Nie Zheng insists that he set out alone so as to insure that news of his dangerous endeavor not leak out.

Sima Qian describes the actual assassination of Xia Lei in only ten Chinese characters: "Nie Zheng went straight in, ascended the steps, and stabbed Xia Lei to death."[33] Nie Zheng performs the dire deed so easily precisely because he does not intend to escape—he is quite willing to give his own life to take the life of his patron's enemy! But before Nie Zheng is captured or killed by the troops surrounding the slain Xia Lei, he uses the skill he has acquired as a dog butcher and "skins his own face, gouges out his eyes and disembowels himself." This incredible act of self-mutilation, carried out so that no one can identify his body and continue the cycle of revenge, is presented as evidence of fanatical devotion and courage. The ruler of Han, the murdered Xia Lei's lord, subsequently exposes Nie Zheng's body in the market and offers a reward to anyone who can identify him.

The versions of this story in *Intrigues* and *Records of the Historian* are so similar up to this point that they must derive from the same source. The story, as summarized above, also contains themes familiar to Sima Qian's readers: unrecognized talent, responsibility to one's parents, the debt of loyalty owed to someone who truly knows and appreciates one's abilities, and the courage to die— indeed, to throw one's life away in a moment of supreme courage. But the story of Nie Zheng continues, and suddenly Sima Qian's version swerves from that of *Intrigues*. We begin with the latter version:

> Zheng's elder sister heard of this and said, "My younger brother is extremely virtuous. I cannot value my own body and destroy my younger brother's name. This was not my brother's intention." She then went to Han, looked at him and said, "What courage! A nobility of spirit exceeding Ben and Yu and higher than Cheng Jing![34] Now he is dead and has no name. His parents have already died, and he has no brothers. This has been for me. Now I cannot bear to value myself and not raise aloft my brother's name."

> So she embraced the corpse and cried over it, saying, "This is my younger brother Nie Zheng of Shenjing Village in Zhi." Then she also committed suicide at the foot of the corpse.

> When the people of Jin, Chu, Qi, and Wei heard of this, they said, "Not only was Zheng capable, but his older sister was also a noble woman!" That Nie Zheng's name is known in later generations is because his sister did not fear the punishment of being minced and mixed with sauce in order to raise aloft his name.[35]

Sima Qian's version of the story of Nie Zheng's sister and her courageous identification of Nie Zheng's mutilated corpse reads as follows:

> When Zheng's elder sister, Rong, heard that someone had stabbed to death the grand minister of Han, that the criminal had not been captured alive, that the state did not know his name, and that they had exposed his body and displayed with it as reward one thousand pieces of gold, she sighed and said, "Could this be my brother? Alas, Yan Zhongzi knew and appreciated my younger brother."
>
> Immediately she arose and went to the market of Han, and the dead man was indeed Zheng! She embraced the corpse, cried out in deep sorrow and said, "This is the one known as Nie Zheng of Shenjing Village in Zhi."
>
> Those walking about in the market and all the multitudes said, "This man killed the grand minister of our state, and the king has displayed a reward of one thousand pieces of gold for his name. Has the lady not heard this? How dare you come to identify him?"
>
> In response, Rong said, "I have heard this. Still, the reason Zheng accepted indignity and cast himself among the peddlers in the market was that his aged mother, fortunately, had no illness, and I had not yet married. My parent, in accord with her heaven-appointed years, has left the earth, and I have already married. Now, Yan Zhongzi sought out and raised up my younger brother from the midst of affliction and insult and treated him with favor and kindness! What could he do? A gentleman surely will die for one who knows him. Now, because I am still alive, he mutilated himself to cut off pursuit. How could I fear the punishment of death and eternally obliterate a virtuous younger brother's name?"
>
> This greatly startled the people of the Han market. Then she cried out to heaven, sighed in deep sorrow, and died at the side of Zheng's body. When the people of Jin, Chu, Qi, and Wei heard of this, they all said, "Not only was Zheng capable, but his older sister was a noble woman. If Zheng had truly known that his elder sister had unyielding determination, and that she would not worry about the disaster of having her own corpse exposed but would certainly pass across one thousand *li* of danger in order to disclose his name, and that both elder sister and younger brother would die in the market of Han, then he would surely not have dared to entrust himself to Yan Zhongzi. Yan Zhongzi can be called one who knows others and is able to obtain gentlemen."[36]

Sima Qian's version, in addition to being more expansive than that of *Intrigues*, puts the bravery of Nie Zheng's sister much more at the center of the narrative. In the *Intrigues* version cited above, an *unnamed* elder sister hears of the exposed corpse and goes to the market of Han, where she gives a speech praising her brother's virtue. Then, after identifying the corpse and assuring her brother's immortality, she commits suicide. Her bravery, to be sure, is revealed and recognized by all, but in *Intrigues* she does not upstage her brother and become the dominant character in the narrative.

Sima Qian changes this. First of all, the heroine is given a name—Rong. Secondly, when she identifies the corpse, she carries on a dialogue with the people in the market, a dialogue not recorded in *Intrigues*. Often in *Records of the Historian* the voice of the crowd, or a disinterested third party, indicates the "correct" reaction to an event and is a guide to appropriate reader response. That is, the reaction of the reader to Rong's bravery should be, like that of the crowd, incredulity at her willingness to expose herself to certain death in order to identify her brother. Third, Rong gives a speech in which she explains that Nie Zheng, once freed from responsibility by the death of his mother and the marriage of his sister, was bound to offer his life for someone who had known and appreciated him. But just as her brother was bound to die for Yan Zhongzi, so she is now bound to die for her brother. Such a commentary, in the form of Rong's speech, is quite unnecessary except to make as explicit as possible those elements of the narrative Sima Qian does not want overlooked. Sima Qian provides the reaction of the audience (and also the appropriate reaction of the reader): they are "greatly startled." The people of other states who subsequently hear this story, as in the *Intrigues* version, not only proclaim Rong a noble woman but suggest that Nie Zheng had underestimated his sister. Had Nie Zheng known and appreciated her, as Yan Zhongzi knew and appreciated him, he would not have behaved so rashly!

Here, as elsewhere in *Records of the Historian*, a curious or ambiguous element of a story is expanded and emphasized. The whole point of the initial delay in Nie Zheng's mission was to fulfill his obligation to his mother. His self-mutilation, in much the same spirit, was to protect his sister, and perhaps his patron as well, from retaliation. But he failed to foresee the nobility of his own sister. Insofar as Sima Qian's version raises doubts about Nie Zheng, those doubts do not concern the fact that he murdered Xia Lei, but only that he did not fully "know and appreciate" his own sister! He was not as perceptive as Yan Zhongzi in recognizing the greatness of another. Thus, in Sima Qian's version Rong emerges unequivocally as a hero, but some doubt is raised by the voice of the crowd as to whether Nie Zheng knew others as well as he was known.

The shift in Sima Qian's emphasis as he narrates the story takes on particular interest because it is Rong's action that makes the narrative possible. Had she failed to identify her brother, neither his name nor his story could have been known. By carving the skin from his face and plucking out his eyes, Nie Zheng had literally effaced himself from the pages of history and could only have been transmitted to posterity as an anonymous hero—and in China, as we have seen, it is transmission of the *name* that brings salvation. Rong negates the effacement and, through disclosing the corpse's past, becomes the attendant of the historian. Nie Zheng, without his sister Rong, however courageous his actions, would have been one of the nameless heroes Sima Qian bemoans in his "Traditions of Bo Yi," those unknown ones who happened not "to become attached to the tale of a racehorse."[37] We should not be surprised, therefore, that Sima Qian, who writes in large measure to preserve the names of the past, enhances Rong's role in his narrative.

Besides this issue of the effacement and revelation of the hero, and the critical part played by the historian in this process, there are additional reverberations of Sima Qian's own situation in this narrative. The story of Nie Zheng, as told in both *Intrigues* and *Records of the Historian*, is a tale of extreme behavior. Nie Zheng not only fulfills his duty "to one who knows him" but also plunges into a macabre scene of self-mutilation and suicide, and Sima Qian, who usually portrays actual death scenes with the most economical language possible, describes this grotesque moment with unusual detail. Nie Zheng is obviously willing to accept not only the destruction of his body, but the disappearance of his name—he has no concern for history, only concern for loyalty. It is his sister who redeems his name and makes possible, before her own suicide, the inscription of both of their names upon the pages of history.

Sima Qian is a historian who has refused suicide, at least until the names of the past are preserved. In this decision to make names known, he is Rong, the elder sister of Nie Zheng, and becomes morally superior to those who rush too quickly into death and anonymity. But in the guilt-ridden lines of Sima Qian's letter to Ren An, written in the last years of his life, we sense ambivalence and doubt about his own decision to refuse suicide, suffer castration, and await the vindication of history: "If even the lowliest slave or maidservant can commit suicide," writes Sima Qian to his imprisoned friend, "How could one like me not manage to do what had to be done?"[38] This troubling question, despite Sima Qian's tortuous attempts at an answer, is not entirely stilled. Like many other courageous figures in *Records of the Historian*, Nie Zheng becomes the enticing but unchosen alternative; for he was willing, unlike Sima Qian, to accept annihilation from both the present life and the pages of the past in one glorious moment of firm resolve.

As we have seen in this first example, there is ample room in the dramatic and sometimes dark tales of *Intrigues* for Sima Qian to engage those issues that resonate with his own peculiar story. Our second example is one of the most direct confrontations in *Records of the Historian* with the issues of dishonor, impossible choices, and death. Lu Zhonglian, a famous Warring States diplomatist immortalized in a "Traditions" chapter (chapter 83), once wrote a letter to a beleaguered Yan general. The letter, which effectively summarizes issues of great concern to Sima Qian, appears in both *Intrigues* and *Records of the Historian*. While the two versions have minor differences throughout, Sima Qian's version of the final impact of the letter once again diverges from the version in *Intrigues*.

Lu Zhonglian was a man from the state of Qi. Sima Qian describes him as "fond of the curious," the very words Yang Xiong later used to describe Sima Qian himself. Lu Zhonglian's skillful diplomacy assisted the state of Zhao to relieve Qin's siege of the Zhao capital of Handan. But the episode which concerns us here occurred many years later, well after Lu Zhonglian had achieved great fame. A Yan general, whose name is not recorded, had captured the Qi city of Liaocheng. However, the general had been slandered in his home state of Yan and dared not leave Liaocheng to return to Yan. Thus, the general held the captured city for over a year despite various attempts by the powerful state of Qi to dislodge him. Lu Zhonglian, who was serving Qi, finally wrote a letter to the general, attached it to an arrow, and shot the arrow into the city. Sima Qian includes the entire letter in his account of this event, a letter that has become deservedly famous for its persuasive power. It begins with the argument that the general is showing neither loyalty, courage, nor wisdom by holding Liaocheng so tenaciously:

> I have heard that a wise man does not go against the times and repudiate advantage, that a courageous gentleman does not shrink from death and destroy his name, and that a loyal minister does not put himself first and put his ruler last. Now you, sir, have acted on a single moment's anger and have shown no concern that the king

of Yan has no minister. This is not loyalty. You will bring yourself
to death and lose Liaocheng, and your power will not extend to Qi.
This is not courage. Your achievements will fail and your name
will be destroyed so that later generations will have no reason to
praise you. This is not wise. A hereditary lord will not take one as
minister nor will a wandering persuader make a record of one who
has these three characteristics. Therefore, a wise man does not
calculate twice, and a courageous gentleman does not shrink from
death. Now, with regard to life or death, glory or insult, honor or
disgrace, respect or lowliness, this time will not come again. I hope
you, sir, will calculate thoroughly and not be of the common herd.

After his moralistic argument and an injunction to the general
to ponder carefully the critical decision before him, Lu Zhonglian
goes on to outline the actual military situation. The state of Qi, as
Lu Zhonglian analyzes it, has neutralized its enemies and will soon
turn full attention toward Liaocheng. The general is warned that he
cannot possibly withstand such pressure. Moreover, the general's
home state of Yan is in disorder and will not be able to support him
should Qi launch a full-scale assault.

Following this description of the general's hopeless situation,
Lu Zhonglian presents him with two alternatives. The first is to
return to Yan with his "chariots and troops intact," where his
friends "will raise their hands" and praise him for his achievements.
The second alternative is to surrender to Qi, which will, according
to Lu Zhonglian, reward his surrender with the gift of a fief. Having
presented these "attractive" alternatives, Lu Zhonglian turns back
to the question of principles. And like so often in Chinese rhetoric,
principles are discussed in terms of historical precedents:

I have heard that one who adheres to a petty principle will not be
able to achieve a glorious name; and one who detests a petty shame
will not be able to establish a great merit. Previously, Guan Yiwu
shot an arrow at Duke Huan and struck his belt hook. This was
usurpation. Abandoning Gongzi Jiu, he was unable to die. This was
cowardice. He was bound up and put in fetters. This was insult. A
hereditary lord will not take as minister, and people from the same
hometown will not even associate with one who has done these
three acts. If Guanzi had been imprisoned in darkness and had not
come forth, or if he had died and not returned to Qi, then his name,
after all, would have been that of a disgraced man, one of lowly
actions! Even servants would be ashamed to share their names
with him, how much less the common crowd! Although Guanzi
was not ashamed that he was bound in ropes, he was ashamed that

the empire was not regulated. He was not ashamed that he did not
die with Gongzi Jiu, but he was ashamed that his authority would
not extend to the feudal lords. Therefore, he combined the faults of
these three acts, but he became the leader of the five hegemons.
His name was raised high in the empire, and the glory illuminated
neighboring states.[39]

Master Cao was a general of Lu. In three battles he was defeated
three times and lost land amounting to five hundred *li*. If Master
Cao's plan had been not to look back, and if he had considered not
returning but had cut his throat and died, then, his reputation
would not have avoided being that of a defeated army and a captured general! But Master Cao rejected the shame of three defeats
and drew back to lay plans with the ruler of Lu. Duke Huan
subjected the empire and gathered the feudal lords. When Master
Cao relied on the duty of his one sword, and, pointing it at the heart
of Duke Huan atop the sacrificial altar, his expression did not
change and the tone of his speech did not grow confused. What he
had lost in three battles, he restored in a single morning. The
empire was startled, the feudal lords frightened, and his authority
reached to Wu and Yue.[40]

It was not that two gentlemen like these were unable to complete
a small act of integrity and carry out a small principle. But they
considered that by killing themselves or losing their lives, by
breaking off from this world and annihilating themselves from
later times, their merit and reputation would not be established.
This was not wise. Therefore, they got rid of their resentment over
feeling anger and, by the end of their lives, established a name.
They rejected the principle of anger and established the merit that
will last through generations. Therefore, their work vies to be
passed along with the three kings, and their names will only wear
out together with heaven and earth. I hope you, sir, will select one
of these alternatives and carry it out.[41]

With this injunction to choose between one historical figure
who suffered the shame of imprisonment but came forth to assist
his former enemy and another figure who suffered repeated military
defeats but fought on and finally achieved honor, Lu Zhonglian ends
his letter. There are very minor differences in the content of this
letter as found in *Intrigues* and in *Records of the Historian*. However, the description of the general's reaction to the letter is radically different in each of the two versions. *Intrigues* concludes
simply as follows:

The Yan general said, "I have respectfully heard your command."
Thereupon, he dismissed his troops, turned his quiver upside

down, and departed. Consequently, what relieved the state of Qi and saved the commoners from death was the Zhonglian's persuasion.[42]

In Sima Qian's *Records of the Historian*, the result of the letter is described in entirely different terms:

> When the Yan general saw Lu Lian's [i.e., Lu Zhonglian's] letter, he wept for three days. Hesitant, he could not make his own decision. He wished to return to Yan, but he had already broken with Yan and feared he would be punished. He wished to surrender to Qi, but the captives he had killed among the people of Qi were exceedingly numerous, and he feared that after he had already surrendered, he would meet with disgrace. Deeply distressed, he said, "Rather than be put to the blade by others, it is better to do it myself." Thereupon, he killed himself. Liaocheng was thrown into disorder. Tian Dan [a Qi general] consequently massacred the people of Liaocheng. Returning, Tian Dan spoke to Lu Lian and wished to give him a title. But Lu Lian fled into seclusion along the edge of the sea and said, "Rather than be rich and submit to others, I would be poor and follow my own inclinations."[43]

As a comparison of the two conclusions shows so clearly, *Intrigues* is largely concerned with Lu Zhonglian's power of persuasion. With his skilled argumentation, Lu Zhonglian dissuades the general from continuing to hold Liaocheng, and once this argument has its desired result, the narrator rapidly concludes the passage, telling us very little of the ultimate outcome. However, *Records of the Historian* shifts the focus from Lu Zhonglian to the general himself and describes in detail the general's impassioned response to the letter, a response that consists of tears, indecision, and ultimately suicide.

The historical accuracy of Sima Qian's more dramatic version has been questioned. Wu Renjie (fl. 1178), for example, notes that Lu Zhonglian's basic intention was not to push the beleaguered general into suicide but merely to induce the troops to withdraw from Liaocheng. He goes on as follows: "Moreover, having advised the general to keep intact the people of Liaocheng, could he [i.e., Lu Zhonglian] bear to sit and watch [Dan] massacre them? *Intrigues* has achieved the truth while *Records of the Historian* cannot be believed."[44]

Here, then, the frequently criticized *Intrigues* gets the applause of the historically-minded critic, while the oft-praised *Records of the Historian* is disparaged as inaccurate. Such a conclusion is, of course, troubling to defenders of Sima Qian as a historian. Wang Shumin, one of those defenders, may indeed be correct to claim that Sima Qian must have had some textual basis for his description of the end of the siege of Liaocheng.[45] However, the fact remains, as Wu Renjie has correctly noted, that Sima Qian's ending, whatever its ultimate source, raises serious questions. The goal of Lu Zhonglian's argument, as presented in both *Intrigues* and *Records of the Historian*, is to encourage the general to choose between two alternatives, surrendering to Qi or returning to Yan. He assures the general that either of these two courses of action will bring admiration, reward, and the opportunity to establish his name.

Since the entire letter appears in *Intrigues* as an example of clever argument, the conclusion seems appropriate: the general is persuaded by Lu Zhonglian's powerful arguments and simply leaves the city. We are not told whether he returned to Yan or proceeded to Qi. In the *Intrigues* narrative the general is not the focus of attention at all; we need only know that Lu Zhonglian's letter achieved its goal—what finally happened to the general is of little consequence.

Sima Qian's version changes the narrative's center of gravity. Lu Zhonglian presents two alternatives to the Yan general, both involving short-term shame but holding the possibility of long-term glory. The general, however, chooses an entirely different alternative . . . suicide. We have already noted Sima Qian's peculiar and understandable interest in this topic, and hence a story where such an outcome has been chosen over other attested narrative possibilities (i.e., that of *Intrigues*) assumes particular interest.

A key to Sima Qian's version of the story of Lu Zhonglian and the Yan general can perhaps be found in the fact that the general is left unnamed in both *Intrigues* and *Records of the Historian*. Despite the preservation of his story, the general's name has fallen into the darkness of the unrecorded past. In his letter, Lu Zhonglian warned the general of this very possibility: "One who adheres to a small principle will not be able to achieve a glorious name." Sima Qian, of course, saw his own dilemma in precisely the same terms— suicide and avoiding shame, in his case, was the "petty principle," while living on through shame and trial to "achieve a glorious name" provided the nobler alternative. Sima Qian's analysis of Wu Zixu, it will be remembered, is similar—Wu Zixu did not follow the "small principle of dying" at his father's side but lived on to fulfill loftier duties. Sima Qian, like Wu Zixu, Guanzi, and Cao Mo, was unwilling "to break off from this world and disappear from later times." The Yan general, by way of contrast, made just such a choice and becomes, by his choice, Sima Qian's alter ego, a case study of "the road not taken."

Lu Zhonglian's persuasion, as presented in *Records of the Historian*, may have one desired outcome, the end of the occupation of Liaocheng, but neither of the alternatives presented so "attractively" to the Yan general is accepted. Sima Qian removes one problem inherent in the *Intrigues* version, the general has no name because he could not accept shame, but he creates another problem: Lu Zhonglian's persuasion, at least in part, fails. But Sima Qian, I suspect, is more interested in the general's reaction to his dilemma than in Lu Zhonglian's artful persuasion, and his version shifts our attention, at least temporarily, from Lu Zhonglian to the indecision, tears, and eventual suicide of the nameless general.

The sister of Nie Zheng, to whom Sima Qian grants a name, chose the right moment to die. Her death came after she had revealed the name of her brother; her fame is linked to a self-sacrificing decision to grant fame to another. She is, in a sense, the transmitter who has completed the task of revealing the past and is now free to die. But the Yan general, unlike Rong, dies only to save himself from shame. The issue that concerns Sima Qian in these two stories is how and when to die, an issue he addresses directly elsewhere: "One who knows he will die is certain to be courageous. It is not the act of death that is difficult; it is the management of death that is difficult."[46] Of course, the struggle with this very issue of how and when to die informs Sima Qian's letter to Ren An: "Man assuredly has a single death. Sometimes it is as heavy as Mount Tai; and sometimes it is as light as a swan's feather. It is the way one uses it that makes the difference."[47]

In the two examples given above, Sima Qian's narrative, though apparently based upon "*Intrigues,*" swerves at precisely those points where he discovers the contours of his own life and experience. While Sima Qian uses "*Intrigues*" abundantly, and while his own text is profoundly shaped by this problematic source, these earlier narratives can be rewritten and their literary power "enhanced" in accord with the peculiar interests of the Han historian himself. Traditional scholars of *Records of the Historian* might fret about the historical accuracy of such "enhancements," as in the case of the Yan general's suicide and the massacre of Liaocheng, but the truth may be that Sima Qian's great work, particularly the "Traditions" section, is less history than a collection and reworking of earlier sources that appealed to him as much for literary richness as for historical accuracy.

Despite the fact that so much, perhaps most, of Sima Qian's history of the dramatic Warring States period depends upon *"Intrigues,"* there are striking exceptions to this pattern. Zheng Liangshu's list of the "Traditions" chapters concerning Warring States figures and his conservative estimate of the number of lines drawn directly from *"Intrigues"* indicates significant variation from chapter to chapter. Some chapters (69, 70, 71, 72, 78, 79, 80, 83) are based entirely or largely upon *"Intrigues,"* others show less dependence (73, 75, 76), and some appear to have no dependence at all (74, 77, 81, 82).[48] Among this last category, one chapter is particularly interesting because it concerns a character who might almost be called "paradigmatic," the son of the duke of Wei, otherwise known as "Lord Xinling."[49] This figure, whom I shall call Lord Xinling and who will be called simply Gongzi (son of a duke) in several of the translations below, is mentioned briefly in a few episodes in *Intrigues,* but with one possible exception of only one or two lines, *Intrigues,* at least as it exists today, is not the basis of Sima Qian's account.[50]

I have used the term "paradigmatic" in reference to Lord Xinling because he is an exemplar of a virtuous type for whom Sima Qian feels obvious affinity. In his "Self-Narration," where Sima Qian gives a one-sentence summary of each of the 130 chapters of *Records of the Historian,* he describes Lord Xinling as "Able with wealth and honor to associate with the poor and lowly, worthy but able to submit to the unworthy." Sima Qian reiterates this theme at the conclusion of the "Traditions" of Lord Xinling with the claim that it was Lord Xinling's remarkable ability to associate freely with men of much lower status that granted him preeminence among his peers:

> Among the various nobles of the empire, there are those fond of gentlemen. Nevertheless, Lord Xinling's [reputation] as one who made contact with recluses of crags and caves and who was not ashamed to associate with those beneath him has its basis. That his name is at the top of the feudal lords is not without reason.[52]

Indeed, Lord Xinling, in Sima Qian's account, is portrayed as a man who honors and accepts talent wherever he finds it. He is the model of the man who, in the words of Confucius, "does not worry about whether others know and appreciate him, but worries about whether he knows and appreciates others."[53]

Although the prodigious power, which Lord Xinling builds and holds for a time, is based entirely upon his appreciation and use of talented retainers, Sima Qian's account of this figure also exemplifies the unhappy fate that so often comes to men of his type: despite his appreciation for others, Lord Xinling is not fully appreciated in return and eventually falls victim to jealous slanderers. This issue, as we have seen in chapter 1 above, is central to Sima Qian's writings about himself; for he was, in his own view, an unappreciated victim of his own appreciation for Li Ling's stellar military service. But his story also exemplifies the opposite side of this theme. He is not fully appreciated, in spite of his appreciation for others, and he eventually becomes the victim of slander. The "Traditions" of Lord Xinling thus has a peculiar interest as a powerful tale on this problem set squarely in the Warring States period but apparently not deriving, like many other such stories, from "Intrigues."

One final, and perhaps less apparent way in which Sima Qian identifies with the hero of this "Traditions" chapter, is that Lord Xinling, as we shall see, uncovers talent. Men of worth are brought to light through his willingness to condescend and appreciate others. In this respect, he is an analogue to the historian, particularly a historian like Sima Qian, who sees his primary duty as making a record of "enlightened lords, worthy rulers, loyal ministers, and gentlemen who died for duty."[54]

As is the case with so many of the stories Sima Qian has drawn from "Intrigues," it is very difficult to read the "Traditions" of Lord Xinling without a strong impression that one is reading fiction. This impression arises not as much from glaring historical errors and inconsistencies, such as Maspero finds in the Su Qin narrative, as from the very way in which this narrative unfolds. Characters are portrayed in such extreme fashion as to become almost caricatures, and the situations depicted in the story are carefully and cleverly contrived to illustrate those virtues Sima Qian would advocate. The story of Lord Xinling, although not found in today's Intrigues, is entirely consistent with the more imaginative accounts of that much maligned source. The truth may be, as both Henri Maspero and the great Hu Shi have suggested, that there was a wealth of popular romances circulating during the Warring States and early Han periods, and these romances may have gripped the imagination of the Han historian so as to find a place on the more respected and enduring pages of "orthodox history."[55]

As so often in Sima Qian's writings, the first episode of the "Traditions" of Lord Xinling points toward the dominant traits of

the central character and establishes the major themes that are to
shape the ensuing narrative:

> Gongzi [Lord Xinling] was playing chess with the king of Wei.
> From the northern border came the message that the warning
> towers had been lit, and it was reported that "the bandits of Zhao
> have arrived and are about to enter our boundaries." The king of
> Wei put down his chess pieces and wished to summon the great
> ministers to make plans, but Gongzi stopped the king and said,
> "The king of Zhao is only hunting, he is not behaving as a bandit."
> He went on playing chess as before. The king was afraid, and his
> mind was not in the game.
>
> After a short period of time, another message was transmitted from
> the northern regions: "The king of Zhao is only hunting and is not
> behaving as a bandit." The king of Wei was startled and asked,
> "How did you, Gongzi, know this?" Gongzi said, "Among my
> retainers is one who is able to spy out the secret affairs of the king
> of Zhao. He reports to me all of the movements of the king of Zhao.
> I therefore knew it."
>
> After this, the king of Wei feared Gongzi's worthiness and ability
> and dared not entrust Gongzi with the government of the state.[56]

We learn here that Lord Xinling's possession of skilled retainers
grants him an almost supernatural power—Lord Xinling speaks the
very same words that the king's messenger will speak later! Confucian political theory, as is so often noted, assigns great weight to
attracting the service of men of merit as a corrective to the leader's
own limited knowledge and virtue. But this Confucian ideal is
spoiled by the realization, found repeatedly in Sima Qian and numerous later writers as well, that the very perspicacity of wise
retainers invariably arouses fear and jealousy in those it intends to
help: "After this," we are told, "the king of Wei feared Gongzi's
worthiness and ability."
    As the story of Lord Xinling unfolds, we are provided with
example after example of the benefits he receives from his patronage
of talented people. First, there is the famous story of Hou Ying. Lord
Xinling had heard that Hou Ying was a "recluse gentleman," and
despite Hou Ying's initial rudeness to his would-be patron, Lord
Xinling treats this aged and impoverished gatekeeper with perfect
politeness. Hou Ying eventually repays his virtuous patron by giving
the advice that will enable Lord Xinling to relieve the Qin siege of
Handan and win fame among the feudal lords. Second, there is the

brief story of the wife of the king of Wei, who returns Lord Xinling's earlier favor of avenging her enemy and steals the tally that the king of Wei uses to convey orders to General Jin Bi. This tally eventually will allow Lord Xinling to assume control of the army that marches to Handan. Third, there is Zhu Hai, the recluse-butcher, whom Hou Ying recommends to Lord Xinling as a "worthy no one in the world has been able to know and appreciate." Zhu Hai accompanies Lord Xinling to the camp of General Jin Bi and kills him when Jin Bi fails to recognize the authority of Lord Xinling's tally. Fourth, there is the unnamed retainer who warns the victorious hero against pride and thus prevents him from falling into incorrect behavior. Finally, there are the gambler Mao and the porridge-maker Xie, who wisely advise Lord Xinling to return to Wei and no longer ignore the perilous condition of his own home state. Reliance upon such men of worth enables Lord Xinling "to shake the world."[57]

Lord Xinling's moment of greatest glory comes with his defeat of the armies of Qin and his rescue of the Zhao capital of Handan. This victory wins him the approbation of the king of Zhao and the admiration of another famous "master of retainers," Lord Ping Yuan: "The king of Zhao bowed twice and said, `From ancient times there has not been a worthy equal to Gongzi.' From this time on, Lord Ping Yuan did not dare compare himself to this man."[58] Nevertheless, the threat to Lord Xinling has already been signalled in the very first episode of the chapter—men of real talent and virtue inevitably attract suspicion and jealousy. And this jealousy is stirred, as so often in Sima Qian, by villainous slanderers:

The king of Qin worried about it [i.e., the astounding success of Lord Xinling]. Thereupon, he sent ten thousand catties of gold to Wei to seek out the retainers of Jin Bi[59] and cause them to slander Gongzi to the king of Wei, saying, "Gongzi fled [his own state] and has been abroad for years. Today he is a Wei general, and the generals of the feudal lords are all subordinate to him. The feudal lords only hear about Gongzi of Wei and do not hear about the king of Wei. Gongzi also desires to avail himself of this time to face south and become king. The feudal lords fear the power of Gongzi and desire to join together and establish him."

Qin frequently caused counter-spies falsely to congratulate Gongzi and ask whether or not he had managed to be established as king of Wei. The king of Wei heard this slander daily and could not but believe it. Afterward, he did indeed send a person to replace Gongzi as general. Gongzi himself knew that again he had been rejected because of slander, and so he resigned office on account of illness

and did not come to court. With his guests and retainers he drank
far into the night, drinking strong wine; and he had many relationships with women. Day and night he drank and made merry for a
period of four years, until finally he became ill from wine and died.
That year King Anxi of Wei, also passed away.[60]

Thus ends the life of one who appreciated others but was not
appreciated himself. No issue in *Records of the Historian* appears
more frequently than this, and no issue brings Sima Qian to greater
despair and hopelessness.

Elsewhere in *Records of the Historian* the same despair and
hopelessness is voiced by a gifted man who was still alive in Sima
Qian's youth, the noted rhetorician and rhapsodist Zou Yang (206–
129 B.C.E.). Although Zou Yang was a man of the Western Han, Sima
Qian places his "Traditions" with Lu Zhonglian and among other
figures belonging predominately to the Warring States period. There
may be some sense to this, for Zou Yang has been classified as
belonging to the School of the Diplomatists, a school that thrived in
the Warring States, and he had been deeply influenced by the rhetoric of "*Intrigues*" both in style and content of argumentation.[61]

Zou Yang was imprisoned by the king of the feudatory state of
Liang as a result of being slandered by Gongsun Gui and Yang
Sheng.[62] From prison he addressed a letter to the King of Liang, a
letter that was successful in gaining his release and is anthologized
in its entirety in *Records of the Historian*. The style of this letter
must have appealed to Sima Qian; after all, Zou Yang "uses forty-
two historical examples to convey his arguments."[63] But ultimately
it must have been the content of the letter, and the familiar echoes
Sima Qian heard therein, that attracted the attention of the Han
historian.

The letter begins with a rejection of the notion that loyalty is
rewarded: "I have heard that loyalty will not go unrewarded and that
sincerity will not meet suspicion. And I always considered this to be
so. But it is merely an empty saying."[64] The reason loyalty goes
unrewarded is that success always invites slander, and most rulers
are not wise enough to brush falsehoods aside: "Therefore, it doesn't
matter whether a woman is beautiful or ugly; if she enters the
palace, she encounters jealousy. And it does not matter whether a
scholar is worthy or wicked. If he enters the court, he encounters
envy." The power of such slander, argues Zou Yang, is overwhelming: "The voices of the multitude melt gold; accumulated slander
destroys bone."[65]

There are, to be sure, examples of wise lords listed in Zou Yang's letter who overcame the natural tendency to reject true loyalty—in fact, his own letter led to his exoneration—and there are also stories in Sima Qian's history of heroic rulers who rewarded ministers justly. Still, the experience of the most memorable figures in *Records of the Historian*, Lord Xinling, Qu Yuan, Confucius, and so on, does not speak well for the end result of worthy and intelligent service. Perhaps the ultimate despair of Sima Qian's text can be found in the historical evidence throughout *Records of the Historian* that his conclusion in the "Traditions of Bo Yi" is indeed correct: there is no real justice.

The issues of Sima Qian's own life, issues we have explored in this chapter as they appear primarily in certain narratives from the Warring States period, spread throughout his vast text. Like Nie Zheng's sister, Sima Qian would redeem himself by spending his life illuminating the heroes of the past. Unlike the Yan general, he would turn his back upon the "petty principle," which makes it impossible to live through shame and redeem oneself. But obviously Sima Qian feels deep despair, a despair signalled in the "Traditions of Bo Yi," that he cannot fully appreciate and glorify all the worthy persons of the past. However, the dilemmas of the would-be second Confucius are inherent in the words of the first Confucius as well: "I do not worry about whether others know and appreciate me; I worry about whether I know and appreciate others." So says a dispassionate Confucius, seemingly resigned to a life of obscurity spent quietly illuminating the virtues of others. "The True Gentleman hates that he might perish from the earth and his name not be praised," says Confucius elsewhere, grasping after an immortality that only comes if one is known and appreciated by others.

The resolution to this conflict is to become appreciated as one who appreciates others. This was the path of Lord Xinling, and, in quite a different fashion, Nie Zheng's sister Rong as well. It is also the chosen path of the Historian, attaching himself, as he says elsewhere, "to the tail of the racehorse." But there remains in Sima Qian's record a gnawing fear that the injustice he traces so often in his narratives, an injustice Zou Yang expresses with such painful directness, will subvert his hopes as well. Just after one of Sima Qian's most affirmative and moving expressions of hope, spoken to his condemned friend Ren An, dark despair gathers again and reveals once more the sharp contrast between Sima Qian's hope for future vindication and his fear that the shame of his present life will somehow, unjustly, continue for "a thousand generations":

When I truly have completed writing this book, I will deposit it in a famous mountain. If it is passed down to the right people and penetrates villages and cities, then I will have repaid the debt from my previous insult. And although I suffered ten thousand mutilations, how could I have regret? . . . Although a hundred generations pile up, the disgrace only deepens. Therefore, each day my bowels twist nine times. At home I am confused as though something has been lost. I go out and do not know where I am going. Every time I think of this shame, sweat always breaks out on my back and soaks my robe.[66]

6

Ideologue versus Narrator

A great wind arose . . . the storm blew against the troops of
Chu, and the troops were in great confusion, broke apart, and
scattered.

—Records of the Historian

When he [Xiang Yu] was about to die at Dongcheng, he still
did not wake up and upbraid his own errors. Instead, he said,
"It is Heaven that is destroying me and not a fault of my
military prowess!"

—Records of the Historian

In the preceding chapters, I try to reveal tensions and ambiguities in
Sima Qian's text, a tendency at times for *Records of the Historian* to
subvert, or at least vastly complicate, its own arguments. In the
introduction, I ascribe this tendency to the enormous literary
breadth of Sima Qian's work. As an encyclopedist of the past, who
would encompass an entire and diverse textual tradition, Sima Qian
found no clear, consistent meaning in history. In addition to this
problem, which is inherent in the nature of the overwhelming task
the Han historian set for himself, I also note certain psychological
tensions that may have simultaneously pulled his narrative in opposite directions. All of this is, of course, not an entirely new argument. Burton Watson, writing thirty years ago, observed that Sima
Qian's "writing, no matter how one forces it, will produce no 'system' of thought."[1] In fact, much of the criticism of *Records of the
Historian* voiced by Chinese scholars has touched, in one way or
another, upon the issue of Sima Qian's historical and philosophical
"inconsistencies."

The whole problem of textual consistency is one of considerable interest to modern literary critics and theorists. Some among them question the consistency of any text and challenge the notion that a single, clear mind is in control of the production of a literary work. But quite apart from this contemporary literary controversy, students of Chinese civilization have frequently noted a tendency towards "fragmentation" in a whole array of Chinese cultural expressions. Whether considering the piecemeal structure of early Chinese mythology, the initiation of a literary tradition with the lyric rather than the epic, the Chinese landscape painting as a "fragment" of nature rather than as a "composition," the poem read as the expression of a single moment rather than as a universal statement requiring a "metaphorical operation," or a whole host of other cultural phenomena, including the organization of history itself, this particular issue appears time and time again in the scholarship on Chinese civilization.[2]

In a highly provocative recent study, David Hall and Roger Ames have addressed the topic of fragmentation and have contrasted a Western emphasis upon "rational and logical order" with a Chinese emphasis upon "aesthetic order." In the latter worldview, they argue, "plurality must be conceived as prior to unity and disjunction to conjunction."[3] A full consideration of the thesis of Hall and Ames would take me far beyond the topic before us, but it is curious that so many Western scholars, as well as Chinese who have studied the Western tradition, discern this "plurality" and "disjunction" throughout the Chinese cultural world. Seen from such a perspective, the inconsistencies and fragmentation of Sima Qian's work, which have been discussed in this and other works, should not surprise us.

Whatever literary or cultural explanations can be offered for such features, we must admit that Sima Qian does invite the reader to seek coherence in his work, for he announces that his purpose is "to examine the boundary between heaven and man, to penetrate the transformations of ancient and modern times, and to form the words of a single school."[4] This statement, which the Sima Qian specialist Ruan Zhisheng analyzes into "three golden phrases," encourages readers to search the pages of Sima Qian's vast text for a clearly organized intellectual argument, for the "words of a single school."[5]

However, before examining Sima Qian's pursuit of the three goals stated in his "golden phrases," it is necessary to comment briefly on the statement itself. First of all, the Chinese word translated "examine" in the quotation above is *jiu* 究, a term literally meaning "to exhaust." *Jiu* connotes a *thorough* study of a particular problem. The word *ji* 際, which I have translated as "boundary," implies not so much a point of separation as a point where things meet or come together. The original meaning of *ji*, according to Xu Shen (30–124 C.E.), is the corner where two walls join.[7] By using this term, Sima Qian promises to elucidate the *interplay* of heaven and man in the structure of history. Finally, my translation of the last of the "three golden phrases" differs somewhat both from Watson and Chavannes. The former takes *yijia*, my "single school," as "one family" and the latter translates the phrase as "un seul auteur."[8] While it is very difficult to prove the superiority of any one of these translations, I have chosen "single school" because it echoes Sima Tan's famous essay on the Six Schools. Sima Tan, as our earlier discussion indicates, attempted with his essay to find a unified ground within the different schools of thought—he was essentially an eclectic who saw Taoism as sufficiently broad to gather in all of the "strengths" of the major schools while eschewing their weaknesses. Sima Qian, I believe, was seeking for the same kind of unified ground within the specific facts of history.[9]

Scholars who have examined Sima Qian's ideas about the "boundary between heaven and man," to quote the first of his golden phrases, have reached quite diverse conclusions. Wen Chongyi, for example, contends that Sima Qian was a faithful follower of Dong Zhongshu and believed, like his master, that there is a perfect correspondence between heaven and man, that everything occurring in one of these spheres must result in a response or an "echo" in the other. Whatever doubts Sima Qian may have expressed concerning the justice of heaven, argues Wen Chongyi, were only temporary and do not negate his overwhelming faith in the doctrine that "heaven and earth are united as one" (*tian di heyi*).[10]

Xu Fuguan disagrees with such an interpretation. He takes note of Dong Zhongshu's famous theory concerning the mutual response of heaven and earth and states categorically that Sima Qian "had been influenced very little by this school of thought." Heaven to Sima Qian is little more than the mystery he uses to explain that which transcends human understanding. It is to be equated with fate, the arbitrary and capricious power that sometimes frustrates human expectations. Although Xu Fuguan does not draw such a comparison, Sima Qian's philosophy of heaven, as Xu Fuguan explains it, is reminiscent of Xunzi.[11] Li Shaoyong does draw such a comparison and labels Sima Qian's philosophy of heaven "materialist."[12]

The source of such radically different interpretations of Sima Qian's notion of heaven is a tension on the pages of *Records of the Historian* between Sima Qian the inheritor of a Mencius–Dong Zhongshu philosophical tradition, which would bind heaven and earth together into a tight system, and Sima Qian the encyclopedic historian and connoisseur of narrative, who perceives and appreciates far too much complexity to sustain such an orderly theory.[13] For example, Sima Qian's essay "The Offices of Heaven" (chapter 27) affirms the doctrine of an intimate and comprehensible relationship between the movement of celestial bodies and man's fate. In this essay, Sima Qian concludes that "There has never been a case when a [celestial] phenomenon first took shape and then a response did not follow it."[14] But however confidently Sima Qian states this as a theory, he does not apply it, as Zhang Dake has observed, to the actual facts of history. An obvious example is provided by his treatment of one of the most important historical events of the past, the rise of the state of Qin and its eventual unification of China. As Sima Qian narrates and contemplates this critical event from the past, any confidence in a fathomable and just heaven, which resonates with the world of man, dissolves, and the historian is left with a notion of heaven as a transcendent force quite beyond human comprehension:

> If we discuss Qin's virtue and propriety, it could not equal Lu and Wei even at their most violent. If we measure the armies of Qin, they do not equal the strength of the Three Jin. Nevertheless, they finally swallowed up the empire. This was not necessarily because of the advantages of a strategic and precipitous terrain. It seems as if it was the assistance of heaven.[15]

Elsewhere, while contemplating the success of Qin and his inability to find sufficient strategic or political reason for that success, Sima Qian exclaims, "How could it not have been heaven? How could it not have been heaven?"[16] Obviously heaven assisted Qin, but Sima Qian can find no justification for such assistance, no natural and comprehensible resonance between a heaven and an earth that "are united into one."

Sima Qian's second goal, "to penetrate the transformations of ancient and modern times," presents similar interpretive problems. The Han historian, as a matter of ideology, espouses a theory of historical cycles, but in his treatment of particular historical episodes, he is not consistently guided by his own theory. Again, this disjunction has led Sima Qian specialists to reach quite opposite conclusions concerning the historian's ideas on the process of change. Some argue that Sima Qian does indeed believe in cyclical transformation, and they frequently cite two passages from *Records of the Historian* to support their interpretation:

1. In the movements of heaven, a period of thirty years constitutes a minor transformation, a period of one hundred years a mid-range transformation, and a period of five hundred years a great transformation. Three great transformations constitute an era. After three eras, there is completion, the formation of a complete cycle.[17]

2. The government of Xia stressed loyalty. When loyalty declined, the small man turned it into crudeness. Therefore, the people of Yin followed it with respect. When respect declined, the small man turned it into superstitious belief in ghosts. Therefore, the people of Zhou followed it with cultural refinement. When cultural refinement declined, the small man followed it with empty show. Therefore, to save empty show there is nothing equal to loyalty. The way of the kings of the three dynasties is like a cycle. It ends and begins again.[18]

The cycles described in these passages would seem to make the process of change into a closed system, rendering real transformation illusory. But, as I have noted, neither of the cycles described above is generally applied in *Records of the Historian* to actual historical events. Thus, modern scholars such as Shi Ding and Xu Fuguan, who have dealt with this issue, dismiss these passages as relatively unimportant in understanding Sima Qian's interpretation of history. In fact, Shi Ding argues that Sima Qian's treatment of the past clearly reflects a belief in "linear historical change and not a theory of historical cycles."[19] The presence of the passages quoted above, Shi Ding implies, indicates that Sima Qian not only is an encyclopedist of narrative, as I have suggested, but is an encyclopedist of theory as well. Thus, Sima Qian quite freely sorts and selects ideas from the past to explain particular events without forging those ideas into a consistently applied ideology of history.

Of course, one need not discover historical cycles in order to advocate the existence of *some* principles of transformation. Ruan Zhisheng, in a very perceptive study of *Records of the Historian*, identifies a number of these principles, which Sima Qian may not have formulated into a coherent philosophy of change but which can at least be regarded as what Hayden White calls "putative laws

of historical explanation."[20] Ruan notes that Sima Qian sometimes
overtly invokes these laws and sometimes simply embeds them in
the events of the story itself. Three of the most significant of these
are:

1. Transformation follows an organic model. For example, a
full flourishing always signals the beginning of decline. "When
objects flourish," says Sima Qian, "then they decay. When the times
reach an extreme, then they shift."[21] This organic conception of
history constitutes the most basic law and leads quite logically to
the next two principles given below.

2. Meaningful transformation, as an organic model implies,
can only be perceived if periods of time, institutions, and human
beings are examined from beginning to end—in Sima Qian's words,
"from end to beginning." Thus, to be a complete and honest record
of transformation, the whole life of the organism must be scruti-
nized. It is no accident, then, that Sima Qian chose to write a
universal history and divided it further into smaller organic units:
annals of particular dynasties or feudal households, historical sur-
veys of certain institutions, human lives, and so on. Sima Qian's
treatment of these units, and his very words, "end to beginning,"
imply that it is often only from the perspective of the end that we
can understand the beginning. In other words, the end is implied in
the beginning.

3. Transformation, the aging of the living organism, is
gradual and usually is not perceived until the process has led to
some startling extreme: "For a minister to kill a ruler or for a son to
kill a father is not a matter of a single morning or evening. Its
gradual [development] has gone on for a long time."[22]

Such principles of transformation, however commonplace, and
Sima Qian's ideas on the boundary between heaven and man, however inconsistent, are components of that "single school" he would
form. The Han historian, as I have indicated earlier, was keenly
aware of the unhappy fracture in culture that had taken place after
Confucius' great act of cultural synthesis. *Records of the Historian*,
the work of the second Confucius, was written with the intention of
forging a new unity. But this unity would not be found in the
"empty words" of theoretical discourse but in the actual events of
the historical record. Sima Qian would provide, as Confucius supposedly had before, a clear guide for posterity. "The Confucians,"
says Sima Qian, criticizing the philosophers of his own time, "make

judgments about principles; and the rhetoricians pursue their [clever] phraseology. They put no effort into gathering up *the end and the beginning of events.*"[23] Sima Qian seems to believe that only attention to the concrete events of history, surveyed in their full temporal range, can lead to a new and resilient school of thought.

Those concrete events of the past are typically realized in narrative, and through these narratives, as we have seen earlier, Sima Qian's work becomes much less, and also much more, than the single coherent school he apparently sought. The literary genius, who sees complexity, contradiction, and ambiguity in the stories he tells, ultimately subverts his own "putative principles"—in a sense, he loses control of the text. A powerful and final example of this claim is provided by one of Sima Qian's most famous and controversial narratives, the account of the epic struggle between Xiang Yu and Liu Bang for control of China.[24] However, before proceeding to an examination of the chapters that describe this struggle (*Records of the Historian*, chapters 7 and 8), two issues should be discussed. The first, which is somewhat tangential to the central issue here, is the much-debated question of why Sima Qian included his chapter on Xiang Yu within the "Basic Annals" section of *Records of the Historian* rather than placing it in "Traditions" or, at the most, in "Hereditary Households." The second issue, a much more serious problem for our present investigation, is the degree to which Sima Qian's account of the Qin-Han transition is simply quoted from the now lost *Spring and Autumn Annals of Chu and Han*.

In one of his many criticisms of Sima Qian, the Tang historiographer Liu Zhiji argues as follows:

> Someone like King Xiang [Xiang Yu] ought to be given a "Traditions" chapter, but his name is taken as the head of a "Basic Annals" chapter. It is not only that [Xiang] Yu was a usurper and a bandit and cannot be the equal of a Son of Heaven, but also, if we look into the narrative of his affairs, it all is a record of words that have been passed down. If we try to call this an "Annals," it is not appropriate.[25]

Thus, Liu Zhiji, and many other scholars who follow his lead, argue that the "Basic Annals of Xiang Yu" is inappropriately classified, just like at least two other chapters that play prominently in our discussion, the "Hereditary Household of Confucius" and the "Traditions of Bo Yi." Xiang Yu never became emperor and was not part of a dynastic line, such scholars contend, and he consequently belongs not in "Basic Annals" but in "Traditions," which is precisely where the later Han historian Ban Gu classifies him.[26] However, as others have noted, Sima Qian's "Basic Annals" section is not restricted to emperors who are part of a legitimate dynastic succession. Rather, Sima Qian "considered that wherever authority in the empire was actually located, then that person was the 'basis' of the empire and thus deserved a 'Basic Annals.'"[27] By placing Xiang Yu among the "Basic Annals," Sima Qian is acknowledging the fact that for six years the Chu general was the primary power in an empire where one dynasty was at an end and no new dynasty had yet appeared.

The second issue is a more critical one. As we have seen previously, Sima Qian often quotes at length, and usually without attribution, from earlier sources. Where those sources are extant, such as in the case of *Zuo Commentary* or *Intrigues of the Warring States*, one can examine the way in which Sima Qian utilized and altered earlier narratives and thereby gain some idea of the relationship in *Records of the Historian* between direct transmission and creativity. But when studying the "Basic Annals" of Xiang Yu and of his opponent Liu Bang, such a methodology runs aground. Ban Gu relates that one of Sima Qian's primary sources for this period was Lu Jia's *Spring and Autumn Annals of Chu and Han*, but unfortunately this important text was lost during the Southern Song (1127–1279).[28] It is impossible, therefore, to know with confidence precisely how much of Sima Qian's story of the fall of Qin and the rise of Han draws directly upon Lu Jia's text. I believe, however, that there is convincing evidence to prove the amount of quotation or close adaptation in *Records of the Historian* from *Spring and Autumn Annals of Chu and Han* does not even remotely equal that from *Intrigues of the Warring States* or *Zuo Commentary*, two texts that we have discussed at some length in the previous two chapters.[29] But such an issue is, in some measure, irrelevant. Sima Qian, as I have suggested elsewhere, is responsible for the narrative choices that have led to the completed text, and those choices, even when they involve little more than quotation from older sources, can be taken to reflect the intentions of the Han historian.

The two "Basic Annals" chapters to which we now turn concern the lives of single individuals and thereby show little formal difference from most of the chapters of the "Traditions" section.[30] While the first of these chapters, "Basic Annals of Xiang Yu," has been deservedly acclaimed as a literary masterpiece, the second,

"Basic Annals of Gaozu," is, in general, an insipid narrative. This difference in the literary merit of these two chapters is of some interest and has analogues elsewhere in *Records of the Historian*. For example, the brilliant "Traditions of General Li" (chapter 109), one of the most vivid and powerful chapters in Sima Qian's text, can be contrasted with the historian's lackluster treatment of two of General Li's contemporaries and fellow generals, Wei Qing and Huo Qubing (chapter 111), whose "Traditions" chapter is made up almost entirely of dry quotations from decrees and memorials that provide very little sense of the personalities of either of these important historical figures. Xiang Yu and General Li were, of course, dramatic figures who ended their lives in defeat, precisely the type of character to stir Sima Qian's imagination, while Liu Bang, Wei Qing, and Huo Qubing were victors but lacked the charisma and "curiousness" (*qi* 奇) that consistently inspired Sima Qian's best prose.

The contrasting portrayal of Xiang Yu and Liu Bang, and the problems of ideology inherent in that contrast, can perhaps be seen most clearly in three places where the two narratives show an obvious and, I think, intentional affinity. The first of these is a moment in the early lives of the two protagonists when each sees the First Qin Emperor, the imposing ruler who had unified the kingdom and ruled with ruthless power. The second consists of two songs, one authored and sung by Xiang Yu in the midst of defeat, and the other authored and sung by Liu Bang in a moment of victorious exultation. The third is the historian's judgment, a formal feature that these two chapters share with other chapters of *Records of the Historian* but that Sima Qian uses in these cases to address a problem central to the two narratives. Our focus in what follows will be upon these three places where the "Basic Annals of Xiang Yu" and "Basic Annals of Gaozu" show such close formal resemblance.

Xiang Yu, as a young man, is taken to see the First Qin Emperor, who is in the region of Guiji conducting one of his frequent, awe-inspiring imperial processions. Sima Qian describes the scene as follows: "Liang (Xiang Yu's uncle) and Ji (Xiang Yu) were watching this together when Ji said, 'That man can be taken and replaced!' Liang covered Ji's mouth and said, 'Do not speak recklessly. The entire clan will be executed!' "[31] Liu Bang also had occasion to see the First Qin Emperor, but unlike Xiang Yu, who witnessed an imperial procession, Liu Bang saw the emperor in the Qin capital of Xianyang. Sima Qian reports his reactions in the following words:

"He (Liu Bang) sighed deeply and said, 'Alas, a great man ought to be like this.' "[32]

By placing these episodes near the beginning of their respective "Annals," Sima Qian points to a fundamental difference in the two central characters that will reverberate throughout the narratives. Xiang Yu is essentially a character of movement, a man of action—he believes that he can "take" (*qu*) and "replace" (*dai*) the powerful emperor; his behavior here and throughout the narrative corresponds to the transitive verb. Liu Bang, by way of contrast, is a character of stasis who is primarily typified not by transitive actions but by states of being, in this case, the state of *being the emperor*. The young Xiang Yu notices the possibility of *action*, the young Liu Bang the glory of a *situation*!

The reckless energy of Xiang Yu, his compulsion to act, which is forecast so succinctly in the episode above, is seen repeatedly throughout his "Basic Annals." This feature enlivens the story and invests it with astonishing literary power. However, even before the episode discussed above, Sima Qian has provided an indication of Xiang Yu's restless character:

> When Xiang Ji [Yu] was young, he studied writing. Although he had not mastered it, he quit and studied swordsmanship. He also did not master this. Xiang Liang was angry at him. Ji said, "Writing suffices to record one's name and that is all. Swordsmanship aims at taking a single man as opponent and is unworthy of study. I would study taking ten thousand men as opponents." So Xiang Liang taught Ji the art of warfare. Ji was very pleased and understood somewhat its essentials, but again, he was unwilling to study it thoroughly.[33]

Sima Qian's description here of Xiang Yu's failure to master writing, swordsmanship, and the art of warfare appears, as the narrative proceeds, to be an indication of this hero's rash temperament rather than a historical fact. After all, within a page or two of this criticism of Xiang Yu's deficient swordsmanship, he single-handedly kills almost one-hundred men in a fight! And, furthermore, the story of Xiang Yu ends with an episode in which the general exhibits astounding martial skill. Such accomplishments hardly accord with the claim that Xiang Yu did not master swordsmanship. Moreover, Xiang Yu's career as a military strategist, although plainly not without error, was in large measure a brilliant one. His ultimate defeat, at least as Sima Qian tells the story, stems much more from impetuosity and excessive passion than from lack of military know-how.

It is precisely this impetuosity and passion, depicted from the first pages of Sima Qian's account, that provoke Xiang Yu's numerous acts of extreme violence. While Liu Bang regularly forgives the inhabitants of areas that resist him, Xiang Yu slaughters everyone who blocks his way. For example, after his first great military victory, he kills all the inhabitants of Xiangcheng, a city that had withstood his seige "with strength."[34] And on the occasion of his second victory, he "attacked Chengyang and slaughtered the inhabitants."[35] Other examples of Xiang Yu's violent energy abound in Sima Qian's narrative. Perhaps the most infamous of these is his devastating attack on Xianyang, the Qin dynasty capital, which Liu Bang had previously occupied and treated with noteworthy moderation: "Xiang Yu led his troops west and destroyed Xianyang. He killed Ziyang, the king of Qin, who had surrendered, and he burned the palaces and buildings of Qin."[36] A further detail of some current interest concerning this notorious event appears in the "Basic Annals of Gaozu," where it says, "Xiang Yu burned the palaces and buildings and dug up the tomb of the First Emperor."[37]

In Sima Qian's narrative, Xiang Yu's dominant passion, as we might presume from his repeated acts of violence, is "fury" (nu), an emotion ascribed to him on several different occasions. This fury leads to a frightening power that few can withstand. Indeed, Xiang Yu's angry eyes and ferocious scolding are enough to send one brave warrior scurrying away in fear, and on another occasion his savage stare and enraged voice cause a pursuing "marquis" and his horse both to be so startled as to flee "for several li."[38]

Liu Bang, as I have noted above, is not so much a character of transitive action as one who is typified by certain states of being. In accord with such a description, he is governed by conservation and destiny. From the very beginning of his account of the conflict between Xiang Yu and Liu Bang, Sima Qian establishes the fact that the latter's status as a future emperor is divinely sanctioned. Liu Bang's eventual victory will come not so much from what he does as what *he is*—a man who has been chosen and therefore *must* possess the necessary qualities of an emperor. For example, Liu Bang, as Sima Qian tells his story, was the result of a miraculous conception, and his physiognomy indicates a glorious destiny.[39] Even in a drunken stupor, dragons swirl above Liu Bang's head, and his "vapor" clearly marks him as the future emperor.[40] Whereas the narrative of Xiang Yu is driven forward by a powerful central actor, the narrative of Liu Bang is, in a sense, complete from the beginning. He *is* the emperor, a fact that is obvious from the first words of his "Basic Annals." The movement in time and space is constrained by destiny and will only confirm what is clear from the outset—Liu Bang's status as the appointed recipient of heaven's mandate.

In accord with the stasis implied in the fact that he is complete from the beginning, Liu Bang is a character who typically protects and conserves. Moreover, when he does act, it is almost always as a result of the advice of others rather than at his own initiative. His treatment of Xianyang, alluded to above, is a splendid example and provides a vivid contrast with the behavior of his rival. Liu Bang enters the city and destroys nothing. Although such behavior, according to one of Xiang Yu's advisors, is contrary to Liu Bang's usual greedy and lascivious nature, Sima Qian nowhere provides a narrative to support the advisor's negative characterization.[41] Instead, Liu Bang, in Sima Qian's account, seals up the imperial treasuries without stealing a single item and refuses to take advantage of the huge Qin harem.[42]

The protection of Xianyang, an act of preservation that resembles virtually everything Liu Bang does, results from following the advice of others. Throughout the narrative, he is almost completely dependent upon the wisdom of his highly gifted entourage of advisors. This characteristic is skillfully shown by the first words Sima Qian has Liu Bang speak on the pages of *Records of the Historian*, "What should I do about this?" (*wei zhi nai he*), an interrogative that he will repeat once more within a single page and again just two pages later.[43] Sima Qian's portrayal of Liu Bang as repeatedly asking for help and as entirely reliant upon the brilliant plans of others reinforces the Confucian doctrine, widespread throughout *Records of the Historian*, that the most successful political leaders follow the counsel of wise advisors. In fact, toward the end of Sima Qian's narrative, Liu Bang himself acknowledges that relying upon the good advice of men of worth, more than any other quality, has led him to victory over Xiang Yu: "These three (Zi Fang, Xiao He, and Han Xin) are all remarkable talents, and I was able to utilize them. This is the reason I obtained the empire. Xiang Yu had the one, Fan Zeng, and was unable to use him, and this is why I captured him."[44] Xiang Yu is a man of action who does not need the opinions of others. He rushes with independence and ferocity to his own self-destruction. Liu Bang, by way of contrast, is a man of destiny who possesses those essential qualities, both of birth and of personality, that will lead him, or allow him to be led, toward what he already is.

The interpretation presented above, which regards one protagonist as active and independent and the other as static and dependent, is not without problems. Sima Qian's portrayal, here as elsewhere, is filled with strange ambiguities and complexities. Xiang Yu, for all his action, is plainly moving forward toward the past. A spokesman of the pre-Qin world, he is intent upon resurrecting Chu power and becoming the "hegemon-king" of a revived state order modelled on the period before the Qin unification. Xiang Yu's turn away from the Qin capital of Xianyang, perhaps his biggest strategic error, represents a rejection of the centralized bureaucratic order instigated by his Qin predecessors.[45] He abandons this key political power base "inside the pass" because of homesickness and an unbecoming "small-town" vanity: "To be wealthy and noble but not return to one's home," he says, "is like wearing embroidery and walking about in the night."[46] Liu Bang, however, represents the newly emergent bureaucratic state. He rewards his loyal followers with fiefs, to be sure, but the rapidity with which he will undermine such local power centers and replace the "loyalists" with his own sons argues that he hardly has in mind a revival of the Eastern Zhou order. Thus, Xiang Yu, the man of action, is a throwback to an earlier era, an anachronism—his action would lead back to that time of swashbuckling heroes before the Qin unification, where he would fit so well.[47] The much less active Liu Bang is moving forward, or being moved forward by his advisors, with a new order.

In addition to this issue of political directions, there are strange and critical moments in the narrative when the character of action and the character of stasis unexpectedly switch roles. Perhaps the most startling example of this is the famous episode of the Hongmen banquet. Liu Bang is enticed to a banquet in Xiang Yu's camp, where he plans to assuage his opponent's anger by apologizing for entering the pass first and seizing Xianyang. The banquet, as Xiang Yu's wise advisor Fan Zeng knows, is a perfect time for action; their enemy, the man blessed with the auspicious imperial aura, is in their hands and can easily be eliminated. Strangely, Xiang Yu, at this critical moment, becomes inactive. Fan Zeng signals him to take action, a signal reminiscent of a signal from his uncle Xiang Liang that evoked a flurry of violence earlier in Sima Qian's narrative, but Xiang Yu this time does not respond.[48]

Later in the banquet, Xiang Yu's inability to act becomes even more apparent when he is paralyzed by Fan Kuai, a loyal follower of Liu Bang, and a caricature of Xiang Yu himself. Fan Kuai, having heard his lord's life is in danger, bursts into the banquet, his "eyes stare in anger," a phrase used elsewhere to describe Xiang Yu, and his hair stands on end. Confronted with this living parody of his

own ferocity, Xiang Yu can only lean on his sword, raise himself to
one knee and say, "Who is this guest?" After the fierce visitor
delivers a scathing verbal attack, Xiang Yu, our man of action, "has
no means to respond."[49] He is, of course, frozen not only by Fan Kuai
but by the hand of destiny.[50]

Meanwhile, Liu Bang quickly acts to escape danger. In one of
the most curious passages in *Records of the Historian*, Liu Bang
leaves the banquet "to go to the toilet." He beckons Fan Kuai to step
outside with him and immediately asks for advice. Fan Kuai compares his master's precarious position, exposed to Xiang Yu's men,
as fish and meat "before blades and chopping blocks." Liu Bang, still
presumably in the toilet, decides to flee and gives his advisor Zhang
Liang a pair of white jade discs to take back into the banquet as a gift
for Xiang Yu and a pair of wine goblets for Fan Zeng:

> At that time the King of Xiang was camped below Hongmen and
> Liu Bang [the Duke of Pei] was camped at Bashang. The two places
> were forty *li* from one another. Liu Bang [the Duke of Pei] left his
> chariots and horsemen and escaped alone on horse with the four
> men, Fan Kuai, Ying the Marquis of Xia, Jin Qiang, and Ji Xin, who
> held swords and shields and ran along on foot. Following the foot of
> Mount Li, they took a secret road through Zhiyang. Liu Bang [the
> Duke of Pei] had told Zhang Liang, "To my camp by this road is no
> more than twenty *li*. When you estimate that I have arrived in
> camp, then go in."
>
> After Liu Bang [the Duke of Pei] had departed and had time to reach
> the camp, Zhang Liang went in and apologized, saying, "Liu Bang
> [the Duke of Pei] could not handle his cups of wine and was unable
> to take leave."[51]

The picture of the banquet in abeyance while the main guest is
in the toilet, carries on a discussion with his advisors, and then has
enough time to travel twenty *li* (approximately six miles) back to his
own camp is, to say the least, a bizarre one! Here we are presented
with a noteworthy juxtaposition of stasis and action, but it is Xiang
Yu in this episode who cannot act, whom the narrator holds in
strange suspension, while Liu Bang makes a hurried escape, a flight
recommended and supported by advisors. Indeed, throughout the
narrative, Liu Bang's most active moments are his escapes, those
recurring moments when he miraculously flees the grip of Xiang
Yu's army. These episodes of escape reinforce the sense of destiny
about Liu Bang, who can never really be threatened since his end is
present in his beginning.

During one of those escapes, Sima Qian portrays the frightened future emperor as throwing his children from his chariot to hasten its speed, an episode that points to another peculiar ambiguity in Sima Qian's narrative. Liu Bang is fleeing before Xiang Yu's troops, and

> Along the road, he met up with Xiao Hui [his son] and Lu Yuan [his daughter]. He loaded them in his chariot and fled. When the Chu cavalry pursued him, Liu Bang [the King of Han] was desperate and pushed Xiao Hui and Lu Yuan out of the carriage. The duke of Teng constantly got down and loaded them up. This happened three times. The duke of Teng said, "Although we are desperate and cannot drive faster, how can you abandon them?"[52]

Liu Bang, heaven's chosen vessel, is described at the start of his own "Annals" as "humane, fond of others, and delighting in generosity."[53] But elsewhere he is chided for "arrogance and rudeness." Xiang Yu, despite his repeated acts of murderous cruelty, is described as "humane and fond of others," the very words used elsewhere of Liu Bang.[54] Obviously ambivalence exists at the very heart of the characterization of the two central actors in these narratives, an inability or unwillingness to provide a consistent portrayal of either Xiang Yu, the vanquished, or Liu Bang, the victor. This problem, however, can only be fully explored as our consideration of the next two "parallel" episodes unfolds.

After winning repeated victories against Liu Bang, Xiang Yu finds his strength mysteriously diminished. Finally, he is surrounded, has lost the support of his fellow countrymen, and knows the end is near. He arises in his tent during the night and sings of his fine steed Zhui and his beloved woman Yu:

> My strength uprooted mountains,
> My energy arched over the world.
> But the time was not right,
> And Zhui does not run.
> When Zhui does not run,
> What else can I do?
> Oh Yu, oh Yu,
> What will be your fate?[55]

Liu Bang also sings a song, and his song is composed not at a moment of defeat but at his moment of greatest happiness. He has returned as a victorious emperor to his old home of Pei. Surrounded by his former neighbors, he teaches his song to the children:

> A great wind arose,
> Clouds flew aloft.
> My power present everywhere,
> I return to my own home.
> Where will I get fierce knights
> To guard the four frontiers?[56]

The contrasting tone of these two songs in part results from the exactly opposite situations of the narrators—one is sung in the midst of defeat and is concerned with "giving up," while the other is a song of a victor who quite naturally hopes for preservation of what has been gained. But there is more to this contrast than the conflicting situations in which they were written. Xiang Yu, true to his active nature, begins with transitive verbs (*ba*, "uproot," and *gai*, "arch over"). He is the actor, bragging of his achievements, and he chooses the grandest possible objects for his action—"mountains" and "the world." He goes on to sing that he has failed, despite his prodigious action, because "the time was not right" (literally, "advantageous"). Here Xiang Yu, as quoted by Sima Qian, evokes a theme that, as we have seen earlier, spreads throughout *Records of the Historian* and later Chinese literature—the times are out of joint and frustrate the efforts of good men. Xiang Yu believes that fate has destroyed him, and he evokes a theme in his song to which he will return later in the narrative.

Whereas Xiang Yu is present as a strong actor in the first two lines of his song, Liu Bang appears in his first two lines through metaphor. The "wind" and "clouds," which are likened to the new Han emperor, "arise" and "fly aloft" quite naturally. With these metaphors, the emperor suggests that his own victory, like dramatic changes in the weather, is a product of transcendent powers. He does not sing of his actions; for his accomplishment, the fact that his "power" is "present everywhere," is an expression of heaven's will.

The two songs also end with opposite concerns. Xiang Yu knows that he has lost the battle and is giving up, relinquishing the most immediate symbols of his great vitality and love for life. His final worry, in harmony with the characterization that he is indeed "humane," is for another: "Oh Yu, oh Yu, What is your fate?" The fact is, from the first pages of his "Basic Annals," one of Xiang Yu's most characteristic actions is giving up, another transitive action (giving up his studies, giving up Xianyang, giving up Yu, etc.), while Liu Bang is ever-conserving. The latter controls the empire, and so in his song he expresses the wish to preserve, "to guard the four frontiers." True to a pattern established early in his "Annals," success for him depends upon finding and conserving men of capability.

These songs appear very close to the end of each protagonist's life and are, in a sense, farewells Sima Qian uses to establish a fundamental distinction between the two dominant personalities of the Qin-Han transitional period. But this distinction appears even more dramatically in the contrast between their deaths. After an astounding final stand, in which he personally slays "several hundred" Han soldiers and proves to his own men that "it is heaven that is destroying me and not a fault of my military prowess," Xiang Yu, facing certain death, takes his most dramatic and ultimate action—he slits his own throat.[57] I have already noted Sima Qian's fascination with suicide, an act that he rejected for himself but that many of his finest literary characters, in a sense his alter egos, perform with sure resolve. The death of the victor, Liu Bang, could not be more different from that of Xiang Yu. In a battle against the rebel Jing Bu, the emperor is hit by a stray arrow. Although a physician assures him that the wound can be healed, he refuses treatment: "Is this not heaven-ordained fate? Since fate exists in heaven, even the physician Bianque would be of no benefit!"[58] The Han emperor, who has been portrayed all along as a man of destiny, accepts his injury passively and refuses to take any action at all. His wound festers, and he dies.

In their final moments, both Sima Qian's Xiang Yu and Sima Qian's Liu Bang speak of fate, the force that, in large measure, has shaped their lives. The issue of the "border between heaven and man," as reflected in the problem of fate, is a major topic of these "Annals" and also appears in Sima Qian's final judgments of the two chapters. With regard to Xiang Yu, Sima Qian confronts the issue directly:

> When [Xiang] Yu turned his back on the pass and embraced Chu, exiled the Dutiful Emperor and established himself on the throne, and then resented the kings and marquises for rebelling against him, it was a calamity! He boasted of his own achievements, promoted his private wisdom and did not take antiquity as his model. He called it the "work of a hegemon-king" and desired to

manage the empire with force. In five years he perished and lost his kingdom. When he died at Dongcheng, he still did not wake up and did not upbraid his own errors! Instead, he said, "Heaven is destroying me; it is not a fault of using troops!" How could this not be absurd indeed![59]

In his judgment of Liu Bang, Sima Qian's comments surprisingly avoid any direct comment upon the emperor himself. Instead, they are directed to the whole problem of the succession of dynasties. Obviously, Liu Bang, who exists and succeeds largely as a result of heaven's will, does not greatly interest Sima Qian as an individual. After briefly expounding the cyclical theory described earlier, whereby the Han had reverted to the "loyalty" of the Xia as a fit replacement for the decline in Zhou "culture," Sima Qian continues:

> The period between the Zhou and Qin can be called "the exhaustion of culture." However, the government of Qin did not change, but, on the contrary, made punishments and laws harsh. Could that not be absurd? Therefore, Han arose, accepted the exhaustion [of Zhou] and transformed it. Causing men to be untiring, they obtained heaven's succession![60]

Both of these judgments seem to indicate that Xiang Yu's failure and Liu Bang's success were not so much "heaven" as "man." The former made a series of disastrous decisions that led to his downfall, and, consequently, his final use of heaven as an explanation for failure is, according to Sima Qian, an absurd self-delusion. Liu Bang's success was the result of his correct perception of what was needed and the unflagging effort of his followers. However, the conclusion drawn from Sima Qian's final judgments, which puts the burden of history squarely on man's shoulders, is not justified by the narrative itself. Once again, as in the case of Wu Zixu, Sima Qian's narrative and formal judgment appear to contradict one another. Liu Bang, as we have seen, was marked from the beginning as heaven's choice, he needs only to follow and yield to inevitability. One can, of course, argue that Sima Qian stresses approval of Liu Bang as an obligatory bow toward a dynastic founder, a bow that should not be taken seriously. There are, after all, miraculous stories throughout *Records of the Historian* concerning the birth of other dynastic founders, and evidence also can be found elsewhere in his work that Sima Qian himself did not place absolute faith in such miraculous accounts.[61] Surely, political discretion required that Sima Qian establish a case for the divine legitimacy of the ruling dynasty. But even if we grant the general logic of such arguments, the sense of inevitability throughout the narratives of Xiang Yu's defeat and Liu Bang's victory is too persistent to be so easily brushed aside. When the man of action, Xiang Yu, is frozen in inactivity, and Liu Bang escapes, or when Liu Bang passively awaits "fate," as at the moment of his death, the reader suspects that in Sima Qian's account inevitable forces, as much as the human decisions praised and condemned in the two judgments, are driving history relentlessly forward.

There are, of course, other striking examples of this force of inevitability that we have so far not noted. On one occasion, Liu Bang is hopelessly surrounded by the troops of Xiang Yu:

> Thereupon a great wind arose from the northwest. It snapped off trees, blew off roofs, and raised sand and rocks. Growing dark, day turned into night. The storm blew against the troops of Chu, and the troops of Chu were in great confusion, broke apart and scattered. Liu Bang [the King of Han] then managed to escape with several tens of cavalry.[62]

Thus, a divine wind blew for Liu Bang just as it was to blow for the English against the Spanish Armada seventeen centuries later. Xiang Yu can fight Liu Bang, but he cannot contend against all nature!

In fact, Xiang Yu must sense almost from the beginning of the struggle with his opponent that his constant and energetic action is doomed, that the force of fate is on the other side. Shortly before the Hongmen banquet, that moment when the restless actor cannot act, his brilliant political advisor, Fan Zeng, tells him: "I have sent men to observe his (Liu Bang's) vapors. In all cases they form dragons and tigers in five colors. These are the vapors of a Son of Heaven. Quickly attack him and do not lose the opportunity."[63] But we know, as Sima Qian's Xiang Yu must have realized, that the very advice to act carries with it the sure knowledge that such action is doomed to fail. Liu Bang *will become* the Son of Heaven, and Xiang Yu will be rightfully remembered as the "frustrated king" (*fen wang*).

The difficulty in locating Sima Qian's boundary between the realm of heaven and the realm of man grows, in part, from a conflict between what I would call "narrative sympathies" and "ideological sympathies." One cannot read Sima Qian's stirring and impassioned account of Xiang Yu, and compare it to his rather bland narrative of Liu Bang, without suspecting that on some level Sima Qian's sympathies are on the side of the "frustrated king." While Xiang Yu is portrayed as cruel and violent, he is also given a nobility and stature that his opponent cannot match. And despite the ostensible cruelty, we should remember that one of Liu Bang's advisors, perhaps giving voice to Sima Qian's own feelings, pronounces Xiang Yu "humane and fond of others." Moreover, Xiang Yu possesses that characteristic of greatest interest to Sima Qian—he is, in the words of his uncle Xiang Liang, "curious" (*qi* 奇). An admiration for such qualities drives Sima Qian's narrative and provides the power that has made the "Basic Annals of Xiang Yu" one of the most widely admired and anthologized pieces of Sima Qian's prose.

Nevertheless, at the end of the chapter, Sima Qian lays down the mantel of the narrator, puts his own story aside, and makes a final comment as a Confucian historian and ideologue on the story he has just told, and these statements, scholars have sometimes claimed, are particularly valuable in reconstructing "the thought of Sima Qian."[64] But an ideological construct based upon the judgments sometimes requires that we ignore the narrative itself. In these two cases, Sima Qian's judgments seem to say that we have here one story of a man who mistakenly blames fate for his personal failures and another story of a man who saw what needed to be done and did it. Such a flat reading of the two narratives, I maintain, is impossible.

No matter how much Sima Qian, the detached moralist, would like to place the burden for success and failure squarely on man, he cannot do so. He returns, more subtly and more powerfully, in the stories of Xiang Yu and Liu Bang to several of the questions that obsess him in the "Traditions of Bo Yi": Where is justice? Does blind heaven provide a script that promiscuously promotes some and destroys others? Can the historian correct that script in any significant way? As we have seen, Sima Qian has deep personal involvement in these questions. That involvement, and the passion it generates, ultimately complicate, perhaps even undermine, his attempt to forge a single school.

The problem of distilling the thought of a consistent philosophy from Sima Qian's writings not only appears in the shifting boundaries between heaven and earth but also with regard to the transition from antiquity to modernity. Perhaps, as stated earlier in this chapter, Sima Qian's notion of historical change basically follows an organic model and therefore requires an examination of an institution or an individual throughout an entire cycle of life. But there are instances of rupture that cannot be forseen from a model of gradual organic change. These are often moments of surprise that the reader could not predict and that give Sima Qian's text such interest. One of these moments is, of course, the Hongmen banquet scene. What is there in Xiang Yu's previous behavior that would lead us to expect such indecision? Other examples abound in *Records of the Historian*: the inexplicable breakdown of the young killer and "tough" Qin Wuyang, which thwarts Jing Ke's assassination of the king of Qin, the sudden and rather humorous "leaping" of Zhao Xiangzi's heart on the way to the toilet, which allows him to escape Yu Rang's trap, and so on.[65] In these cases, and many others, one senses a force of destiny that cuts across organic development and frustrates the predictability inherent in a notion of gradual transformation.[66] It is, of course, precisely such moments that create and empower the story.

Although Sima Qian, true to his ideological roots, may want to present us with a new, coherent synthesis, the records of the past, and his representation of those records in new narratives subvert his effort. Sima Qian's interests as a narrator, and the strong forces feeding those interests, block unity and create a kaleidoscope of characters who are not easily classified and turned into unequivocal examples. When all is said and done, Sima Qian is not a philosopher of history, and he certainly is not a moralist. He is, instead, a literary genius who writes his story as much as history.

Epilogue

Sima Qian lived at a time frequently identified in the minds of art historians with the bronze mirror. These precious objects, with one side of polished metal and the other side covered with a rich and still somewhat mysterious iconography, were used not just for practical purposes but were also precious talismans buried with the dead. The mirror, it was believed, could capture light and illumine the darkness of the tomb, while the symbols on the back may have represented the cosmos and served to orient the spirit on its journey into another world.

In Chinese civilization, the mirror also becomes a metaphor for history. Such a connection first appears in Sima Qian's writings: "To dwell in the present generation but to be intent upon the doctrine of antiquity is a way of providing a mirror for oneself."[1] The *Family Sayings of Confucius*, a text probably collected from older sources within a hundred years or so after Sima Qian's death, elaborates the metaphor: "A clear mirror is a means to examine the form. Turning toward the past is a means to understand the present."[2]

Indeed, more than one thousand years after Sima Qian, another great historian surnamed Sima, Sima Guang (1019–86), wrote the only comprehensive history of China yet to rival the genius of *Records of the Historian*—its title, *A Comprehensive Mirror to Assist Rule (Zizhi tongjian)*. By looking into the mirror of his history, the latter Sima hoped to provide rulers then and thereafter with a clear and useful vision of their own behavior and its inevitable consequences. In accord with such an idea, history in China to the present day is often regarded as the most practical and contemporary of subjects. Indeed, modern Chinese continue to speak of the present through debating the past.

Certainly *Spring and Autumn Annals*, as Sima Qian describes it, is the perfect mirror to discern one's true shape: "Those who

145

govern must know *Spring and Autumn Annals,* or before them will
be slander, and they will not see it; and behind them will be violence, and they will not know."[3] Sima Qian, as an inheritor of the
classical Confucian tradition, would present a mirror as clear as the
masterwork of Confucius, "revealing in actual events" clear principles that "distinguish the suspicious and doubtful, clarify right
and wrong, and settle what was undecided."[4]

In spite of such goals, Sima Qian was stirred, as we have seen,
by motives other than to be a clear conveyor of Confucian morality:
"I am frustrated," Sima Qian once said, "that my heart has that
which it has not completely expressed." As a man who had suffered
much, and who believed that all distinguished literature is born in
suffering, the Han historian not only assembled and attempted to
make sense from the abundant texts of the past but also poured out
sentiments from a heart shaped by a curious and traumatic series of
personal events. Those sentiments, as I have tried to show, profoundly shape *Records of the Historian* and impart to it some of the
same questions and ambiguities that can be seen in the text of Sima
Qian's life.

Central to Sima Qian's portrayal of his own experience, as we
have seen above, is a complicated relationship to authority. The
memory of his father urging him to follow Confucius strengthened
his resolve, he tells us, to withstand the brutal punishment of
another authority, Emperor Wu. His father, in this tangle, becomes
the primary authority and leads him to a rather extreme emphasis
upon filial duty. In a provocative and important article, entitled
"Selfhood and Otherness," Tu Wei-ming tries to show how filial
obedience in Confucian thought is subordinated to self-realization
so that disobedience to one's father, at least in some circumstances,
can be justified.[5] I would not in general dispute Tu's gentle construction of filial piety, but Sima Qian, I believe, is moved by more
extreme expressions of this virtue than Tu's model would approve.
We have already examined the narrative of the two Wu brothers,
Shang and Yun, who each lived and died under a heavy burden of
filial obligation. An even more startling example of such duty appears in the "Hereditary Household of Kang Shu of Wei" (chapter
37). The story is of Duke Xuan of Wei (r. 718–700 B.C.E.) and his two
sons and is rewritten by Sima Qian from *Zuo Commentary.*

A close comparison of the two versions, one in *Zuo Commentary* and the other in *Records of the Historian,* will not concern us
here, although such a comparison demonstrates critical differences
between the lapidary *Zuo* accounts and the more clearly motivated

stories of *Records of the Historian*.[6] The critical point of current concern is that this is a story of an unworthy father, Duke Xuan, who conspires to murder his son, the rightful heir to the dukedom of Wei. Duke Xuan orders criminals to ambush and kill any traveller who approaches them with a white banner, a banner he then gives to his heir. A loyal half brother discloses the conspiracy, but the heir does nothing to avert the calamity. "To go against a father's command and seek to live," he says, "is not right." This filial son is not like the mythical Emperor Shun, whom Tu Wei-ming applauds for not being "submissive to the brutality of his father." But the story is even more extreme than this. The half-brother tries to save the heir's life by snatching away the white banner and riding into the ambush first himself. He is killed, but the heir insists on dying too: "The one you ought to have killed is I," he protests to the criminals. In his final judgment on this tale, Sima Qian applauds the heir for "hating to damage his father's intent," and exclaims, further, "How sad this is!"[7]

Sima Qian's comments display two interrelated and critical facets of his historiography: first, the echoes of his own past continually wrap around his accounts of the past; and second, his involvement with his stories is as much emotional as intellectual. Sima Qian is no Thucydides, "objectively" constructing a rational account of the past. He presents himself as fully human and is, I believe, profoundly entangled in his history.

Founded as much by the heat of personal anxiety as by the cold facts of the past, Sima Qian's mirror is a distorted and cloudy one. The "doctrine of antiquity" that he has given us is not easily discerned. In fact, the contours of greatest interest in his mirror are often the contours of stories, and such stories consistently derive power and continued interest from their narrative and moral complexity. We so frequently return to *Records of the Historian*, as we return to other of the world's great classics, because this text is as difficult and confusing as life itself. The clouds in Sima Qian's mirror are the patterns of a full and intricate human being and are, thereby, the clouds that in one way or another trouble us all.

Appendix: Chronology of Sima Qian's Life

Year	Major Events in the Life of Sima Qian	Relevant Events in Han History
145 B.C.E.	Sima Qian born near Longmen along the western bank of the Yellow River probably in Hancheng county of modern-day Shanxi province.	
141		Emperor Wu ascends the throne at the age of sixteen.
140	Sima Tan, Sima Qian's father, begins serving the Han court as Duke Grand Astrologer.	
136	Sima Qian says in his "Self-Narration" that "At the age of ten I could recite ancient texts."	Academicians for the Five Classics are formally established.
135		The pro-Taoist Empress Dou dies.
126	Sima Qian says that "At the age of twenty I travelled in the area of the Yangtze and Huai Rivers. I ascended Mt. Guiji and explored the Cave of Yu." Elsewhere, Sima Qian	

Year	Major Events in the Life of Sima Qian	Relevant Events in Han History
	indicates that his travels were extensive (see Zheng Haosheng, pp. 39–40).	
124	Begins service as Gentleman of the Palace (*Langzhong*).	
123		Capture of a "White Unicorn."
122		Execution of Liu An, the Prince of Huainan and sponsor of eclectic Taoism.
111	Sent by Emperor Wu as a part of an expedition to the southwest regions of Ba and Shu to help create five new commanderies.	
110	Death of Sima Tan near Luoyang and his final injunction to his son.	Emperor Wu performs the *feng* and *shan* sacrifices at Mount Tai.
108	Succeeds his father as Prefect Grand Astrologer.	
104	Completes work on new calendar, which is proclaimed in this year.	
99	Accused of "defaming his superior" for supporting the failed general Li Ling.	Small force led by General Li Ling is defeated by the Huns.
98	Undergoes punishment of castration in the "Silkworm Chamber."	
96	Rehabilitated and appointed Prefect Palace Secretary (*Zhong shu ling*).	
95		Another "White Unicorn" captured.
93/91?	Writes his famous "Letter in Response to Ren An"	

Year	Major Events in the Life of Sima Qian	Relevant Events in Han History
	explaining why he chose to remain alive and undergo punishment rather than commit suicide.	
91		Famous "Black Magic Case."
87		Death of Emperor Wu.
86	Death of Sima Qian(?).	

Notes

Introduction

1. *Lun yu jijie* (hereafter, *LY*), *SBBY* ed., 6:7.

2. Jean Levi, *Le Fils du ciel et son annaliste* (Paris: Gallimard, 1992), p. 10.

3. Sima Qian's precise dates are a subject of some controversy. There are two theories concerning his date of birth. The first, supported by Wang Guowei, Liang Qichao, Zheng Haosheng, and others, puts his birth in 145 B.C.E. The second, held by Guo Moruo and Li Changzhi, gives his birth as 135 B.C.E. The evidence for either position is meager. Unless additional information comes to light, it is difficult to go beyond Zheng Haosheng's 1956 essay, which argues in favor of 145. See "Sima Qian shengnian wenti de shangque," appended to Zheng's *Sima Qian nianpu* (revised edition, Shanghai: Commercial Press, 1956). A more recent summary of arguments concerning Sima Qian's dates, also favoring 145, is found in Zhang Dake, *Shi ji yanjiu* (Lanzhou: Gansu People's Press, 1985), pp. 74–120.

4. *Shi ji* 130, p. 3292. All quotes from *Shi ji* (hereafter, *SJ*) are to the "Mainland punctuated edition" (Beijing: Zhonghua, 1959). A complete translation of Sima Qian's "postface" is found in Burton Watson's excellent study, *Ssu-ma Ch'ien, Grand Historian of China* (New York: Columbia University Press, 1958). I have used my own translations throughout unless otherwise noted.

5. *SSJZS* ed. (rpt., Taibei: Yiwen, 1973), vol. I, p. 6a.

6. For this story, see Wang Jia (d. 324 C.E.), *Shi yi ji*, *SKQS* ed., 2:2a–b.

7. This particular story, which appears in Li Daoyuan (d. 527 C.E.), *Shui jing zhu*, *SBCK* ed., 4:2a, becomes the source of the idiom "to bump one's head at Dragon Gate" and "to leap over Dragon Gate," meaning respectively to fail and to pass the civil service examination. For more information and tales about Longmen, see *Han cheng xian zhi*, Qianlong 49 (1784), 1:10a–11b.

8. *SJ* 130, p. 3293.

9. For some observations on this issue, see my article "Ssu-ma Ch'ien's Conception of *Tso chuan,*" *JAOS* 112:2 (April-June, 1992), pp. 295-301.

10. On the Han capital of Chang'an, see Wang Zhongshu, *Han Civilization,* translated by K.C. Chang (New Haven and London: Yale University Press, 1982), pp. 1-28.

11. The cosmological and religious significance of the early Chinese city is the subject of Paul Wheatley's, *The Pivot of the Four Quarters: A Preliminary Inquiry into the Origins and Character of the Ancient Chinese City* (Edinburgh: Edinburgh University Press, 1971).

12. Xiao Tong, *Wen Xuan or Selections of Refined Literature, Volume One: Rhapsodies on Metropolises and Capitals,* translated by David Knechtges (Princeton: Princeton University Press, 1982), p. 101.

13. (1949; rpt., Taibei: Kaiming, 1976), pp. 4-5.

14. Ibid., p. 23. A slight variant of Li Changzhi's scheme can be found in Wen Chongyi, who analyzes a conflict in Sima Qian between a bright, happy youth and a very depressed, grim middle- and old-age. See "Lun Sima Qian de sixiang," *Shi ji lunwen xuanji,* ed. by Huang Peirong (Taibei: Chang'an, 1982), pp. 41-42.

15. *LY* 6:7b (6.27); 9:4a (9.11); and 12:5a (12.15).

16. *The Trouble with Confucianism* (Cambridge, Mass.: Harvard University Press, 1991), p. 41.

17. *Poetry and Personality: Reading, Exegesis, and Hermeneutics in Traditional China* (Stanford: Stanford University Press, 1991), p. 11.

18. *Zhuangzi,* SBBY ed., 10:13b-14a.

19. Some argue that the report of the execution of the scholars is "almost certainly fictional." See Derk Bodde, "The State and the Empire of Ch'in," *The Cambridge History of China,* volume 1: *The Ch'in and Han Empires, 221 B.C.-A.D. 220,* edited by Dennis Twitchett and Michael Loewe (Cambridge: Cambridge University Press, 1986), pp. 95-96.

20. "Liang Han bo shi jiafa kao," *Liang Han jingxue jin gu wen pingyi* (Taibei: Dongda, 1983), p. 169.

21. *SJ* 6, p. 258. For greater detail on the history of the Office of the Academicians, see Qian Mu, "Liang Han bo shi", pp. 165-233.

22. See Wu Hung, *The Wu Liang Shrine: The Ideology of Early Chinese Pictorial Art* (Stanford, California: Stanford University Press, 1989), pp. 148-56.

23. Watson, *Ssu-ma Ch'ien;* Edouard Chavannes, *Les Mémoires historiques de Se-ma Ts'ien,* vol. 1 (1895; rpt., Paris: Librairie d'Amérique et

d'Orient, 1967); Li Changzhi, *Sima Qian*; and Zhang Dake, *Shi yi yanjiu.* Happily, a complete English translation of *Records of the Historian*, which promises to be an exhaustive study as well, is currently in preparation under the direction of Professor William Nienhauser of the University of Wisconsin.

24. Wang Guowei, "Tai shi gong xingnian kao," *Guantang jilin*, vol. 11 (rpt., Shanghai: Guji, 1983); and Zheng, *Sima Qian nianpu.*

25. For a somewhat lengthier introduction to this structure, see my "Shih-chi" in *The Indiana Companion to Traditional Chinese Literature*, ed. by William Nienhauser (Bloomington: Indiana University Press, 1986), pp. 689–94.

26. *SJ* 62, p. 2136.

27. *Ssu-ma Ch'ien*, pp. 120–22.

28. Liu Zhiji (661–721), the great Tang scholar of historical writing, notes that "In the case of *Springs and Autumns*, the *zhuan* explains a 'classic' (*jing*). In the case of *Records of the Historian* and *History of the Han*, the *zhuan* explains an 'annal' (*ji*)." Thus, in Liu's mind, the "Basic Annals" constitutes the backbone of *Records of the Historian* and the "Traditions" (*lie zhuan*) are explanatory or supplementary. See *Shitong tongshi* (A Comprehensive Explanation of *A Study of Historiography*) (rpt., Taibei: Liren, 1980), p. 46. See also Chen Shih-hsiang, "An Innovation in Chinese Biographical Writing," *Far Eastern Quarterly* 13 (November 1953): 44–62.

29. See the explanation in Xu Fuguan, in "Lun *Shi ji*," *Zhongguo shixue shi lunwen xuanji*, vol. 3 (Taibei: Huashi, 1980), pp. 136–37.

30. *SJ* 61, p. 2121.

31. *HS* 30, p. 1714.

32. Ibid.

33. Takikawa Kametarō, "Shiki sōron," *Shiki kaichū kōshō* (1934; rpt., Taibei: Hongshi, 1986), p. 105. For a defense of Chu Shaosun, see Li Changzhi, *Sima Qian*, pp. 194–99.

34. See, for example, the arguments of A. F. P. Hulsewé in "The Problem of the Authenticity of *Shi-chi* Ch. 123, The Memoir on Ta Yüan," *T'oung Pao* 40.1-3 (1975): 83–147. Hulsewé's arguments have been answered in part by Kazuo Enoki, "On the Relationship Between the *Shih-chi*, Bk. 123 and the *Han-shu*, Bks. 61 and 96," *Memoirs of the Research Department of the Toyo Bunko* 41 (1983): 1–32.

35. *Mémoires*, vol. I, pp. ccix–ccx.

36. New York and London: W. W. Norton & Co., 1992.

1. The Frustration of the Second Confucius

1. Wolfgang Bauer, *Das Antlitz Chinas: Die autobiographische Selbstdarstellung in der Chinesischen Literatur von ihren Anfängen bis Heute* (Munich: Carl Hanswer Verlag, 1990), p. 79.

2. Ban Gu's account of Sima Qian is found in *HS* 62, pp. 2707–39.

3. The "Self-Narration," found in *SJ* 130, is translated by Watson (*Ibid.*, pp. 42–57). The "Letter in Response to Ren An" is found in *HS* 62, pp. 2725–36. Useful translations of the letter are: Chavannes, *Mémoires*, vol. I, ccxxvi–xli; Watson, *Ssu-ma Chien*, pp. 57–67; and J. R. Hightower in *Anthology of Chinese Literature from Early Times to the Fourteenth Century*, edited by Cyril Birch (New York: Grove Press, 1965), pp. 95–102. The precise dating of the letter is a problem. Early commentators insist that Ren An was executed for his involvement in the famous succession crisis and witchcraft case of 91 B.C.E. Thus, Chavannes dates the letter to this time (*Mémoires*, p. xlii). This date, however, contradicts certain information found in the letter itself. Watson thoroughly reviews all available evidence and places the letter to Ren An in the eleventh lunar month of 93 B.C.E. (*Ssu-ma Ch'ien*), pp. 194–98.

4. For a good summary of the important role of this classic in the Han, see Pi Xirui, *Jingxue lishi*, with notes by Zhou Yutong (1961; rpt., Taibei: Hanjing wenhua shiye, 1983), pp. 41–42. It was not long after Sima Qian that one Han dynasty apocryphal text could quote Confucius as stating that "My ideas are in *Spring and Autumn Annals*, and the actions I recommend are in the *Classic of Filial Piety*" (ibid., p. 42).

5. *SJ* 38, p. 1610. For Takikawa's comment, see *SKKC*, 38:7 (p. 609). If Takikawa's surmise is correct, then Sima Qian is breaking apart the analogy, widespread in the Han, between the father-son and the ruler-minister relationship, and is attaching greater importance to the former. On this point, see Xu Fuguan, "Tai shi gong de sixiang beijing ji qi shixue jingshen," *Shi ji lunwen xuanji*, p. 17.

6. The title *tai shi gong* has frequently been translated as "Grand Historian." Chavannes was correct, I believe, to render the term as "Duc grand astrologue." It is a variant of the title *tai shi ling*, a position in the Han bureaucracy translated by Hans Bielenstein as "Prefect Grand Astrologer." See *The Bureaucracy of Han Times* (Cambridge: Cambridge University Press, 1980), p. 19. On the equivalence of the two offices, see *Zhongguo shixue shi cidian* (Taibei: Minwen, 1986), p. 30

7. *SJ* 130, p. 3288.

8. The quotation is taken from *Zhuangzi*, SBBY ed., 10:14a. However, this particular chapter (chapter 33) may be from as late as the first century

of the Han dynasty. See A. C. Graham, *Chuang Tzu: The Inner Chapters* (London: George Allen & Unwin, 1981), p. 257.

9. Kung-chuan Hsiao's explanation of the "decline" into disunity is an accurate reflection both of this belief and of the ambivalence that continues to characterize Chinese descriptions of this intellectually lively period. See *A History of Chinese Political Thought*, trans. by Frederick Mote (Princeton: Princeton University Press, 1979), pp. 437–38.

10. As is well-known, even Hanfeizi's aggressive Legalism, which made a deep impression on the First Qin Emperor, was deeply influenced by both Taoism and Confucianism and is, therefore, partially a product of synthesis. Sima Qian himself saw such a close relationship between Laozi and Hanfeizi that he put their "Traditions" in a single chapter (*SJ*, chapter 63). This synthesis of Taoism and Legalism is to become the Huang-Lao Taoism so popular in the early Han. By way of contrast, Liu An's *Huainanzi* is a splendid example of synthesis, but Liu himself plotted revolt against Emperor Wu and possibly regarded his book as the textual basis for a new, revolutionary political order.

11. *Xunzi, SBBY* ed., 3:7b–17b (chapter 6). A careful English translation of this important chapter can be found in John Knoblock, *Xunzi: A Translation and Study of the Complete Works* (Stanford: Stanford University Press, 1988), pp. 212–29.

12. Ibid., 8a, 8b, etc.

13. 10:13a–23b (chapter 33). For an English translation, see Watson, *Ssu-ma Ch'ien*, pp. 362–77, and A. C. Graham, *Chuang Tzu*, pp. 274–85.

14. Qian Mu's analysis of this text is particularly interesting. He sees Lü Buwei's work as an attempt to use the eclecticism and richness of Eastern culture (represented by the states of Lu and Qi) to combat the legalistic and rather militaristic philosophies of the north and west (particularly the "three-Jin"), which had been carried to Qin originally by Lord Shang and others. See his fascinating analysis of this issue in *Qin Han shi* (rpt., Taibei: Dongfang, 1985), pp. 4–11.

15. *SJ* 85, p. 2510. Compare *Lü shi chun qiu, SBBY* ed., 12:9.

16. Kung-chuan Hsiao notes that *"Huai-nan Tzu (Huainanzi)* took form just as the Han period burgeoning of Huang-Lao doctrines reached its peak and was on the verge of declining, and as the Confucian school was beginning to win the court's admiration" (*Chinese Political Thought*, pp. 572–73).

17. *Shi ji yanjiu*, p. 7. See also Wu Zhongkuang in "Xian Qin xueshu sixiang de lishixing zongjie," *Sima Qian he Shi ji*, ed. by Liu Naihe (Beijing: Beijing Press, 1987), p. 200. For some speculation on the possible relationship between Sima Qian and Dong Zhongshu, see my "Tangles and Lacu-

nae: A Few Aspects of Ssu-ma Ch'ien's Portrayal of His Intellectual Antecedents," *Chen Qilu yuanshi qizhi rongqing lunwenji* (Taibei: Xuesheng,
1992), pp. 439–50.

18. *SJ* 130, p. 3289.

19. One can contrast the highly cynical interpretation of the reigns of
Emperors Wen and Jing presented in Li Changzhi, *Sima Qian*, pp. 126–27,
for example, with the picture given by Qian Mu, *Qin Han shi*, pp. 60–63.

20. Kung-chuan Hsiao divides his study of Han political thought into
three periods. The watershed for the first two, which concerns us here, is
141 B.C.E. Before this, "Huang-Lao doctrines flourished" . . . and even the
Confucians "were subject to their inevitable influences"; while after this,
"the Confucians had thrown off the bridle of Huang-Lao and were in sole
possession of the age's esteem" (*Chinese Political Thought*, p. 412). In other
words, the Confucians, under Emperor Wu, completed an intellectual conquest similar to the political conquest of the First Qin Emperor eighty years
before. There is some controversy over the exact extent of this "conquest."
For two somewhat different perspectives, see Homer Dubs, "The Victory of
Han Confucianism," *History of the Han Dynasty*, vol. II (American Council
of Learned Societies, 1944), pp. 341–53; and Benjamin Wallacker, "Han
Confucianism and Confucius in Han," *Ancient China: Studies in Early
Civilization*, ed. by David T. Roy and Tsuen-hsuin Tsien (Hong Kong: The
Chinese University Press, 1978), pp. 215–28. As Yu Qiding notes in one of
the most thorough studies of this problem, however ambiguous and limited
the "Confucian victory" might have been in the political realm, Confucianism did gain control at this time of the official educational structure. See
Yu's *Xian Qin Liang Han rujia jiaoyu* (Beijing, 1987), p. 92.

21. Sima Tan is quoting *Xiao jing, SBBY* ed., 3b.

22. *SJ* 130, p. 3295.

23. *SJ* 130, p. 3296.

24. *Mengzi Zhao zhu, SBBY* ed. 14:7a (7B:38). Jia Yi says, "I have heard
that from Yu on down five hundred years passed and Tang arose. From Tang
on down more than five hundred years passed and King Wu arose. Therefore, the appearance of a sage-king takes five hundred years as its chronological period" (*Xin shu, SBBY* ed., 1:8a). Sima Qian refers to the importance
of the five-hundred-year period elsewhere in *Records of the Historian*,
where it is called the period of "a great transformation" (*SJ* 27, p. 1344). Li
Shaoyong argues that the notion of such a cycle is related to the theory of
the five processes (*wu xing*) (*Sima Qian zhuanji wenxue lun gao*
[Chongqing: Xinhua, 1987], p. 68).

25. *Chun qiu Zuo zhuan zhu*, ed. by Yang Bojun (Beijing: Zhonghua,
1981), Ai 14, p. 1680.

26. *SJ* 130, p. 3295.

27. *SJ* 130, p. 3296.

28. See the account of Sima Qian himself as translated by Burton Watson, *Ssu-Ch'ien*, pp. 57–67. Chavannes discusses the entire episode in his *Les Mémoires historiques*, vol. I, pp. xxxvi–xliv. The best account of Li Ling's ill-fated expedition is Michael Loewe's "loose translation" of *HS* 54: "The Campaigns of Han Wu-ti," *Chinese Ways in Warfare*, eds. Frank A. Kierman, Jr. and John K. Fairbank (Cambridge, Mass.: Harvard University Press, 1974), pp. 119–22.

29. *HS* 62, p. 2730. The name "Silkworm Hall" comes from the fact that this room was dark and warm, like a room where silkworms are grown "to avoid wind and cold." The reason for the reduction of the punishment to castration is something of a mystery. Lü Xisheng has discussed possible provisions for this change under Han law and concludes that Sima Qian himself would have had to petition for such a reduction. See "Sima Qian gongxing xiyi," *Zhongguo shi yanjiu* 4 (1983): 68.

30. *HS* 62, p. 2736.

31. This demand is stated emphatically in *Classic of Filial Piety*, which says, "The trunk, limbs, hair of the head, and skin are received from our parents. We dare not to harm them" (*Xiao jing*, 3b). The necessity to return the body to the grave whole is also alluded to in *LY* 8:1b (8.3).

32. *HS* 62, p. 2727.

33. *Sima Qian*, p. 50. See also the numerous examples of Sima Qian's regard for the authority of Confucius given in ibid., pp. 43–50.

34. *SJ* 130, p. 3299. Hu Sui, it should be noted, is an actual historical figure who worked with Sima Qian on the calendar revision announced in 105 B.C.E. and initiated in 104 B.C.E. Sima Qian comments on Hu Sui in *SJ* 108, p. 2865, describing him as "correct of heart and deeply devoted." Whether the dialogue with Hu Sui recorded in the "Self-Narration" ever took place or not is, of course, impossible to say.

35. He is, of course, somewhat disingenuous in such a claim. *Records of the Historian*, as many scholars have observed, is filled with direct and implied criticisms of Emperor Wu and his policies. For example, Sima Qian presents a clear description and ringing indictment of the economic and political breakdown of his own time in chapter 29 of *Records of the Historian*, translated by Burton Watson as "The Balanced Standard," *Records of the Grand Historian of China*, Number LXV of the Records of Civilization (New York: Columbia University Press, 1971), vol. 1, pp. 79–106.

36. *SJ* 130, pp. 3299–3300.

37. *LY* 7:1a (7.1).

38. *Gongyang zhuan, SSJZS* ed., Ai 14.

39. *SJ* 28, p. 1387; and 130, p. 3300.

40. *SJ* 130, pp. 3319–20.

41. *SJ* 130, p. 3319.

42. Cf. *SJ* 130, p. 3300 and *HS* 62, p. 2735.

43. "The Scholar's Frustration: Notes on a Type of Fu," *Chinese Thought and Institutions,* ed. by John K. Fairbank (Chicago: Chicago University Press, 1957), pp. 310–19.

44. The translation is from James Robert Hightower, "The Fu of T'ao Ch'ien," *HJAS* 17 (1954): 198. There is also some question as to whether this rhapsody is indeed the work of Sima Qian. Tao Qian (365–427 C.E.) accepted the attribution as do a number of modern scholars. See Zhao Xingzhi, "Sima Qian fu zuo de pingjia," *Sima Qian: qi ren ji qi shu* (1960; rpt., Taibei: Chang'an, 1985), pp. 170–86.

45. *SJ* 130, p. 3300.

46. *SJ* 130, p. 3295.

47. See *SJ* 61, p. 2125: "If it is not just, he does not put forth energy." It is in this same sense that the term appears in *LY* 7:4a–4b (7.19).

48. See the discussion on this word family in Wang Li, *Tongyuan zidian* (rpt., Taibei: Wenshizhe, 1982), p. 525.

49. *SJ* 84, pp. 2481, 2486, 2490. I have adapted slightly the excellent translation of this piece by David Hawkes, *Ch'u Tz'u: The Songs of the South* (Oxford: Clarendon, 1959), pp. 12–13.

50. For some interesting ideas on Sima Qian's use of the Qu Yuan myth, see Laurence A. Schneider, *A Madman of Ch'u: The Chinese Myth of Loyalty and Dissent* (Berkeley: University of California Press, 1980), pp. 17–24.

51. See Chavannes, *Mémoires,* vol. I, pp. xliii–xliv.

52. The term I have translated here as "despondent," *yi yu* 抑鬱, means literally "to push down and block up" (*HS* 62, p. 2725). The first character of this compound, *yi,* is defined in *Shuo wen jie zi* as "to press down." The character seems to derive from an ancient form in which a hand pushes someone into a kneeling position. See Xu Shen, *Shuo wen jie zi gulin,* ed. by Ding Fubao (rpt., Taibei: Commercial Press, 1976), pp. 4429b–30b. The second character, *yu,* originally means "trees growing thickly," but comes to mean "blocked up" (ibid., p. 2685b).

53. *HS* 62, pp. 2727–28.

54. *HS* 62, p. 2733. *Yin* originally meant "to draw a bow." See *Shuo*

wen, p. 5769a–69b. *Jue* is often used in ancient Chinese to mean "open up a channel" so that water can flow freely. See examples in Zhu Junsheng (1788–1858), "Tongxun dingsheng" commentary reproduced in *Shuo wen jie zi gulin*, p. 5015a.

55. *SJ* 7, p. 336.

56. *SJ* 109, p. 2876.

57. *SJ* 86, pp. 2532–33.

58. *HS* 62, p. 2733.

59. *HS* 62, p. 2735. A propros of this issue Eric Henry has explained that "The principal reason for the popularity of suicide in early China was that it was a demonstration of sincerity or integrity, a way of making one's innermost self known to others." He goes on to note that suicide may be unnecessary if temporary disgrace is offset by long-range honor. See his "Motif of Recognition," *Harvard Journal of Asiatic Studies* 47.1 (June 1987): 13.

60. *HS* 62, pp. 2733–35.

61. *HS* 62, p. 2735.

62. Li Changzhi attempts just this (*Sima Qian*, pp. 151–206).

63. See "Han wenxue shi gangyao," *Lu Xun quanji*, vol. 8 (Beijing: Renmin, 1963), p. 308. "Encountering Sorrow" is, of course, the great lyrical poem of Qu Yuan setting forth, according to the traditional interpretation, his complaint against his ruler for ignoring the loyal service and wise advice he offered.

64. *SJ* 130, p. 3312.

65. See *Shi tong tongshi*, p. 238.

66. *Shi ji pinglin*, ed. by Ling Zhilong (1576; rpt., Taibei: Diqiu, 1992), p. 61:1b. Zhang Dake labels the chapter "a prefatory, eulogizing essay" and says it is no different in form from the prefaces to the "Charts." See his *Shi ji quanti xinzhu* (Xi'an: Sanqin, 1990), p. 1315. Compare Fan Zhonggui, "Shi ji Bo Yi lie zhuan cheng 'qi zhuan yue' kaoshi," *Dalu zazhi* 18.5 (March 1959): 1–3.

67. Indeed, some suspect that the relatively brief "tradition" portion of this chapter is quoted directly from some other source. On this see Qu Yingsheng, "Shi ji lie zhuan yi Bo Yi ju shou zhi yuanyin," *Dalu Zazhi* 12.3 (February 1956): 28–32. Wang Shumin rejects such a notion and argues that Sima Qian's story of Bo Yi and Shu Qi is pieced together from references in such sources as *Zhuangzi*, *Lü shi chun qiu*, and *Han shi waizhuan*. See *Shi ji jiaozheng* (Taibei: Academia Sinica, 1982), vol. 7, p. 1995.

68. *SJ* 61, p. 2121.

69. On these figures, see *Zhuangzi*, 9:16a (chapter 28).

70. *SJ* 61, p. 2121.

71. *SJ* 61, p. 2122. The quotation from Confucius appears in *LY* 5:6b (5.23).

72. Ibid. "Neglected poem" refers to an ancient poem that has not been gathered in *Classic of Poetry*.

73. For an English-language summary of several of these variations, see Sarah Allan, *The Heir and the Sage* (San Francisco: Chinese Materials Center, 1981), pp. 108–17.

74. *SJ* 61, p. 2123. Shen Nong is a mythical ruler of the distant past. Yu is a dynastic title under which the legendary Shun (traditional dates: 2255–2206 B.C.E.) reigned, and Xia is the dynasty that followed (traditional dates: 2205–1766 B.C.E.).

75. *MZ* 2:13a (1B.9). For a translation, see D. C. Lau, *Mencius* (Hong Kong: The Chinese University Press, 1984), Vol. I, p. 39.

76. The debate was between Master Huang and Yuan Gu and is discussed in detail by Kung-chuan Hsiao as an example of the conflict between Legalism and Confucianism in the early Han (*Chinese Political Thought*, pp. 456–57). The original report of the debate is found in *SJ* 121.

77. *SJ* 61, p. 2123.

78. This adage appears in *Laozi*, ch. 79 and also in *Shuo yuan*, where it is attributed to Confucius (*SBCK* ed.), 10:17a. For further variants, see Shi Zhimian, *Shi ji huizhu kaozheng dingbu* (Taibei: Huagang, 1976), p. 1070, and Wang Shumin, *Shi ji jiaozheng*, p. 2000.

79. *SJ* 61, p. 2125.

80. *LY* 15:7b (15.39).

81. *LY* 7:3a (7.24).

82. *LY* 9:7a (9.27).

83. Some commentators believe this is an allusion to *Laozi*, which says, "When the state is in disorder, there are loyal officials" (chapter 18). Just as close is a statement attributed to Qu Yuan in *SJ* 84, p. 2486.

84. *SJ* 61, p. 2126.

85. *SJ* 61, p. 2127.

86. *SJJZ*, p. 2008.

87. *SJ* 61, p. 2127.

88. Ibid.

89. *SJ* 61, p. 2127.

90. In an important article, Xu Fuguan has traced the transformation from a religious to a humanistic historiography in ancient China. The earliest scribes (the so-called *zuo ce*, "makers of registers") were priests who performed an entirely religious function. The office of the astrologer-historian (*shi*), as reflected in *Zuo Commentary*, still shows a primarily religious function and includes such duties as offering prayers, managing divinations, managing the calendar, explaining calamities, presenting imperial commands, and managing genealogies. Xu traces the gradual humanization of this institution from mid-Zhou into the Han but states that "in this Chinese spirit of humanism can be seen the characteristics of a religion." He notes that gradually the judgment of the historian (who is now much more a "historian" than an "astrologer") becomes a substitute for the judgment of gods and also replaces god as the one who ultimately, through the power of the writing brush, grants immortality. See the provocative article "Yuan shi—you zongjiao tongxiang renwen de shixue chengli," *Zhongguo shixue shi lunwen xuanji*, pp. 1–72.

91. *SJ* 61, p. 2127.

92. This hope, to create "a single school," is expressed in "Letter in Response to Ren An" and will be the subject of chapter 6 below.

2. Sima Qian's Confucius

1. Wang Anshi, "Kongzi shi jia yi," *Linchuan xiansheng wenji*, SBTK ed., vol. 46, pp. 71:11b–12a (455–56).

2. Zhao Yi, *Gaiyu congkao* (Taibei: Xinwenfeng, 1975), vol. I, 5:2b.

3. *SJ* 130, p. 3319.

4. *LY* 2:1a (2.1): "Governing with moral power is just like the North Star. It keeps its place and the myriad stars circle it." *Laozi*, SBBY ed., 1.6 (chapter 11): "Thirty spokes share a single hub."

5. Liao Dengting says, "Those who have held the greatest power are given 'Basic Annals,' those who extended [their influence] over a long period of time, are called 'Hereditary Households'; and those who in power are not as great as those in 'Basic Annals,' and in duration are not as long-lasting as 'Hereditary Households,' are called 'Traditions'" (quoted in *SKKC*, 47:2). On this topic, Zhu Dongrun adds, "During the Zhou-Han Period, whoever was able to circle the north star or share the hub and act as a minister of a state, one whose service resembled 'the arms and legs of the ruler,' was put by Sima Qian in 'Hereditary Households.' It did not matter whether or not they founded a fief, or whether or not they continued on [as a family] through generations." See "Shi ji ji biao shu shi jia zhuan shuo li," *Shi ji*

lunwen xuanji, p. 367.

6. *SJ* 130, p. 3310. See Zhu's explanation for including Confucius in this section in *"Shi ji"*, p. 367.

7. This particular view of Confucius' political mission is standard *Gongyang* doctrine. We should not forget that Sima Qian may have been a student of Dong Zhongshu, the premier *Gongyang* scholar of his age and was, at any rate, thoroughly familiar with the great scholar's doctrines. On the Han interpretation of the political mission of Confucius, see "Kongzi yu Chun qiu," *Liang Han jingxue,* pp. 235–83.

8. *Kaoxin lu* (rpt. Taibei: Shijie, 1968), p. 1:4.

9. *Confucius and the Chinese Way* (1949; rpt. New York: Harper & Row, 1960), p. 245.

10. Ibid., p. 248.

11. Cui, *Kaoxin lu.* Qian Mu has considered the life of Confucius in several places. Most noteworthy is his masterful *Xian Qin zhuzi xinian* (2nd ed., Hong Kong: University of Hong Kong Press, 1956), pp. 1–88. Chavannes' work on this chapter is typically impressive. He also includes a short "Note Additionelle," in which he briefly considers the difficult task that faced Sima Qian as he wrote a biography of Confucius (*Mémoires,* vol. 5, pp. 283–445). I should note that there have been more positive appraisals of Sima Qian's work on Confucius than those noted above. Kaizuka Shigeki, for example, says that Sima Qian "put his whole heart into his writing on Confucius.... It might well be argued that of the 130 chapters of the 'Historical Records,' this section secures the most remarkable effect." *Confucius,* trans. by Geoffrey Bowas (London: George Allen & Unwin Ltd., 1956), p. 43.

12. There are three versions of *Analects* mentioned during the Han: an "ancient script" version in twenty-one chapters, which was supposedly found in a wall in Confucius' mansion during the reign of Emperor Jing (r., 157–141 B.C.E.), a Qi version in twenty-two chapters, presumably stemming from a Qi exegetical tradition, and a Lu version in twenty chapters, which derived from a Lu State tradition. Chavannes argues, against several Chinese interpreters, that Sima Qian used the Lu version of *Analects* and not the "ancient script" version. Qu Wanli believes, at any rate, that these two versions were very closely related and stood in opposition to the Qi version, which contained a number of passages not in the Lu text. The texts were then edited by Zhang Yu in the last years of the Former Han. Zhang followed the Lu version but did select some "good portions" of the Qi version. On this subject see He Yan's preface to *Analects* in *Lun yu jijie,* xu (preface), 1a–1b. See also Qu Wanli, *Xian Qin wen shi ziliao kaobian* (Taibei: Lianjing, 1983), p. 384.

13. *LY* 13:3b (13.10).

14. *SJ* 47, 1924.

15. This is illustrated in a recent book on early Confucianism: Robert Eno, *The Confucian Creation of Heaven* (Albany: SUNY Press, 1990), p. 83, where Eno discusses a passage from *Analects* (7.23) that "makes little sense unless one accepts contextual material found in the *Shih-chi*."

16. Zhao 7, pp. 1295–96.

17. Ding 1, p. 1527.

18. Ding 10, pp. 1578–79.

19. Ding 12, pp. 1586–87.

20. Ai 11, p. 1665.

21. Zhao 20, p. 1422; and Zhao 29, p. 1504.

22. Ai 14, p. 1682.

23. There are four episodes in *Discourses of the States* concerning Confucius, as well as several other passages in which Confucius simply comments on some contemporary event. Of the four episodes, Sima Qian uses three: *Guo yu*, SBBY ed., 5:7a–7b (cf. *SJ* 47, p. 1912), where Ji Huanzi finds a sheep in an earthenware crock, provoking a lecture by Confucius on the names of various prodigies (*guai*); *Guo yu*, 5:10b–11b (cf. *SJ* 47, pp. 1912–13), in which Confucius identifies a huge bone as belonging to one of the "spirits" (*shen*) which Yu gathered at Guiji Mountain; and *Guo yu*, 5:11b–12a (cf. *SJ* 47, p. 1922), where Confucius identifies an arrow found in a dead bird as coming from a far-off tribe called Sushen. In none of these episodes does Confucius appear as the rationalist described in *Analects*, but he also includes the above episodes from *Guo yu*, where Confucius does indeed discuss prodigies (*guai*—5:7a–7b) and spirits (*shen*—5:10b–11b). In the only other Confucius episode in *Guoyu*, Ji Kangzi sends Confucius' disciple Jan You to offer the Master a fief (5:12b–13b). This episode is not used in Sima Qian's account, although Ji Kangzi does talk to Ran You about inviting Confucius (See *SJ* 47, p. 1934).

24. *Shina keigaku shi ron*, tr. by Jiang Xia'an as *Zhongguo jingxue shi* (1934; rpt., Taibei, 1986), pp. 60–70.

25. 2:4:4a–5b.

26. Chapter 6, 3:6:14a–14b. In chapter 14 there are several accounts of discussions between Confucius and Lao Dan in which the former is befuddled and the latter is portrayed as a paragon of wisdom who freely attacks such Confucian doctrines as humaneness, duty, the study of the Six Classics, and so on.

27. For example, Yan Ying's attack before Duke Jing upon Confucius (*SJ* 47, p. 1911) is drawn from *Yanzi chun qiu*, SBBY ed., 7:8:12a–12b or

Mozi, SBBY ed., 9:39:14b–15a, and the account of the execution of the vice-director Mao (*SJ* 47, p. 1917) most likely is drawn from *Xunzi*, 20:1b (chapter 28).

28. *SJ* 47, p. 1927.

29. *Shuo yuan, SBBY* ed., 13:2a–2b.

30. *SJ* 47, p. 1909. For the *Xunzi* passage, see 19:27:11a.

31. Watson, too, takes issue with Creel (*Ssu-ma Ch'ien*, pp. 167–68).

32. On the portrayal of Confucius in the Han apocryphal texts, see the invaluable study of Jack Dull, "A Historical Introduction to the Apocryphal Ch'an-Wei Texts of the Han Dynasty," Ph.D. dissertation, University of Washington, 1966, pp. 516–26.

33. The unnatural union referred to here is an interpretative problem. Sima Qian says that "He (a personal name), the father of Confucius, and Confucius' mother, a girl of the Yan clan, *ye he* 野合 and gave birth to Confucius." *Ye he*, would at first glance, seem simply to mean "copulated in the wilds," but this is an interpretation that seems to embarrass most commentators, who contend that *ye he* means "unnatural union" and refers to the great difference in age between Confucius' mother and father, an age gap that is contrary to ritual requirements (see commentary under *SJ* 47, p. 1906). Cui Shi (1852–1924) suggests that the text is probably referring to a mysterious impregnation that took place while the couple was in the fields at an altar praying to have a son. Thus, the line after the one in question speaks of praying at an altar on Ni Mound and should actually precede the one concerning the mysterious union (*Shi ji tan yuan* [Beijing: Zhonghua, 1986], p. 146). Whether the couple made love in the wilds, or Confucius' mother was impregnated miraculously at an altar on Ni Mound, or there was something illicit about the relationship, such as an inappropriately large difference in age, the union was indeed unnatural in *some* way.

As a child, Confucius plays with ritual vessels (see *SJ* 47, p. 1906). The prophecy of his future greatness is drawn by Sima Qian from *Zuo Commentary*, Zhao 7, p. 1295.

34. *SJ* 47, p. 1909. For the notion that the passage is displaced, see *SKKC* 47:13. Wang Shumin believes, as I do, that the text is "a general discussion of events to follow" (*SJJZ*, vol. 6, p. 1730).

35. See Cui Shi, *Shi ji tan yuan*, p. 152.

36. *SJ* 47, pp. 1916–17. The sources are *Xunzi*, 4:8:2a–b and *Lü shi chun qiu, SBBY*, ed. 16:10a.

37. *SJ* 47, p. 1915.

38. There is controversy as to precisely what kind of position is meant here by Chinese *xiang* 相, which can mean "prime minister" or simply "to

assist." The word is repeated in the version found in *Records of the Historian*, and Cui Shu says, "What the *Zuo Commentary* calls *xiang* refers to assisting with ritual. It does not mean he was prime minister ... probably *Records of the Historian* mistakenly takes *xiang* as 'prime minister'" (*Kaoxin lu*, 2:22). But Yang Bojun, distinguished modern commentator of *Zuo Commentary*, suspects that "prime minister" is the intended meaning. He quotes Quan Zuwang as follows: "When it says he was *xiang* at Jiagu, it truly is a proof that Confucius was prime minister. In the Spring and Autumn period, there was no position more important than that of prime minister. Wherever it says one acted in the position of '*xiang*'-ing his ruler, it is nothing other than acting as prime minister. But in Lu, during the reign of the twelve dukes beginning from Duke Xi, all those who served the ruler as prime minister were from the three (ducal) clans. The prime minister of Lu could only be from a ducal clan. But at that time, on account of the Yang Hu rebellion, Confucius had been elevated from commoner status into the position. Thus, they were using him in such a position contrary to usual practice" (Yang, p. 1577). One thing is fairly certain, Sima Qian himself considers Confucius' service as prime minister to be a central event in the life of the Master. The event is not only mentioned in the "Hereditary Household of Confucius" but is referred to elsewhere in the text. See for example, "The Hereditary Household of Wu Taibo": "In the fifteenth year [of King Helu of Wu] Confucius acted as prime minister in Lu" (*SJ* 31:15a); "The Hereditary Household of Chu": "In the sixteenth year [of King Zhao of Chu] Confucius acted as prime minister in Lu" (*SJ* 40:20b); and so on. For further evidence, see Wang Shumin, vol. 6, p. 1742.

39. Ding 10, pp. 1577–79.

40. *Guliang Commentary* says, "The men of Qi arose to the clamor of drums and wished to use this opportunity to seize the Duke of Lu" (*SBBY* ed., Ding 10, 19:7a). Takikawa claims that, "The Duke Astrologer (Sima Qian) exaggerates and loses the true picture" (*SKKC*, 47:28).

41. Yanzi probably died well before 500 B.C.E. See Qian Mu, "Xian Qin zhuzi", pp. 10–11.

42. In Sima Qian's account Yanzi is presented as a jealous rival to Confucius who, upon hearing that his duke might offer Confucius a position, attacks the sage bitterly. Confucius is represented by Yanzi as arrogant and profligate. In addition, Yanzi goes on to say, "Over many generations, one cannot exhaust his studies; and over years, one cannot comprehend his ritual" (*SJ* 47, p. 1911). This particular episode appears in the "anti-Confucians" sections of the *Spring and Autumn Annals of Master Yan* (*Yanzi chun qiu*), chapter 8, and *Mozi*, chapter 39. Chavannes has proven, I believe, that the *Yanzi* redaction is the earlier of these two accounts (vol. V, p. 306). Sima Qian has plainly drawn on these older sources but has modified them significantly. Cui Shu strenuously attacks Sima Qian for including such an obviously false episode in his history—an episode that he believes entirely

misrepresents Yanzi and is obviously a product of the Warring States period: "It is very clear that this passage comes from the mouth of a person of the Warring States period [probably a Mohist, he has argued earlier]. Its wording is superficial and crude like that of a Warring States, Qin, or Han piece, and does not at all resemble the narrative style of *Zuo Commentary* or *Mencius*" (see *Kaoxin lu*, 1:32).

43. *SJ* 47, p. 1915.

44. *Guliang Commentary*, however, says, "Their heads and feet came out through different doors," indicating that they were beheaded rather than cut apart at the waist (Ding 10, 19:7a–7b).

45. Such as Cui Shu, *Kaoxin lu*, 2:23. Wang Shumin believes that the action of the marquis of Qi was indeed insulting to Lu, but then adds that "beheading the performers does seem rather excessive!" (*SJJZ*, vol. 6, p. 1744).

46. See *MZ*, *SBBY* ed., 6:13a (3B.9).

47. *SKKC*, 47:2.

48. *SJ* 47, p. 1918. Homer Dubs, arguing that this event could not have caused Confucius' departure, reconstructs a different and somewhat more plausible scenario. He suggests that the real reason, which had to do with the Master's forcing the great clans to dismantle their city-castles, carried political implications that Emperor Wu would have considered dangerous. Thus, Sima Qian supposedly suppressed the actual story. See Dubs, "The Political Career of Confucius," *JAOS* 66 (1946): 273–82.

49. *SJ* 47, p. 1911.

50. "Someone slandered Confucius to Duke Ling of Wei. Duke Ling caused Gongsun Yujia to accompany him [Confucius] in his comings and goings. Confucius was afraid that he would be accused of an offense by him" (*SJ* 47, p. 1919).

51. "In the autumn (492 B.C.E.) Ji Huanzi fell ill. They took him in a cart to look at the city of Lu. He sighed deeply and said, 'Previously this state almost flourished.' He looked back and said to his successor Kangzi, 'As soon as I die, you will certainly become prime minister of Lu. When you are prime minister of Lu, you must summon Zhongni (Confucius).' Several days later Hanzi died. Kangzi succeeded to his position. After the burial was completed, he wished to summon Zhongni. Gong Zhiyu said, 'Previously my former lord used him but did not persist to the end. Finally, he was ridiculed by the feudal lords. Now if you use Confucius, and cannot persist to the end, then we will again be ridiculed by the feudal lords'" (*SJ* 47, p. 1927).

52. See this somewhat lengthy episode that follows Confucius' release from the distress in the region of Chen and Cai in *SJ* 47, p. 1932.

53. *SJ* 47, p. 1942.

54. "When Zigong reported the facts [of the description] to Confucius, Confucius laughed with delight and said, 'Although the exterior form is the last thing [of importance], that I resemble a dog in a house of mourning is indeed so! Is indeed so!'" (*SJ* 47, pp. 1921–22). In the account of this episode in *Han shi waizhuan*, Confucius is not amused by the description and disclaims its accuracy. See *HSWZ* 9, translated by Robert Hightower in *Han shih wai chuan*, Harvard-Yenching Institute Monograph Series, vol. XI (Cambridge: Harvard University Press, 1952), pp. 306–8.

55. *SJ* 47, p. 1924. Sima Qian is quoting Confucius' words from *LY*, 13:3b (13.10).

56. The first such episode occurs when Confucius, who is in mourning shortly after the death of his mother, wishes to accept an invitation from the powerful Ji clan to attend a banquet. He originally wants to go but Yang Hu dissuades him from attending (*SJ* 47, p. 1907). In 501 B.C.E. Gongsun Buniu revolted against the Ji clan and invited the assistance of Confucius. The latter wanted to serve Gongsun Buniu but was restrained by his disciple Zilu (*SJ* 47, p. 1914—compare *LY* 17:2b–3a [17.5]). Boxi revolts several years later in the state of Zhao and invites Confucius. Again, he wishes to go and serve the upstart rebel, and again it is Zilu who dissuades him (*SJ* 47, p. 1924—compare *LY* 27:3b–4a [17.7]).

57. This sentence includes a grammatical structure that indicates Sima Qian is passing along information of which he is not certain (*SK CC*, 47:14). I have discussed this passage in my paper "Takikawa Kametarō's Comments on Chapter 47 of *Shih Chi*," *Di erjie Zhongguo yuwai hanji guoji xueshu huiyi lunwenji* (Taibei: Lianjing, 1989), pp. 995–1007.

58. *SJ* 47, p. 1909.

59. *SJ* 63, p. 2140.

60. Cui Shu is particularly harsh: "This is probably based upon a tradition, passed down among the followers of Laozi and Zhuangzi, that Confucius discussed ritual with Laozi. It has been expanded and distorted in order to degrade Confucius and promote their own theories. That [Sima Qian's] 'Hereditary House of Confucius' does not investigage this but erroneously utilizes the tradition is indeed misguided" (*Kaoxin lu*, 1:21). Lu Shunzhi, a Ming commentator, has an explanation of this passage that reveals how much interpretative effort some Confucians spent to explain away the Laozi episodes. Noting that Laozi did not believe in ritual and that Confucius lived in a state "where the ritual was complete," he wonders "why Confucius would go so far to seek ritual of Laozi." He concludes that Confucius' real intent was to make Laozi "submit and bring him back to ritual" (*Shi ji pinglin*, p. 47.3).

61. See *Li ji Zheng zhu*, SBBY ed., 6:7:6a and 12a–13b; and *Kongzi jia yu*, SBBY ed., 3:11:1a–2b.

62. One of the most extended pieces of this type is found in "The Traditions of Fortune Tellers" (chapter 127). This piece is almost all a lengthy diatribe by a certain Sima Jizhu delivered to Song Zhong and Jia Yi. Sima Jizhu argues that "The True Gentleman dwells in lowly obscurity in order to avoid the masses and hides himself in order to avoid human relationships" (*SJ* 127, pp. 3215–20). For a translation of the entire chapter, see Watson, *Records*, vol. II, pp. 468–75.

63. Two such episodes appear in *LY* 28:2a–3b (18.5, 18.6). The first is Confucius' famous encounter with Jie Yu, the Madman of Chu; and the second is Zilu's discussion with the "Agriculturalists" Zhang Ju and Jie Ni. Cui Shu says that these passages "do not resemble something that could come from the hands of Confucius' disciples" (*Kaoxin lu*, 3:14). Both of these episodes are included in Sima Qian's "Hereditary Household of Confucius" (*SJ* 47, p. 1933 and 47, p. 1929).

64. Roland Barthes is only one modern critic who asks us to forsake the old notion of the "single voice": "We now know that the text is not a line of words releasing a single 'theological' meaning (the 'message' of an Author-God) but a multi-dimensional space in which a variety of writings, none of them original, blend and clash. The text is a tissue of quotations drawn from the innumerable centers of culture." *Image, Music, Text* (New York: Hill and Wang, 1977), p. 146. This blending of a tissue of quotations is even more striking in the Chinese tradition where one's personality so very often takes form around the books one reads. The Chinese scholar voraciously digests the past, and his own prose could hardly be other than a space in which the numerous, and often conflicting, voices of the past "blend and clash."

65. The *locus classicus* is a very brief statement in *Analects*: "They (Confucius' party) ran out of dried provisions in Chen. The followers were ill and none were able to arise. Zilu, filled with resentment, saw [Confucius] and said, 'The True Gentleman also has affliction?' The Master said, 'The True Gentleman is firm in his affliction. The petty man, if afflicted, is reckless'" (*LY* 15:1b [15.2]). Mencius adds to this by noting, "That the gentleman was in difficulties between Chen and Cai was because he had no friends at court." *MZ* 14:5b (7b:18). See *Mozi*, 9:15b–16a (chapter 39); *Xunzi*, 20:4b (chapter 28); *Zhuangzi*, 7:11a (chapter 20), 9:15a (chapter 28), and elsewhere; and *Lü shi chun qiu*, 14:15b.

66. Located in modern-day Anhui province, just southwest of Haoxian. On this identification, see Qian Mu, *Shi ji diming kao*, p. 367.

67. The quotation is from Mao poem no. 234. See *Mao shi Zheng jian*, SBBY ed., 15:13b.

68. This is a reference to the same Bo Yi and Shu Qi discussed in chapter 1 above. Prince Bigan was the uncle of the last ruler of the Shang, the notorious Zhou. Sima Qian tells his story as follows: "Zhou became increasingly debauched and disorderly and would not stop. The viscount of Wei frequently remonstrated, but Zhou did not listen. The grand preceptor and the vice preceptor made plans to depart. Bigan said, 'One who acts as a minister must struggle [to change his sovereign] to the point of death.' Thereupon he sternly remonstrated with Zhou. Zhou became angry and said, 'I have heard a sage's heart has seven cavities.' He cut open Bigan to look at his heart" (SJ 3, p. 108).

69. My reading of this passage follows Wang Shumin, SJJZ, vol. 6, p. 1768.

70. SJ 47, pp. 1930–32.

71. MZ 14:5b (7b:18); see Lau, p. 293.

72. Kaoxin lu, 3:16–18.

73. Sima Qian's account provides a context for LY 7.22: "Confucius left Cao and went to Song, he was practicing ritual with the disciples under a large tree. The grand marshal of Song, Huan Tui, wished to kill Confucius. He pulled up the tree, but Confucius moved. A disciple said, 'You should make haste [to leave]!' Confucius said, 'Heaven has produced virtue in me. What can Huan Tui do to me?'" SJ 47, p. 1921.

74. SJ 47, p. 1919.

75. "Thereupon Confucius left Chen and passed through Pu. Just at that time, the Gongshu clan used Pu as a base for rebellion, and the people of Pu detained Confucius. Among his disciples was a certain Gongliang Ru, who accompanied Confucius with five private chariots. He was tall and worthy, and he possessed courage and strength. He said, 'I formerly was following the Master when he met difficulty in Kuang. Now, once again, we encounter difficulty here. It is simply fate! If I again with the Master encounter difficulty, I wish to fight and die.' He fought with great intensity. The people of Pu were afraid ... and sent Confucius out through the east gate" (SJ 47, p. 1923).

76. SJ 130, p. 3320.

77. SJ 47, p. 1935.

78. See The Hero With a Thousand Faces (Princeton: Princeton University Press, 1968), p. 193.

79. SJ 74, p. 2345.

80. SJ 130, p. 3295.

3. The Six Arts and *Spring and Autumn Annals*

1. On this, see *Zhou li Zheng zhu, SBBY* ed., 10:7b.

2. The wording here is translated from Yu Qiding's excellent study, *Xian Qin Liang Han rujia jiaoyu,* p. 26. Yu mentions three critical transformations in the history of Chinese education. The first "starts in the Spring and Autumn and Warring States period and culminates in the middle years of the Western Han." It is a change from the "aristocratic education that took the Western Zhou Six Arts as basic content to the scholar-official education that took the Confucian Six Classics as basic content" (ibid., p. 1).

3. The precise relationship during the early Han between the classical art of ritual and extant texts dealing with ritual is a subject of some controversy. On this subject, see the illuminating discussion of Xu Fuguan, *Zhongguo jingxue shi de jichu* (Taibei: Student Bookstore, 1982), pp. 161–68.

4. A comprehensive history of the Confucian canon, one of the most important institutions in Chinese civilization, is yet to be written in English. Some very insightful and interesting comments, however, can be found in John B. Henderson, *Scripture, Canon, and Commentary: A Comparison of Confucian and Western Exegesis* (Princeton: Princeton University Press, 1991), pp. 21–61. On the formation and transmission of the classics in the Han, an excellent study is that of Tjan Tjoe Som, *The Comprehensive Discussions in the White Tiger Hall* (Leiden: E.J. Brill, 1949), pp. 82–178. The rather sketchy history presented here has drawn heavily upon such standard Chinese-language sources as Xu Fuguan, *Zhongguo jingxue,* Zhou Yutong, *Qun Jing gailun* (1948; rpt., Taibei, 1986), and Pi Xirui, *Jingxue lishi.*

5. *LY* 8a, 8b (8.8)

6. "The Master said, '*Poetry,* three hundred in number, can be covered in a single phrase, "in thought have no perverseness."' " *LY* 2:1a–1b (2.2). For a very helpful and thorough study of the developing notion of *Poetry* in *Analects,* see Van Zoeren, *Poetry and Personality,* pp. 52–79.

7. *LY* 7:4a (7.17).

8. *LY* 9:5a (9.14). "Ya" and "song" are two sections of the *Classic of Poetry,* presumably named after two different modes of music. Whether the passage is referring to work on two specific sections of a text or simply upon two types of music which happen to be included in *Classic of Poetry,* is impossible to say.

9. On this general issue, see Xu Fuguan, *Zhongguo jingxue,* pp. 3–7.

10. Duke Xi 27, p. 445. Placing these four Arts together as a primary group is a persistent practice that continues into the Han.

11. Edward Shaughnessy notes an interesting transformation that takes place in *Zuo Commentary* with regard to *Changes*. For the first hundred or so years recorded in *Zuo*, *Changes* is regarded as "a manual of divination." After that, however, the text begins to be cited in *Zuo* as "an ancient wisdom text." It is no accident, Shaughnessy believes, that this change roughly corresponds to the lifetime of Confucius. See, "The Composition of *Zhouyi*," Ph.D. dissertation, Stanford University, 1983, p. 2.

12. On this issue, see the important study of Hong Ye, which appears as a preface to *Combined Concordances to Ch'un-ch'iu, Kung-yang, Kuliang and Tso-chuan*, Harvard-Yenching Institute Sinological Index Series, Supplement 11 (rpt., Taibei: Chinese Materials Research Aids Service Center, 1966). He argues that *Zuo Commentary* assumes *Spring and Autumn Annals* to be nothing other than the old Lu annals and not to be identified with Confucius. Not all agree with Hong's position. Yang Bojun, for example, tries to prove that the author of *Zuo Commentary* considered Confucius to be the compiler of *Spring and Autumn Annals*. However, I am not convinced by his arguments. For Yang's ideas on this subject, see *Chun qiu Zuo zhuan zhu*, p. xxii.

13. Zhao 2, p. 1227.

14. *MZ* 6:13a (3B:9). This whole section of *Mencius* is of the greatest importance in the history of the Confucian tradition. For a translation, see D.C. Lau, pp. 128–33.

15. See *Mozi* 8:2b, 3b, 4a, and 4b. It appears that during the Zhou dynasty, each of the feudal states kept a year-by-year written record of major events in that state.

16. In a critical essay on this issue, Qian Mu reminds us that for much of Chinese history *Spring and Autumn Annals* was considered as Confucius' greatest contribution: "Moreover, when people before the Sui and Tang dynasties honor Confucius, they attach much more importance to *Spring and Autumn Annals* than to *Analects*." See Qian Mu's "Kongzi yu Chun qiu," *Liang Han jingxue*, pp. 235–83.

17. *MZ* 6:14a (3B:9).

18. On this subject, see Pi Xirui, *Jingxue Lishi*, p. 55.

19. *Xunzi* 4:7a (chapter 8). Xunzi emphasizes, more than anyone before him, the educational role of these disciplines. In this respect he anticipates the movement in the early Han to define education in terms of a canon. See especially *Xunzi* 1:4a (chapter 1). On the Han obsession with placing the classics into a unified scheme and its broader implications, see John B. Henderson, *Scripture, Canon, and Commentary*, pp. 45–50.

20. *Xunzi* 3:5b (chapter 5) and 19:5b (chapter 27).

21. See Xu Fuguan, *Zhongguo jingxue*, p. 48.

22. *Li ji Zheng zhu*, 15:1a.

23. The text *Zhuangzi* does indeed link Confucius to all the canonical texts and actually uses the term "classic" (*jing*) in describing these works, but the reference is found in chapter 14 of *Zhuangzi*, a highly controversial chapter that might date from as late as the Western Han. The passage in question reads as follows: "Confucius spoke to Lao Dan, saying, `I, Qiu, have put in order *Poetry, Historical Records, Ritual, Music, Changes,* and *Spring and Autumn Annals,* the Six Classics" (5:26a–26b). Xu Fuguan notes that this chapter frequently uses the expression "Three August Sovereigns" (*san huang*), a term that first appears elsewhere in *Records of the Historian.* Thus, he concludes that "this is not material that can be accepted as evidence for the history of classic studies" (*Zhongguo jingxue,* p. 42).

24. Sima Qian devotes a chapter to Li Sheng and Lu Jia (chapter 97). He concludes the chapter by noting that "I have read Mr. Lu's *New Sayings* in twelve chapters. Assuredly he was the most skilled rhetorician of the modern age" (*SJ* 97:13b–14a). Xu Fuguan's discussion of this important early Han thinker emphasizes his critical role in the history of classical scholarship and demonstrates that Lu Jia had a particularly close relationship to the *Guliang* tradition of *Spring and Autumn Annals* exegesis (see *Liang Han sixiang shi*, p. 93). He goes on to argue that Sima Qian was influenced by Lu Jia's notion of the political importance of the classics (p. 95).

25. Lu Jia, *Xin yu, SBBY* ed., 1:2b.

26. *Ibid.*, I:3b.

27. For biographical information on Jia Yi, see his "Traditions" in *SJ* 83, pp. 2491–2503.

28. *Xin shu, SBBY* ed., 8:5b–6a. As one might expect, later discussions of the classics tried to buttress the authority of the "five" by linking them to the five processes. Others continued to argue in favor of "a classificatory scheme based on six." See Henderson, *Scripture, Canon, and Commentary,* p. 49.

29. Kung-chuan Hsiao, who gives a very lucid explanation of Jia Yi's philosophy, does not believe that Legalism was a strong influence upon Jia Yi and emphasizes the influence of Mencius. See *Chinese Political Thought,* pp. 473–83. *Records of the Historian* does, however, state that Jia Yi was versed in the writings of Shen Buhai and Lord Shang, two prominent Legalist thinkers. On the philosophical inclinations of several major early Han political figures, Yu Qiding's observation bears repeating: "Lu Jia, Jia

Yi, Zhao Cuo, and other famous early Han thinkers had all been influenced in the realm of political thought by Taoism and Legalism, but their educational perspective was completely Confucian" (*Xian Qin Liang Han rujia jiaoyu*, p. 94).

30. Derk Bodde, "The State and Empire of Ch'in," *The Cambridge History of China*, Volume 1: *The Ch'in and Han Empires, 221 B.C.–A.D. 220*, ed. by Denis Twitchett and Michael Loewe (Cambridge: Cambridge University Press, 1986), p. 73.

31. This brief sketch of the institution of the academicians utilizes the excellent study of Qian Mu, "Liang Han bo shi."

32. See *HS* 10, p. 313.

33. The precise date of the memorials is a subject of considerable controversy. On this issue, see Tzey-yueh Tain, "Tung Chung-shu's System of Thought, Its Sources and Its Influence on the Scholars," Ph.D. dissertation, University of California, Los Angeles, 1974, pp. 49–53.

34. *HS* 56, p. 2532. With only minor adaptations, my translation follows that of Derk Bodde in Fung Yu-lan, *A History of Chinese Philosophy* (Peiping: Henri Vetch, 1937), vol. II, p. 17.

35. *HS* 6, p. 159.

36. See Xu Fuguan, *Zhongguo jingxue*, pp. 76–77.

37. Benjamin E. Wallacker minimizes the impact of Dong Zhongshu's recommendations and suggests that it is unlikely his "strong statement brought great changes during his own lifetime, whatever importance was attached to his writings after his death." See "Han Confucianism and Confucius in Han," *Ancient China: Studies in Early Civilization*, ed. by David T. Roy and Tsuen-hsuin Tsien (Hong Kong: The Chinese University of Hong Kong, 1978), p. 216. For a number of opinions to the contrary, beginning with Liu Xin and Ban Gu and extending to Fung Yu-lan, Wing-tsit Chan, and Timoteus Pokora, see the summary in Tain, "Tung Chung-shu's System of Thought," pp. 1–2. While I do not dispute the contention, articulated most recently by Anne Cheng, that the Han "victory of Confucianism" was "extremely nuanced" (see *Étude sur le Confucianisme Han* [Paris: Collège de France, 1985], p. 22), I accept the traditional view that Dong's memorial was critical to the establishment of the canon as the foundation of state-sponsored education.

38. See Xu Fuguan, *Liang Han sixiang shi*, p. 102 on the general influence of Lu Jia upon Han thought in general. Concerning Dong Zhongshu, see Li Weixiong, *Dong Zhongshu yu Xi Han xueshu* (Taibei: Wenshizhe, 1978), pp. 27–31.

39. Dong Zhongshu also says that "Their [i.e., the Qin] idea was to eradicate the Way of the former kings and govern exclusively with self-

indulgence and recklessness." The "poison handed down" from the Qin "until today has not been destroyed" (*HS* 56, pp. 2504-5).

40. A full translation, I am told, is now in process. For partial translations, see Woo Kang, *Les trois théories politiques des Tch'ouen Ts'ieou: Interprétées par Tong Tchong-chou d'après les principes de l'école de Kong-yang* (Paris: Librairie Ernest Leroux, 1932); Otto Franke, *Studien zur Geschichte des Konfuzianischen Dogmas und der Chinesischen Staatsreligion: Das Problem des Tsch'un-ts'iu und Tung Tschung-shu's Tsch'un-ts'iu fan-lu* (Hamburg: L. Friederichsen & Co., 1920); and Fung Yu-lan, *History of Chinese Philosophy*, pp. 7-87. A clear and concise presentation of Dong Zhongshu's political philosophy can be found in Richard Vuylsteke, "The Political Philosophy of Tung Chung-shu (179-104 B.C.): A Critical Exposition," Ph.D. dissertation, University of Hawaii, 1982. As always, Kung-chuan Hsiao's comments on Dong Zhongshu are illuminating (*Chinese Political Thought*, pp. 484-503).

41. "The common people's pursuit of advantage is like the way water runs downhill. If you do not use education to damn up [this pursuit], who can stop it?" (*HS* 56, p. 2503). This passage alludes to *MZ* 1.9b (IA:6), but in his constant emphasis upon the transforming power of education, Dong Zhongshu is reminiscent of *Xunzi*.

42. *HS* 56, p. 2508.

43. *HS* 56, p. 2512.

44. *Chun qiu fan lu*, *SBBY* ed., 1:2:8b.

45. *Chun qiu fan lu*, 6:16:2b.

46. *Chun qiu fan lu*, 1:1:3b. See also Tain's succinct summary of the major principles of this "constitution" ("Tung Chung-shu's System of Thought," pp. 186-94).

47. *SJ* 121, p. 3128.

48. According to Sima Qian, Hu Wusheng, a scholar from the state of Qi who became an academician under Emperor Jing, was one of those responsible for transmitting the *Gongyang* tradition: "Those in Qi who speak of *Annals*," Sima Qian adds, "for the most part received [their knowledge] from Hu Wusheng" (*SJ* 130:12a). Others dispute Dai Hong's claim and believe that the *Gongyang Commentary* took written form long before the early Han. See Xu Fuguan, *Zhongguo jingxue*, p. 178 and *Liang Han sixiang shi*, pp. 317-28. On this topic, see also Anne Cheng, *Confucianisme Han*, pp. 69, 109.

49. See Xu Fuguan, *Liang Han sixiang shi*, pp. 326-29. The fact that the notion of *yin* and *yang* does not appear in *Gongyang Commentary* is evidence that the tradition of *Gongyang* exegesis, whenever it might actually have assumed textual form, is one that predates the spread of this idea

throughout the world of Chinese thought. I should note here that a recent article has argued that those portions of *Chun qiu fan lu* containing traces of the five processes are not by Dong Zhongshu. See G. Arbuckle, "A Note on the Authenticity of the *Chunqiu Fanlu*," *T'oung Pao* 75 (1989): 236–44.

50. On this relationship, see Jack Dull, "Apocryphal Texts of the Han Dynasty", pp. 28–29.

51. *Chun qiu fan lu*, 3:4:5b.

52. *Chun qiu fan lu*, 3:5:10a. Here, I have adapted slightly the translation of Derk Bodde (Fung, *History of Chinese Philosophy*, p. 75).

53. See, for example, Li Changzhi, *Sima Qian*, p. 117 and Xiao Li, *Sima Qian pingzhuan* (Jilin: Jilin wenshizhe, 1986), p. 36.

54. *SJ* 47, p. 1935.

55. Ban Gu says that the collection, as it came from the hand of Confucius, was one hundred chapters in length. See *HS* 30, p. 1706.

56. *SJ* 47, p. 1936.

57. Sima Qian is quoting a passage from *LY* 9:5a (9.14) discussed previously.

58. *SJ* 47, p. 1937.

59. I have merely adapted here the translations of the various sections of *Book of Changes* from Wilhelm/Baynes, *The I Ching*, Bollingen Series XIX (Princeton: Princeton University Press, 1967), p. xix.

60. For example, Sima Zhen (*SJ* 47, p. 1937) and Chavannes (V, 400–401) follow the first interpretation, while the modern-language translator Zhang Ziliang follows the second (*Baihua Shi ji* [Taibei: Lianjing, 1985], vol. II, p. 752.)

61. On Ban Gu's belief that Confucius wrote the "Ten Wings," see *HS* 30, p. 1704.

62. *SJ* 47, p. 1937.

63. See p. 49 and n. 9 above.

64. *SJ* 47, p. 1943. The quotation is from *MZ* 6:13a (3B:9).

65. *Chun qiu fan lu*, 6:17:3a. Watson has discussed the phrase *kong yan*, which I have translated as "theoretical words," and argues that both Sima Qian and Dong Zhongshu thought Confucius did use "theoretical words" in *Spring and Autumn Annals*. See Watson, *Ssu-ma Ch'ien*, pp. 87–89 and p. 211 (n. 67). I agree but believe the sense here is that an exclusive use of "theoretical words" is not as good as providing actual historical illustrations.

66. It is, in fact, the usual position occupied by *Changes* in the Old-Script School lists. On the significance of such order, see Zhou Yutong, *Jing jin gu wen xue* (1926; rpt., Taibei: Shangwu, 1985), pp. 5–12.

67. *SJ* 130, pp. 3297–98. My summaries and translations of this section owe a great deal to the excellent work of Burton Watson and only differ in regard to minor points (*Ssu-ma Ch'ien*, pp. 50–53).

68. The book in question was entitled *Gongyang Dong Zhongshu zhi yu* (*Dong Zhongshu Decides Court Cases from Gongyang*). This book was reported to include descriptions of 232 cases. Only a few of these cases are preserved in various encyclopedias and collections. For a succinct summary of the history of this text, see Li Weixiong, pp. 15–17.

69. For a recent discussion of Sima Qian as a *Gongyang* partisan, see Wu Ruyu, *Shi ji lun gao* (Jiangsu: Jiaoyu chubanshe, 1986), pp. 1–17.

70. The Joint-Harmony is, according to one interpretation, the period when the Duke of Zhou and the Duke of Shao managed the Zhou government (841–828 B.C.E). On this rather problematic period see Cho-yun Hsu and Katheryn M. Linduff, *Western Chou Civilization* (New Haven and London: Yale University Press, 1988), pp. 144–46.

71. *SJ* 14, pp. 509–10. This is, of course, a reference to *Zuo Commentary*, a book that Sima Qian always calls by the name above. In fact, Sima Qian's use of this title supports the theory that *Zuo Commentary*, as it is known today, was not originally written as a commentary at all, but as an independent history of the Spring and Autumn period. Sima Qian, however, indicates that he believed it was primarily an exposition of the words of Confucius, presumably words found in *Spring and Autumn Annals*.

4. Dying Fathers and Living Memories

1. *SBBY* ed., 12:2b.

2. *SJ* 14, p. 509.

3. *Shuo wen jie zi gulin*, p. 5817b.

4. *LY* 6:7b (6.24).

5. *Shitong tongshi*, p. 1.

6. Ibid., p. 19.

7. I have briefly discussed these issues in my article "Liu Chih-chi on Ssu-ma Ch'ien," *Di yijie guoji Tangdai xueshu huiyi lunwenji* (Taibei: Xuesheng, 1989), pp. 36–53.

8. This particular notion, which Westerners often disparage as a "fragmented" worldview, finds parallels throughout the traditional Chinese cultural world. Andrew Plaks, for example, has noted the lack of a "center" in the Chinese literary character, "an uncertainty that keeps them from presenting or even tending towards an unequivocal self-image." See his "Towards a Critical Theory of Chinese Narrative," *Chinese Narrative: Critical and Theoretical Essays*, ed. by Andrew Plaks (Princeton: Princeton University Press, 1977), p. 340. On the larger philosophical issue, see David Hall and Roger Ames, *Thinking Through Confucius*, pp. 17–21.

9. The term *"ununterbrochener Fluss,"* as a characteristic of traditional Western narrative distinguishing it from the narrative of China, is drawn from Jaroslav Průšek's seminal article "History and Epics in China and the West," *Chinese History and Literature* (Prague Academia, 1970), pp. 17–34.

10. Hardy's article is a very sober and useful introduction to Sima Qian's "multiple narratives" ("Can an Ancient Chinese Historian Contribute to Modern Western Theory? The Multiple Narratives of Ssu-ma Ch'ien," *History and Theory* 33.1 [1994]: 22–38).

11. *Sima Qian sojian shu kao* (Shanghai: Renmin, 1963), pp. 3–21. Another study, that of Lu Nanqiao, also lists eighty-one sources. See "Lun Sima Qian ji qi lishi bianzuan xue," *Sima Qian: qi ren ji qi shu*, pp. 93–125. Ruan Zhisheng counts eighty-eight sources in "Tai shi gong zenyang souji he chuli shiliao," *Shumu jikan* 7.4 (March 1974), pp. 17–35.

12. This important chapter has recently been the subject of two English-language studies: Joseph Roe Allen III, "An Introductory Study of Narrative Structure in *Shiji*," *Chinese Literature: Essays, Articles, Reviews* 3 (1981): 31–66; and David Johnson, "The Wu Tzu-hsü Pien-wen and Its Sources: Part I," *Harvard Journal of Asiatic Studies* 40.1 (1980): 93–156, and "Part II," *HJAS* 40.2 (1980): 465–503. Allen's study, the best introduction available to the narrative style of *Records of the Historian*, is an application of Robert Scholes and Robert Kellogg's well-known study of narrative (see *The Nature of Narrative* [New York: Oxford University Press, 1975]), Allen illustrates his conclusions with an in-depth analysis of two chapters, the "Traditions of Wu Zixu" (chapter 66) and the "Traditions of General Li" (chapter 109). Although I emphasize certain portions of the Wu Zixu narrative not discussed in depth by Allen, his work has been useful to me and is occasionally cited in what follows. Johnson's study, unlike that of Allen, is not primarily concerned with *Records of the Historian* but with a ninth- or tenth-century "transformation text" (*bianwen*) of the Wu Zixu tale found at Dunhuang. However, in the course of tracing sources for this later text, Johnson has much of interest to say about the version of Wu Zixu found in *Records of the Historian* and its antecedents.

13. *SJ* 67, p. 2199; 70, p. 2300; 83, p. 2471; and 66, p. 2183. As one example of a highly positive evaluation of Wu Zixu in a late Zhou text, note the following passage from *Xunzi*, where he is placed alongside the great Duke of Zhou and the oft-praised Guan Zhong: "King Cheng's treatment of the Duke of Zhou was such that there was no occasion where he went forth and did not heed him. He knew those whom he should honor. Duke Huan's treatment of Guan Zhong was such that in state affairs there was no occasion where he went forth and did not use him. He knew those who could bring advantage. But Wu had Wu Zixu and was not able to use him. That the state came to destruction was because they turned against the Way and neglected a worthy" (17:11a [chap. 24]). Bigan was a virtuous minister of the evil King Zhou, the last ruler of the Shang dynasty. King Zhou had Bigan's heart ripped out as punishment for the latter's righteous remonstrations (see *SJ* 3, p. 108). Wu Zixu was often paired with Bigan. In *Zhuangzi*, for example, Robber Zhi ridicules these two figures: "When the world talks about loyal ministers, we are told that there are none to surpass Prince Bigan and Wu Zixu. Yet Wu Zixu sank into the river and Bigan had his heart cut out. These two men are called loyal ministers by the world, and yet they ended up as the laughingstock of the empire" (Watson, *The Complete Works of Chuang Tzu*, p. 330).

14. Grant Hardy demonstrates the degree to which Sima Qian's "Chronological Chart of the Twelve Feudal Lords" relies upon *Zuo Commentary*. Hardy's work on the "Charts" is a highly important attempt to unravel the relationship between ancient China's two most important ancient histories ("The Interpretive Function of *Shih chi* 14, 'The Table by Years of the Twelve Feudal Lords,' " *JAOS* 113.1 [1993]: 14–24).

15. As we shall see, this same historical episode appears in an account of a Wu Zixu speech preserved in the "Hereditary Household of Wu Taibo." It is somewhat surprising, however, that Sima Qian says nothing about the Shao Kang story in his "Basic Annals of Xia." This "oversight" has elicited considerable criticism and discussion (*SKKC* 2:45–46).

16. *Jia* is identified as *Mallotus japonicus*, a tree often used to make coffins. It is probably just such a use that Wu Zixu, foreseeing the future fall of the state of Wu, had in mind.

17. David Johnson traces precisely this development. He argues that "The first stories about the puissant yet benevolent Wu Zixu must have been oral, but written accounts of his *gestes* probably appeared very early. As time passed, whole systems of related stories about him developed" ("The Wu Tzu-hsü Pien-wen," p. 94). That is, Wu Zixu, like Su Qin and several other late Zhou figures, became a subject of what Maspero has called a "roman," although these *romans* were probably much more based in a popular, oral world than Maspero thought (see Henri Maspero, "Le roman historique dans la littérature Chinoise de l'antiquité," *Études historiques: Melanges posthumes sur les religions et l'histoire de la Chine*, vol. III [Paris:

Publications de Musée Guimet, 1950], pp. 54–64). I presume that by the time *Zuo* was written there already was a rich body of lore about Wu Zixu and that the *Zuo* author selected from this lore material he thought credible and relevant to his purpose.

18. Sima Qian, as Ban Gu after him, attributes both works to Zuo Qiuming. In his postface, he says, "Zuo Qiuming lost his sight and then we had *Discourses of the States*" (130, p. 3300). In "The Chronological Tables of the Twelve Lords," Zuo Qiuming is listed as author of *Spring and Autumn Annals of Master Zuo* (*SJ* 14, p. 510). Some scholars, such as Jin Dejian, believe that the two books were originally one and had not been divided by Sima Qian's time (*Sima Qian*, p. 5). This is highly unlikely. There are a number of reasons to believe that the two texts are by different authors and were never transmitted as a single work. For a clear Chinese language summary of the arguments, see Qu Wanli, *Xian Qin wen shi ziliao kao bian*, pp. 400–402. An excellent and much more detailed summary of opinions on *Discourses of the States* and its relationship to *Zuo Commentary* can be found in James Pinckney Hart, Jr., "The Philosophy of the 'Chou Yü,'" Ph.D. dissertation, University of Washington, 1973. Hart concludes his survey of earlier opinions with some suggestions of his own. He argues from rather meager evidence, as he himself admits, that *Discourses* and *Zuo* are both based upon an earlier and now lost history of the state of Qin, which must have been written before 440 B.C.E. *Discourses*, Hart believes, is a product of the 3rd century B.C.E. (see p. 248). For more detail, see my "Ssu-ma Ch'ien's Conception of *Tso chuan*."

19. This is convincingly demonstrated by Zhang Yiren in his seminal "Lun *Guo yu* yu *Zuo zhuan* de guanxi," *Guo yu Zuo zhuan lunji* (Taibei: Dongsheng, 1980), pp. 96–101.

20. *Guo yu*, *SBBY* ed., 19:2b.

21. Ibid., pp. 3a–3b.

22. Ibid., p. 4b.

23. Ibid., pp. 4b–5a.

24. Ibid., p. 14a.

25. On this issue, see Qu Wanli, *Xian Qin*, pp. 440–41.

26. Quoted in Zhang Xincheng, *Wei shu tongkao* (rpt., Hongkong: Yulian, n.d.), p. 1016. See Qu Wanli's minor reservations about such an extreme claim in *Xian Qin*, pp. 441–42.

27. See *HS* 30, p. 1741.

28. *Lü shi chun qiu*, *SBBY* ed., pp. 10:8a–8b.

29. Ibid., pp. 14:8a–8b.

30. Ibid., pp. 14:12a–13a.

31. Ibid., pp. 23:5b–6a.

32. Joseph Allen discusses the approval of the fisherman as an example of a method of characterization common in Sima Qian wherein the comment of a third person provides a key to a character. The fisherman "is [in the literary tradition] quintessentially moral. He is an authority on moral integrity . . . and provides the supreme praise of Wu's moral character" ("Narrative Structure in *Shiji*," p. 56).

33. See David Johnson, "The Wu Tzu-hsü Pien-wen," p. 124, where he notes that "I have not seen this incident recounted in any other pre-Sung source on Wu Tzu-hsü." On the subject of the ugly but wise person, see Stith Thompson, *Motif-Index of Folk Literature*, vol. V (Bloomington: Indiana University Press, 1957), pp. 421–22.

34. Certainly David Johnson is correct to note that "Whatever *Lü-shih ch'un-ch'iu*'s source for its material about Wu Tzu-hsü, it was not *Tso-chuan*" ("The Wu Tzu-hsü Pien-wen," p. 123).

35. See, for example, *Guliang Commentary*, Ding 4, and *Gongyang Commentary*, Ding 4. For some important comments on the latter version, see Mark Edward Lewis, *Sanctioned Violence in Early China* (Albany: SUNY Press, 1990), pp. 84–85.

36. *Shi tong*, p. 19.

37. *SJ* 31, pp. 1461–72.

38. *SJ* 40, pp. 1712–16.

39. *SJ* 41, pp. 1740–44.

40. *SJ* 86, pp. 2516–18.

41. Scholarly comments on Sima Qian's use of *Zuo* sometimes have failed to consider the particular format of the section into which *Zuo* has been adapted. "Hereditary Household" chapters typically present in brief fashion the major political events affecting feudal states. Thus, material in *Zuo* that is not directly germane to the politics of a particular state tends to be deleted in Sima Qian's adaptations of that text into the "Hereditary Household" chapters.

42. *Sima Qian chuanxie Shi ji caiyong Zuo zhuan de yanjiu* (Taibei: Zhongzheng, 1981), pp. 74–102. We have already seen one excellent example of Sima Qian's expansion of a *Zuo* narrative in his account of Confucius' participation in the famous Jiagu meeting.

43. Ibid., p. 4.

44. These "extra-historical" forces may be less noticeable in "Hereditary Households," where most of the *Zuo* adaptations appear, than in

"Traditions," generally agreed to be the most "literary" of Sima Qian's sections, and where, for reasons stated above, few *Zuo* passages could be used.

45. Ibid., p. 97.

46. I must emphasize here that by "reshape" I do not mean Sima Qian necessarily reworked the *Zuo* passage without reference to alternative versions of the story that may have existed in his time. Certainly he was familiar with the *Zuo* account, and, given his own announced textual priorities, it must have held considerable sway over him. But whether his "reshaping" is a creative act on his part or the simple selection of another now-lost account, the episode, as far as textual history goes, emerges from his text "reshaped," and he must be held accountable for that new shape.

47. This phrase is somewhat obscure in the original—literally, "For each one of us to follow would be best" (see *Chun qiu Zuo zhuan zhu*, p. 1408).

48. That is, will be so busy trying to counter Yun that they will have no time to eat until it is very late.

49. *Zuo*, Zhao 20, p. 1408.

50. *SJ* 66, pp. 2172–73.

51. *SJ* 40, pp. 1713–14.

52. One of Sima Qian's harshest and most famous critics, the Jin scholar Wang Ruoxu (1174–1243) notices and comments on the discrepancy in the two accounts: "When *Records of the Historian* records the words of Wu Yun, father and son, the 'Traditions' chapter and the 'Hereditary Household' chapter are not uniform. The words came out from a single man's mouth, and the writing comes from a single man's brush. If the words differ, how can the story be believed?" (*Hunan yilao ji, SBCK* ed., vol. 65, 19:1b).

53. *Zuo*, Ding 4, pp. 1547–48.

54. *SJ* 66, pp. 2176–77.

55. *SJ* 31, p. 1466. In the "Hereditary Household of Chu," it says only that he "defiled the tomb of King Ping" (40, p. 1715).

56. See, for example, Shi Zhimian, *Shiji huizhu kaozheng dingbu*, pp. 593–94, who gives a series of other accounts and notes that "in all cases they do not say that he beat King Ping's corpse."

57. This was indeed the perception of some later scholars. Yang Xiong, for example, says, "[Wu Zi]xu caused Wu to make disorder, shattered Chu, entered Ying, whipped a corpse and availed himself of the private dwellings [of the Chu king]. These acts all do not accord with virtue" (*Fa yan*, p. 10:2a).

58. Thus, Allen, translating Li Changzhi's term *"duizhao,"* refers to Wu Zixu and Fuchai as "contrastive foils" ("Narrative Structure in *Shiji,"* pp. 51, 57).

59. *SJ* 66, p. 2178.

60. See *SJ* 66, p. 2178. Cf., 31, p. 1469, and 41, p. 1740.

61. *SJ* 66, p. 2178.

62. Wu Zixu's speech, as reported in the "Hereditary Household of Wu Taibo" is as follows: "Formerly, the ruler of Guo killed Zhen Guan in order to attack Zheng Xun. He destroyed the Emperor Xiang of the Xia dynasty. The Emperor Xiang's concubine, Min, just happened to be pregnant and fled to the ruler of Reng, where she gave birth to Shao Kang. Shao Kang became master of the stables of the ruler of Reng. The ruler of Guo also wished to kill Shao Kang, but Shao Kang fled to the ruler of Yu. The ruler of Yu, thinking of the virtue of Xia, thereupon gave him two daughters as wives and enfeoffed him in Lun. He had ten square *li* of land and five hundred people. Later on, he gathered up the multitudes of Xia and pacified the officials. He sent people to entice him [i.e., the ruler of Guo], and subsequently destroyed the ruler of Guo and restored the achievements of Yu [i.e., restored the Xia dynasty]. He sacrificed to Xia as an equal to heaven and did not neglect ancient duties. Now, Wu is not equal to the strength of the ruler of Guo, and Goujian is greater than Shao Kang" (*SJ* 31, p. 1469).

63. *SJ* 66, p. 2179. Cf., *SJ* 31, p. 1471, and *Zuo*, Ai 11, p. 1664.

64. A text found in *Shu jing* (*Classic of Historical Documents*) (1815; rpt., Taibei: Yiwen, 1955), pp. 9:1a–19a.

65. *SJ* 66, p. 2127.

66. *Shulü*, the name of a fine sword, is also called *shulu* or *tulu*. It is mentioned under the latter name in *Xunzi* 18:5a. For a list of the various names of famous swords in ancient China, see *Guang ya, SBBY* ed., 8a–27b.

67. The Chinese word is *zi* 梓: *catalpa ovata*. This tree was considered the "king of trees" in ancient China and was especially good for making vessels. The commentators insist here, as with the *Zuo* account, where the tree mentioned was the related *jia*, that "vessels" here refers specifically to coffins.

68. *SJ* 66, p. 2180.

69. The chapter then concludes with a brief account of what happened to Sheng, the son of Jian who fled Chu and is therefore the rightful heir to the throne of Chu. It is also a story of revenge that ends with the failure and suicide of Sheng.

70. *SJ* 31, p. 1475. Note that in both *Zuo* and *Discourses* Fuchai hangs himself. In the latter text this makes Wu Zixu's speech about Duke

Ling, a speech not in *Records of the Historian*, a foreshadowing of Fuchai's death.

71. *SJ* 41, pp. 1745–46.

72. *SJ* 66, p. 2183.

73. *HS* 62, p. 2735.

74. John C.Y. Wang finds a didactic pattern in *Zuo Commentary*: "Put very simply, the pattern is this: just as the evil, the stupid, and the haughty will usually bring disaster upon themselves, the good, the wise, and the humble tend to meet their just rewards" ("Early Chinese Narrative: The *Tso-chuan* as Example," *Chinese Narrative*, p. 14).

75. *HS* 62, pp. 2737–38.

76. *Fa yan*, 12:2b.

5. (Wo)men with(out) Names

1. "Vertical and Horizontal" refers to two different alliances advocated by rhetoricians of the Warring States period. The "Vertical" is a north-south alliance between the states of Qin and Chu, directed against Qi, and the "Horizontal" is an east-west alliance of Chu and Qi against Qin. The term "Long and the Short" probably refers not to different alliances, as Watson understands it (*Ssu-ma Ch'ien*, p. 185), but to the method of argumentation used by Warring States persuaders whereby the advantages (the "Longs") and the disadvantages (the "Shorts") of different positions were put forth (*SKKC*, p. 15:3).

2. *SJ* 15, p. 685.

3. The Legalist master Hanfeizi, to cite a single example described in *Records of the Historian*, first comes to the attention of the king of Qin through his writings (*SJ* 63, p. 2155).

4. *SJ* 15, p. 686. Xu Fuguan provides evidence that Sima Qian's description of the Qin records as faulty is an accurate one (see his "Yuan shi," p. 22).

5. Zheng Liangshu, *Zhanguo ce yanjiu*, p. 178.

6. The phrase "*Zuo shi Guo yu*," appearing in this passage, has been taken by some as a single text. In regarding it as a reference to two works, *Zuo Commentary* and *Discourses of the States*, I am following, among others, the punctuation introduced into the text by the editors of *HS* 62, p. 2737, and Chavannes' translation of Ban Biao's comments on *Records of the Historian* as found in *Mémoires*, vol. I, CCXLL.

7. *HS* 62, p. 2737. Ban Gu's "Bibliographic Essay" lists this work in fifteen chapters and states that it, like so many ancient Chinese texts, was "edited by Liu Xiang" (*HS* 30, p. 1714). References to this work, usually containing fewer chapters than the edition noted by Ban Gu, continue to appear down to the Southern Song (1127–1224) when the book was presumably lost.

8. Ban Gu's "Bibliographic Essay" states that this book was written by Lu Jia and occupied nine chapters (*HS* 30, p. 1714). For further details see chapter 6 below.

9. Henceforth, whenever I refer to the sources that became *Intrigues* (that is, the sources used by Sima Qian and eventually gathered together by Liu Xiang), I will write "*Intrigues*," while *Intrigues*, written without quotations, refers to the text as it was edited approximately one hundred years after Sima Qian's death.

10. See "*Zhanguo ce* zuo yu Kuai Tong kao," *Gushi bian*, ed. by Gu Jiegang, vol. 4 (rpt., Taibei: Minglong, 1970), pp. 229–32; and "Ba Jin Dejian xiansheng *Zhanguo ce* zuozhe zhi tuice," ibid., vol. 6, pp. 379–85. The reference in *Records of the Historian* to Kuai Tong says, "Kuai Tong was skilled at the theories of the Long and Short, and, discussing the exigencies and changes of the Warring States period, he made eighty-one chapters" (*SJ* 94, p. 1649).

11. Zheng, *Zhanguo ce yanjiu*, p. 10.

12. For "Diplomatists" as the translation of the name of this school, I have followed Frederick Mote (Kung-chuan Hsiao, *Chinese Political Thought*, p. 42). The name comes from those who advocated the Vertical and Horizontal alliances. The Diplomatists, who were constantly trying to persuade feudal leaders of their various policies, were experts in rhetoric and are sometimes known in English as the "School of Rhetoricians."

13. See Zheng, *Zhanguo ce yanjiu*, p. 17 and James Crump, *Chan-kuo Ts'e* (rev. ed., San Francisco: Chinese Materials Center, 1979).

14. *Zhanguo ce yanjiu*, p. 17.

15. *Chan-kuo Ts'e*, p. 11. Xu Fuguan agrees with such a judgment: "The motive for those who began the compilation of *Intrigues of the Warring States* was neither to admonish others nor to preserve the historical material of this period. Their intention was to utilize the intrigues of power-seekers and the clever rhetoric of that time as material for wandering persuaders" ("Lun *Shi ji*," p. 73).

16. As quoted in Zhang Zhengnan, *Zhanguo ce chutan* (Taibei: Commercial Press, 1984), p. 214.

17. The Confucian distaste for judgments made on the basis of "mere profit" is, of course, well known. See, for example, *LY* 4:4a (4.16):

"The True Gentleman understands duty; the small man understands profit."

18. See *Zhanguo ce, SBBY* ed., "Xu hou," 2a. I have used here Crump's excellent translation of this passage, *Chan-kuo Ts'e*, p. 6. Crump gives the opinions of several other traditional Chinese scholars towards *Intrigues.* Typical of these is the comment of Luo Kefei (fl. ca. 1090): "those who read the book should admire the effectiveness of its persuasions and overlook the baseness of its subject matter so that they are moved only by the rhetoric itself" (p. 7).

19. Zheng Liangshu, *Zhanguo ce yanjiu*, pp. 27–28. On the "conservative" nature of this estimate, see also pp. 182–83.

20. It is, of course, difficult to get precise percentage figures for the second of these sources because Sima Qian usually adapts *Zuo Commentary* quite freely, as we have seen, whereas he quotes "*Intrigues*" almost verbatim. Part of the reason for adapting *Zuo Commentary*, as Zheng notes, was linguistic: "With regard to language, we know that the Gentleman Grand Astrologer often used the modern language of the Han dynasty to translate more obscure older books. For example, when the Gentleman Grand Astrologer quoted *Ancient Historical Documents (Shang shu)* or *Zuo Commentary*, in order to make them easier for readers of his time, he often translated the difficult vocabulary into simple contemporary language. This is something everyone knows. The language of *Intrigues* is simpler and so Sima Qian did not have to 'translate' " (Zheng, *Zhanguo ce yanjiu*, p. 184).

21. On this issue, see Chen Zhi, "*Tai shi gong Shu ming kao*", *Shi ji lunwen xuanji*, pp. 199–206.

22. On Wang Feng, see, Michael Loewe, "The Former Han Dynasty," *The Cambridge History of China*, vol. 1: *The Ch'in and Han Empires, 221 B.C.–A.D. 220*, ed. by Denis Twitchett and Michael Loewe (Cambridge: Cambridge University Press, 1983), p. 215.

23. "Heavenly Offices" refers to the celestial luminaries.

24. *HS* 80, pp. 3324–25.

25. On the historicity of the Su Qin account, see Henri Maspero, "Le roman historique," who argues that the account of Su Qin in *Records of the Historian* derives from a political *roman* composed in the third century B.C.E. and "has no more place in a history of China than d'Artagnan of Alexander Dumas would have in a history of seventeenth-century France" (pp. 61–62). While I would not be so hasty as Maspero to discount the possibility that the Su Qin story has some historical basis, certainly the account in *Records of the Historian*, as Maspero shows, is largely fictional.

26. Quoted in *Gujin tushu jicheng*, vol. 327, p. 28.

27. *SJ* 18, p. 878. Sima Qian's standards as a "careful" historian have been much praised. Zhou Hulin, for example, quotes the passage from the *Analects* cited above and states enthusiastically that "The Gentleman Grand Astrologer possessed just that characteristic!" He then gives a number of examples where Sima Qian shows great caution in his treatment of the records of the past (Zhou Hulin, *Sima Qian yu qi shixue* [Taibei: Wenshizhe, 1987], pp. 194–97).

28. *LY* 2:4b (2.28).

29. *New York Review of Books* 35:5 (31 March 1988), p. 23. I would like to thank Professor Joseph Allen of Washington University for bringing this article to my attention.

30. "It is always interesting, and always instructive," says Ernest Jones in a valuable statement of the obvious, "to note the respects in which he [i.e., a poet] changes elements in the story" ("The Death of Hamlet's Father," in *Literature and Psychoanalysis*, ed. by Edith Kurzweil and William Phillips [New York: Columbia University Press, 1983], p. 34).

31. This fact has not escaped notice. Huang Zhen (fl. 1040 C.E.) criticizes Sima Qian for immortalizing assassins. Yu Rang, Huang Zhen thinks, is indeed a worthy man gaining revenge for his lord, but "the rest were stupidly committing murder and were themselves going contrary to human feeling" (*Huang shi ri chao, SKQS*, "Masters Section" [*zi bu*], vols. 707–8, p. 46:47a).

32. There are several good translations of this story. See, in particular, *Selections from Records of the Historian*, trans. by Yang Hsien-yi and Gladys Yang (Beijing: Foreign Languages Press, 1979), pp. 389–92.

33. *SJ* 86, p. 2424.

34. Ben is Meng Ben and Yu is Xia Yu, both valiant knights from the reign of King Wu of Qin (697–677 B.C.E.). Cheng Jing is a heroic knight who supposedly lived in Qi during the Spring and Autumn period.

35. *Zhanguo ce*, 27:7a–7b. "Being minced and mixed with sauce" is a reference to one of the most feared punishments of ancient China. Her suicide, of course, was to avoid such a terrible fate.

36. *SJ* 86, pp. 2525–26.

37. *SJ* 61, p. 2127.

38. *HS* 62, p. 2733.

39. This account substantially supplements the picture of Guanzi, a famous Spring and Autumn period prime minister of Qi, found in his "Traditions" (see *SJ* 62, pp. 2131–34). Guanzi was originally a tutor to Jiu, one of the sons of Duke Xi (730–698 B.C.E.) of Qi. After the duke's death, Guanzi assisted Jiu in an attempt to seize the throne but lost out to another

son who is known to history as Duke Huan. Although Guanzi had fought against Duke Huan, the latter was favorably impressed with the former's abilities and made him his chief minister. On Guanzi see Sidney Rosen, "In Search of the Historical Kuan Chung," *Journal of Asian Studies* 35.3 (May 1976): 431–40.

40. The story of Cao Mo's intimidation of Duke Huan and the recovery of Lu lands is found in *SJ* 86, pp. 2515–16.

41. *SJ* 83, pp. 2467–68.

42. *Zhanguo ce*, 13:2a–3b.

43. *SJ* 83, p. 2469.

44. See quotation in *SKKC*, 83:18.

45. *SJJZ*, vol. 8, p. 2487.

46. This appears in Sima Qian's judgment at the end of the "Traditions of Lian Po and Lin Xiangru" (*SJ* 81, p. 2451). The translation is somewhat problematic. "Management of death" translates Chinese *chu si* 處死, a term that has been variously understood (see, for example, Yang and Yang, Records of the Historian, p. 151: "It is not hard to die, only hard to face death"). The translation I propose here is the same as the vernacular interpretation of Wu Shaozhi, *Baihua Shiji* (*Vernacular Records of the Historian*) (Tainan: Xibi, 1988), p. 521. On "management" or "control" for *chu*, see *Zhongwen da cidian*, 33505, items 7 and 12.

47. *HS* 62, p. 2732.

48. See the statistics for each chapter in Zheng, *Zhanguo ce yanjiu*, pp. 179–82.

49. Some editions of *Records of the Historian* label chapter 77 the "Traditions of the Son of the Duke of Wei," others as the "Traditions of Lord Xinling." The former is more likely to be Sima Qian's original title (Shi Zhimian, *Shiji huizhu*, p. 1264). The name comes from the fact that he is the son of Duke (or King) Zhao of Wei (r. 295–277 B.C.E.) and younger brother of Duke (or King) Anxi (r. 276–243 B.C.E.).

50. For *Intrigues* references, see 10:7a, 20:6b, 21:5b, and 25:6a–7a. The one exception, although not counted by Zheng Liangshu concerns Lord Xinling's murder of Jin Bi (25:6a) and the advice that "there are some things you cannot forget, and some things you must forget" (cf. *SJ* 77, p. 2382).

51. *SJ* 130, p. 3324.

52. *SJ* 77, p. 2385.

53. *LY* 1:5a (1.16).

54. The quotation is taken from Sima Tan's final injunction to his son, spoken on his deathbed in Luoyang (*SJ* 130, p. 3295).

55. On the existence of such romances, see Dr. Hu Shi's important "Shuo Shi," originally published in 1958 and reprinted in *Zhongguo shixue shi lunwen xuanji*, vol. I, ed. by Du Weiyun and Huang Jinxing (Taibei: Huashi, 1980), pp. 1–6.

56. *SJ* 77, pp. 2377–78.

57. *SJ* 77, p. 2384.

58. *SJ* 77, p. 2381. Lord Ping Yuan was himself a man famous for his appreciation for men of talent. Sima Qian tells the following extreme story about him: "The loft of Lord Ping Yuan's home overlooked a commoner's home. In the commoner's home there was a cripple who limped out to draw water. One of Lord Ping Yuan's beautiful women, who lived in the loft, looked down and laughed at him. The next day the cripple came to Lord Ping Yuan's gate and requested, 'I have heard that you treat gentlemen well, and that the reason scholars come here from great distances is that you value gentlemen and do not value concubines. I unfortunately am hunch-backed, and one of my lord's harem looked down upon me from the loft and laughed at me. I wish to obtain the head of the one who laughed.' Lord Ping Yuan laughingly responded, 'Fine.' After the cripple left, Lord Ping Yuan jokingly said, 'Look at this fool! He wishes, on account of a single laugh, to kill one of my beauties. Is that not excessive!' And in the end, he did not kill her. After a year, more than half of his guests and the retainers at his gate had gradually departed. Lord Ping Yuan considered this strange and said, 'I, Sheng, have not once dared to be impolite in my treatment of you gentle-men. Why have so many left?' One of his retainers came forward and said, 'Because you, lord, did not kill the one who laughed at the cripple, we consider you fond of sensual beauty and not fond of gentlemen. So they have departed.' Lord Ping Yuan thereupon beheaded the beauty who had laughed at the cripple and himself went to his gate and presented it to the cripple and apologized to him. Afterwards, his retainers gradually returned" (*SJ* 76, pp. 2365–66).

59. It will be remembered that Lord Xinling was responsible for the death of the Wei general Jin Bi.

60. *SJ* 77, p. 2384.

61. On his classification as one of the Diplomatists, see *HS* 30, p. 1739. Concerning the issue of the influence from "*Intrigues*" upon his style, see Eva Chung, "A Study of the 'Shu' (Letters) of the Han Dynasty (206 B.C.– A.D. 220)" (Ph.D. diss., University of Washington, 1982), pp. 277–79. She says that she relies for much of her information upon an unpublished paper of Prof. David Knechtges.

62. See *HS* 47, p. 2210; 49, p. 2276; and 51, p. 2353.

63. Eva Chung, not I, has counted the allusions ("A Study of the 'Shu' (Letters)," p. 277).

64. *SJ* 83, p. 2470.

65. *SJ* 83, p. 2473.

66. *HS* 62, p. 2736.

6. Ideologue versus Narrator

1. *Historian of China*, p. 151.

2. The bibliography on these issues is an enormous one, and I indicate here only a few relevant works. A very important article of broad implications is, of course, Jaroslav Průšek, *Chinese History and Literature*, pp. 17–34. Derk Bodde has spoken of the "fragmentary and episodic" nature of Chinese mythology, although he does seem to believe that there was an original but now lost "unity" (see "Myths of China" in *Mythologies of the Ancient World*, ed. by Samuel Noah Kramer [Garden City: Anchor Books, 1961], pp. 370, 76). Anne Birrell, on the contrary, sees the "amorphous, untidy" nature of Chinese myth as predigested and more authentic than those drawn into a unity like in such Western texts as *Iliad* and *Odyssey* (*Chinese Mythology: An Introduction* [Baltimore: Johns Hopkins University Press, 1993], pp. 17–18). For the characterization of Chinese landscape painting given above, see Michael Sullivan, *The Arts of China* (Berkeley: University of California Press, 1984), p. 156. Concerning the Chinese lyrical poem as the expression of a nonfictional moment, see Stephen Owen, *Traditional Chinese Poetry and Poetics* (Madison: The University of Wisconsin Press, 1985), pp. 12–53. The term "metaphorical operation" is taken from Owen, pp. 23–24. Charles S. Gardner, in his classic study of Chinese historiography, refers to the "primitive" nature of Chinese historical writing where "respect for the integrity of texts is so strong... that often no attempt is made to harmonize the documents which are thus brought into juxtaposition" (*Chinese Traditional Historiography* [Cambridge, Mass.: Harvard University Press, 1938], p. 71).

3. See *Thinking Through Confucius*, p. 136. Of course, this feature of Chinese philosophy was noticed very early and was considered by some a "failure." An important, if somewhat dated, article is Homer Dubs, "The Failure of Chinese to Produce Philosophical Systems," *T'oung Pao* 26 (Leiden, 1929): 98–109, in which he attacks H. Hackmann's claim that the nature of the Chinese language does not allow systematic philosophy. Dubs goes on to attribute the Chinese "failure" to Chinese "practical attitudes," the neglect of the Chinese to develop "mathematics as a pure science," and the too early establishment of Confucianism as an authoritarian state philosophy. In his brilliant study of classical Chinese philosophy, A.C.

Graham argues against extreme claims such as those of Dubs by noting that "the ancient Chinese are very much more rational than they used to look." But Graham goes on to summarize the Chinese attitude toward rational systems by noting that "reason is for questions of means; for your ends in life listen to aphorism, example, parable, and poetry . . . it is inevitable that on the Chinese scale of value the wise dicta of Confucius and Lao-tzu are primary, the practical rationality of Mo-tzu and Han Fei is secondary" (*Disputers of the Tao* [La Salle, Illinois: Open Court, 1989], p. 7).

4. *HS* 62, p. 2735.

5. "Shi lun Sima Qian suoshuo de `tong gujin zhi bian,'" *Zhongguo shixue shi lunwen xuanji*, vol. III, p. 185. Zhang Dake also provides a detailed analysis of each of these phrases (*Shi ji yanjiu*, pp. 22–35).

6. See *Shuo wen jie zi gulin*, p. 3295b.

7. Ibid., p. 6516.

8. Watson, *Ssu-ma Chien*, p. 66; Chavannes, *Mémoires*, p. cxxxvii.

9. My argument here is drawn from Bai Shouyi's "Shuo `Cheng yijia' zhi yan," *Sima Qian he Shi ji* (*Sima Qian and Records of the Historian*), ed. by Liu Naihe (Beijing: Anping, 1987), pp. 31–40. Zhang Dake holds essentially the same position. He argues that Sima Qian's intention was to "comprehend thoroughly the teachings of the one hundred schools in order to establish a new, unified system of thought" (ibid., p. 30).

10. "Lun Sima Qian de sixiang," *Shi ji lunwen xuanji*, pp. 37–41.

11. "Lun Shi ji," *Zhongguo shixue shi lunwen xuanji*, vol. III, pp. 88–95. Xunzi's classic statement is found in his "Essay on Heaven" (ch. 17—*SBBY*, 11:9a–15a), in which, for example, he says: "To produce without acting and to obtain without seeking, this is what is meant by the office of heaven. Therefore, although the way of heaven is deep, this man will not put deep thought on it; although it is great, he will not use his ability for its investigation; although it is mysterious, he will not scrutinize it— this is what is meant by refraining from contesting with heaven. Heaven has its seasons, Earth has its wealth, Man has his government. The foregoing is what is meant by being able to form a triad with heaven and earth. To give up that wherewith one can form such a triad and to desire to know those with whom he forms a triad is to be led into error." *The Works of Hsün-tzu*, trans. by Homer Dubs (London: Arthur Probsthain, 1928), pp. 174–75.

12. Li Shaoyong, *Sima Qian zhuanji*, p. 24.

13. Zhang Dake has discussed this incongruity and notes that while Sima Qian at times is inclined towards the notion of "the Mandate of Heaven" and "his teacher" Dong Zhongshu's theories, "in his concrete narration of the movement of history and in his evaluation of human

beings, one sees no shadow of the theory of the Mandate of Heaven" (Zhang, *Shi ji yanjiu*, p. 25).

24. *SJ* 27, p. 1349. Cf. Chavannes, "il n'arrive jamais qu'une apparition céleste se produise sans être suivie d'un événement qui y corresponde en effet" *(Mémoires*, vol. III, p. 408).

15. *SJ* 15, p. 685.

16. *SJ* 16, p. 760.

17. *SJ* 27, 1344.

18. *SJ* 8, pp. 393–94.

19. "Lun Sima Qian de tong gujin zhi bian," *Sima Qian yanjiu xin lun* (Beijing: Henan Renmin, 1982), p. 40.

20. See *Metahistory* (Baltimore: Johns Hopkins University Press, 1973), p. 11.

21. *SJ* 30, p. 1442. As has been noted by others, Sima Qian's praise of the flourishing of his own time can be regarded as a warning of impending decline. Emperor Wu's policies may have brought Han power to a high point, but the seed of decline, according to the "organic model," is always hidden within the moment of greatest glory.

22. *SJ* 130, p. 3298. I am indebted here to Ruan Zhisheng's ("Shi lun Sima Qian") excellent article and the abundant textual examples he provides.

23. *SJ* 14, p. 511.

24. In *Records of the Historian*, Liu Bang is variously called either the Duke of Pei, the King of Han, or Gaozu (The Grand Ancestor). For the sake of simplicity, I will call him "Liu Bang," but when translating from Sima Qian himself, I provide in brackets the name Sima Qian actually uses.

25. *Shi tong tongshi*, p. 46. Elsewhere, Liu Zhiji says, quite emphatically, "Xing Yu was a usurper and a bandit . . . how is it one could taboo his name and call him 'King'" (ibid., p. 42).

26. See *HS* 31, where Xiang Yu is put in a "Traditions" chapter with another anti-Qin rebel, Chen She.

27. The quote is from Zhang Zhao. For this and further discussion, see *SKKC* 7:2.

28. For Ban Gu's statement, see *HS* 62, p. 2737. In a note found in the preface to *Collected Explanations of Records of the Historian (Shi ji jijie)*, Sima Zhen, who has undoubtedly seen *Spring and Autumn Annals of Chu and Han*, tells us its general scope: "It records the first uprisings of the Xiang clan and the Grand Ancestor of the Han, and it speaks of affairs from

the time of [emperors] Hui and Wen." For an excellent summary of the history of this text and an interesting argument that it was originally known as *New Sayings* (*Xin yu*), a title presumably shifted somewhat later to another text by Lu Jia, see Jin Dejian, *Sima Qian*, pp. 320–27.

29. The first piece of evidence for such a conclusion is a statement of the ever-opinionated Liu Zhiji, who lived at a time when *Spring and Autumn Annals of Chu and Han* was extant and had obviously examined the text closely. He compares the two texts and notes that "when we examine what [Sima] Qian has written, he is constantly differing from the older [source]" (*Shitong tongshi*). Liu Zhiji knows that Ban Gu has listed *Spring and Autumn Annals of Chu and Han* as a primary source of *Records of the Historian*, and he is surprised that Sima Qian deviates so frequently from Lu Jia's account.

A second piece of evidence, which supports my conclusion, is provided by examining the references to *Spring and Autumn Annals of Chu and Han* in the three commentaries to *Records of the Historian* that were compiled before Lu Jia's text was lost. If, Sima Qian's text closely follows *Spring and Autumn Annals of Chu and Han*, we would expect this fact to be reflected by frequent references in these commentaries to the earlier source. However, the three commentaries, as found on the 150 pages of the "Basic Annals of Xiang Yu" and "Basic Annals of Gaozu" (Bona Edition), contain only ten references to *Spring and Autumn Annals of Chu and Han*. This in no way compares to the frequency of the same commentators' references to *Intrigues of the Warring States* in those cases where it is the source of Sima Qian's narratives. For example, in those portions of "Traditions of Assassins" (chapter 86) drawn from *Intrigues*, the three commentators in question refer to the earlier source approximately one and one-half times per page! I believe that the commentators show so little concern for those inevitable minor differences between the text and its "source" precisely because the two accounts are so different as not to invite the kind of careful comparison that is warranted by accounts drawn from *Intrigues*.

Third, if one compares the few extant fragments of *Spring and Autumn Annals of Chu and Han* with the corresponding portions of *Records of the Historian*, one is struck by how little the two sources agree. A particularly striking example is provided by Xiang Yu's famous "Song of Gaixia," which is entirely different in the two sources. Furthermore, *Spring and Autumn Annals of Chu and Han* preserves a detailed and lively account of Liu Bang's entry into the pass that is not paralleled at all in Sima Qian (for a collection of fragments from *Spring and Autumn Annals of Chu and Han*, see Hong Yixuan, *Jingdian jilin*, *Baibu congshu* edition, ch. 10).

Finally, if we examine Ban Gu's statement about Sima Qian's sources, we discover that he employed three different verbs to indicate the type and degree of reliance upon earlier texts. For *Zuo Commentary* and *Discourses of the States*, the verb is *ju* 據 "to rely upon," a verb that reflects quite accurately the kind of adaptation we noted in chapter 4 above. In the case of *Intrigues* and *Genealogical Origins*, the verb is *cai* 採 "to select' or "to quote." Again, this complies with what we have seen in chapter 5 above. But Ban Gu says that Sima Qian *shu* 述 "transmitted" or "narrated" *Spring and Autumn Annals of Chu and Han*. This implies, I believe, that he utilized the earlier source but did not quote from it extensively. Instead, he narrated the same events found in that earlier work but felt free to alter his own version as other sources or his own literary sensitivities might dictate.

30. On this similarity Li Shaoyong notes: "In reality, the seven 'Basic Annals,' from the 'Basic Annals of the First Qin Emperor' on, all record the activities of a single emperor and have no major difference from the 'Traditions' that record the biographies of a single man" (*Sima Qian*, p. 5). It is this feature of the "Basic Annals of Xiang Yu" that troubles Liu Zhiji.

31. *SJ* 7, p. 296.

32. *SJ* 8, p. 344.

33. *SJ* 7, p. 295.

34. *SJ* 7, pp. 299–300.

35. *SJ* 7, p. 302.

36. *SJ* 7, p. 315.

37. *SJ* 8, p. 376. This is of current interest precisely because scholars inside and outside of China await the excavation of the central tomb of the First Qin Emperor, an event that might disclose the amount and type of damage inflicted by Xiang Yu.

38. The first episode involves the "skillful Han cavalryman and archer Loufan" (*SJ* 7, p. 328), and the second episode is just before Xiang Yu's death when he confronts a pursuer, the marquis of Chiquan (*SJ* 7, p. 334).

39. "His parent, Dame Liu, once was resting on the hillside above a great swamp. She dreamt that she encountered a god. At that time, there was thunder and lightning, and the sky darkened. When the Grand Duke [her husband] went to look, he saw a dragon above her. Consequently, she was pregnant and gave birth to Liu Bang [Gaozu]. Liu Bang [Gaozu], as a man, had a high bridge to his nose and a dragonlike countenance. He had beautiful whiskers and seventy-two black spots on his left thigh" (*SJ* 8, pp. 341–42).

40. *SJ* 8, p. 343.

41. *SJ* 7, p. 311.

42. See *SJ* 7, p. 311 and 8, p. 362.

43. His first words, to the reader who is perusing *Records of the Historian* from beginning to end, appear in the "Basic Annals of Xiang Yu" (*SJ* 7,

pp. 311, 314).

44. *SJ* 8, p. 381.

45. *SJ* 7, p. 315.

46. *SJ* 7, p. 315. This statement leads an unnamed character to exclaim, "People say that men of Chu are simply monkeys with caps. Truly it is so!" When Xiang Yu hears this, he boils the speaker alive.

47. In his history of the Qin-Han period, Nishijima Sadao supports such an interpretation. Discussing the system established by Xiang Yu, he says, "This system denied the prefecture-county system established by the Qin. It is entirely a revival of the condition of feudal division" (*Baihua Qin Han shi*, p. 54). Lao Gan, in his history of the Qin-Han period, notes that Liu Bang accepted the basic changes brought about by Qin: "After becoming the King of Han, he completely changed to a Qin-style organization" (*Qin Han Shi* [Taibei: Zhongguo wenhua, 1986], p. 21).

48. I am referring here to Xiang Yu's first dramatic act: "In a moment, Liang signalled Ji with his eyes and said, 'You can indeed act!' Thereupon, Ji drew his sword and cut off the head of the governor" (*SJ* 7, p. 297).

49. *SJ* 7, p. 313.

50. Professor Stephen West writes that he has "often thought that the 'Basic Annals of Xiang Yu' could be read as a binary structure of impetuosity and indecision" (private communication).

51. *SJ* 7, p. 314.

52. *SJ* 7, p. 322.

53. *SJ* 8, p. 342.

54. *SJ* 8, p. 381. Such criticism appears in his own "Annals" and not just elsewhere. There is a passage, however, in the "Traditions of Favorites and Sycophants" (chapter 125) where the Duke of Pei is described as "extremely violent and contentious" (*SJ* 125, p. 3191). Xu Fuguan believes that this passage reveals Sima Qian's true feelings about the Duke of Pei's personality ("Tai shi gong de sixiang beijing ji qi shixue jingshen," *Shi ji lunwen xuanji*, p. 27).

55. *SJ* 7, p. 333. The song appears quite differently in a fragment of *Spring and Autumn Annals of Chu and Han*:

> The soldiers of Han already invade the land—
> On all four sides the sounds of Chu songs.
> The plans and energy of the Great King finished,
> How will my concubine live on?

See Hong Yixuan, *Jingdian jilin*, p. 2b.

56. *SJ* 8, p. 389.

57. *SJ* 7, p. 336.

58. *SJ* 8, p. 391. Bianque was a highly skilled physician of the Warring States period. His "Traditions" are found in *SJ* 105, pp. 2785–94.

59. *SJ* 7, p. 339.

60. *SJ* 8, pp. 393–94.

61. The "Basic Annals of the Yin" states that the dynastic founder's mother, Jian Di, became pregnant by swallowing an egg dropped by a "black bird" (*SJ* 3, p. 91). The mother of the founder of the Zhou dynasty conceived by stepping in the footprint of a giant (*SJ* 4, p. 111). The mother of the founder of the Qin imperial line, like the forerunner of the Yin before her, swallowed an egg dropped by a black bird (*SJ* 5, p. 373).

62. *SJ* 7, p. 322.

63. *SJ* 7, p. 311.

64. Ruan Zhisheng, for example, says that the basic materials for reconstructing Sima Qian's thought are the "Self-Narration," the judgments (*tai shi gong yue*) and Sima Qian's occasional intrusions into the narrative (as occurs in the "Traditions of Bo Yi") ("Shi lun Sima Qian", p. 186).

65. Both of these examples are drawn from the "Traditions of the Assassins" (*SJ* 86, pp. 2534, 2521).

66. In fact, Sima Qian seems obsessed elsewhere with those little, "insignificant" events that have, in a totally unpredictable way, enormous impact upon the course of history. Note, for example, his comment on this very fact at the conclusion of his "Traditions of the Jesters" (chapter 126): "Chunyu Kun looked up at heaven and laughed out loud, and King Wei of Qi [as a result] exercised great power. Meng shook his head and sang, and a carrier of firewood was enfeoffed. Zhen looked out over the balustrade and called out loudly, and the guards were reduced by half. How could this not be extraordinary!" (*SJ* 126, p. 3203).

Epilogue

1. *SJ* 18, p. 878.

2. *Kongzi jiayu, SBBY* ed., p. 7:4a.

3. *SJ* 130, p. 3298.

4. *SJ* 130, p. 3297.

5. *Confucian Thought: Selfhood as Creative Transformation* (Albany: SUNY Press, 1985), pp. 113–30.

6. Both the *Zuo Commentary* version and the *Records of the Historian* version can be found in Burton Watson, *The Tso Chuan: Selections from China's Oldest Narrative History* (New York: Columbia University Press, 1989), pp. 13–15.

7. *SJ* 37, p. 1593.

Glossary

The glossary of Chinese words and terms appearing below does not contain the names of authors and books listed in the bibliography, nor does it contain items found within quotations from common Chinese works and hence readily accessible through consulting the original from the appropriate citation.

ben ji ("Basic Annals")　本紀
bianwen ("transformation texts")　變文
Bigan　比干
bo shi ("academicians")　博士
bo shi guan ("office of academicians")　博士官
Cai (state)　蔡
Chang'an (city)　長安
Chen (state)　陳
Chen Renxi　陳仁錫
Chen She　陳涉
Chu (state)　楚
Chu Shaosun　褚少孫
chuan ("transmit")　傳
Dai Hong　戴宏
FanYuqi (=General Fan)　樊於期
Fan Kuai　樊噲
fu (rhapsody)　賦
Fuchai (king)　夫差
Gaozu　高祖
Gongliang Ru　公良孺
Gongsun Gui　公孫詭
Gongzi　公子
Goujian (king)　句踐

gu wen ("old script")　古文
Gu Yanwu　顧炎武
Guanzi　管子
gudian ("classical")　古典
Guiji (place-name)　會稽
Han (dynasty)　漢
Han (state)　韓
Handan　邯鄲
Helu (king)　盧閭
Hou Gong　侯公
Hou Ying　侯嬴
Hu Sui　壺遂
Hu Wusheng　胡毋生
Huan Tui　桓魋
Huang Zhen　黃震
Hui (emperor)　蕙
jia (*Mallotus japonicus*—type of tree)　檟
Jiagu (place-name)　夾古
Jin (state)　晉
Jin Bi　晉鄙
jin wen ("new script")　今文
jing ("classic")　經
Jing (emperor)　景
Jing Ke　荊軻
Jishi (place-name)　積石
Jixia (place)　稷下
junzi ("True Gentleman")　君子
Kong Anguo　孔安國
kong yan ("empty words")　空言
langman ("romantic")　浪漫
li ("ritual")　禮
Li Guang　李廣
Li Ling　李陵
Li Si　李斯
Liang (state)　梁
Liao Dengting　廖登延
lie zhuan ("Traditions")　列傳
Liu An　劉安
Liu Bang　劉邦

Liu Xiang　劉向
Longmen (place-name)　龍門
Lu (state)　魯
Lu chun chiu　魯春秋
Lu Zhonglian　魯仲連
Lun heng　論衡
Lü Buwei　呂不韋
Meng Xizi　孟釐子
nian biao ("Chronological Charts")　年表
Nie Zheng　聶政
nu ("fury")　怒
Ping Yuan　平原
Pu (place-name)　蒲
Qi (state)　齊
Qin (state and dynasty)　秦
Qing (dynasty)　清
Qu Yuan　屈原
Ren An　任安
Rong　榮
Shandong (modern province)　山東
shi ("poetry")　詩
Shi jing　詩經
shi jia ("Hereditary Households")　世家
shu ("Treatises")　書
shu ("historical documents")　書
Shu jing　書經
Shun (mythical sage-king)　舜
Sima Guang　司馬光
Sima Tan　司馬談
Sima Zhen　司馬貞
song (section of *Classic of Poetry*)　頌
Song (state)　宋
Su Qin　蘇秦
Tai (mountain)　泰
tai shi gong ("Duke Grand Astrologer")　太史公
tai shi ling ("Prefect Grand Astrologer")　太史令
Tang (dynasty)　唐
ti ("fraternal respect")　弟
tian di heyi ("heaven and earth are united as one")　天地合一

Wang Feng　王豐

Wang Shizhen　王世貞

Wei (state)　衛

Wei (river)　渭

Wen (emperor)　文

wen ("culture")　文

Wu (state)　吳

Wu (emperor)　武

Wu Renjie　吳仁傑

Wu Yue chun qiu (*Spring and Autumn Annals of Wu and Yue*)
　吳越春秋

wu xing ("five processes")　五行

Xia (dynasty)　夏

Xiang Yu　項羽

Xianyang　咸陽

xiao ("filial piety")　孝

Xiao He　蕭何

xingren ("official receptionist")　行人

Xinling　信陵

xiongnu (northwestern barbarians)　匈奴

Xu Shen　許慎

Xuan (Han emperor)　宣

xulie ("to put in order, to arrange")　序列

ya (section of *Classic of Poetry*)　雅

Yan (state)　燕

Yan Hui　顏回

Yang Hu　陽虎

Yang Sheng　陽生

Yanzi　宴子

Yao (mythical sage-king)　堯

yi ("duty")　義

yijia ("single school")　一家

Ying (Chu capital)　郢

Yu (mythical sage-king)　禹

Yu Rang　豫讓

yue ("music")　樂

Yue (state)　越

Yue jing　樂經

Yue jue shu (*Book of the Culmination of Yue*)　越絕書

Yumen (place-name) 禹門
Zeng Gu 曾固
Zengzi 曾子
Zhang Yan 張宴
zhi sheng ("ultimate sage") 至聖
Zhou (dynasty) 周
Zhu Hai 朱亥
zhuan ("tradition, transmission") 傳
Zhuangzi 莊子
zhuzi bai jia ("Various Masters and Hundred Schools") 諸子百家
Zichan 子產
Zongheng jia ("School of Diplomatists") 縱橫家
Zou Yang 鄒陽
zuo ("produce, create") 作
Zuo Qiuming 左丘明
Zuo shi chun qiu 左氏春秋

Bibliography

Abbreviations Used Below

SBBY *Si bu bei yao* 四部備要

SBCK *Si bu cong kan* 四部叢刊

SKQS Si ku quan shu 四庫全書

SSJZS Shisan jing zhu shu 十三經注疏

Western Sources

Allan, Sarah. *The Heir and the Sage.* San Francisco: Chinese Materials Center, 1981.

Allen, Joseph Roe III. "An Introductory Study of Narrative Structure in *Shiji.*" *Chinese Literature: Essays, Articles, Reviews* 3 (1981): 31–66.

Arbuckle, Gary. "A Note on the Authenticity of the *Chunqiu Fanlu.*" *T'oung Pao* 75 (1989): 226–34.

Barthes, Roland. *Image, Music, Text.* New York: Hill and Wang, 1977.

Bauer, Wolfgang. *Das Antlitz China: Die autobiographische Selbstdarstellung in der Chinesischen Literatur von ihren Anfängen bis Heute.* Munich: Carl Hanser Verlag, 1990.

Bielenstein, Hans. *The Bureaucracy of Han Times.* Cambridge: Cambridge University Press, 1980.

Birrell, Anne. *Chinese Mythology: An Introduction.* Baltimore and London: Johns Hopkins University Press, 1993.

Bloom, Harold. *New York Review of Books* 35.5 (31 March 1988): 23.

Bodde, Derk. "Myths of China." In Samuel Noah Kramer, ed., *Mythologies of the Ancient World.* Garden City: Anchor Books, 1961.

———. "The State and the Empire of Ch'in." In Denis Twitchett and

Michael Loewe, eds., *The Cambridge History of China, Volume 1: The Ch'in and Han Empires, 221 B.C.–A.D. 220.* Cambridge: Cambridge University Press, 1983.

Campbell, Joseph. *The Hero with a Thousand Faces.* Princeton: Princeton University Press, 1968.

Chavannes, Edouard. *Les Mémoires historiques de Se-ma Ts'ien.* 1895. Reprint. Paris: Librairie d'Amérique et d'Orient, 1967.

Ch'en Shih-hsiang. "An Innovation in Chinese Biographical Writing." *Far Eastern Quarterly* 13 (1953): 44–62.

Cheng, Anne. *Étude sur le Confucianisme Han.* Paris: Collège de France, 1985.

Chung, Eva Yuen-wah. "A Study of the 'Shu' (Letters) of the Han Dynasty (206 B.C.–A.D. 220)." Ph. D. diss., University of Washington, 1982.

Creel, H. G. *Confucius and the Chinese Way.* 1949. Reprint. New York: Harper & Row, 1960.

Crump, James. *Chan-kuo Ts'e.* Revised edition. San Francisco: Chinese Materials Center, 1979.

Dawson, Raymond, trans. *Sima Qian: Historical Records.* Oxford: Oxford University Press, 1994.

De Bary, Wm. Theodore. *The Trouble with Confucianism.* Cambridge, Mass.: Harvard University Press, 1991.

Dubs, Homer. "The Failure of Chinese to Produce Philosophical Systems." *T'oung Pao* 26 (1929): 98–109.

———. "The Political Career of Confucius." *Journal of the American Oriental Society* 66 (1946): 273–82.

———. "The Victory of Han Confucianism." *History of the Han Dynasty,* vol. 2. Baltimore: Waverly Press, 1938.

———, trans. *Works of Hsün-tzu.* London: Arthur Probsthain, 1928.

Dull, Jack. "A Historical Introduction to the Aprocyphal Ch'an-Wei Texts of the Han Dynasty." Ph.D. diss., University of Washington, 1966.

Durrant, Stephen. "Liu Chih-chi on Ssu-ma Ch'ien." *Di yijie guoji Tangdai xueshu huiyi lunwenji* 第一屆國際唐代學術會議論文集 [Proceedings of the First International T'ang Studies Conference]. Taibei: Xuesheng, 1989.

———. "*Shih-chi.*" In William Nienhauser, ed., *The Indiana Companion to Traditional Chinese Literature.* Bloomington: Indiana University Press, 1986, pp. 689–94.

———. "Ssu-ma Ch'ien's Conception of *Tso chuan*." *Journal of the American Oriental Society* 112.2 (1992): 295–301.

———. "Takikawa Kametarō's Comments on Chapter 47 of *Shih chi*. In *Di erjie Zhongguo yuwai hanji guoji xueshu huiyi lunwenji* 第二屆中國域外漢籍國際學術會議論文集 [Proceedings of the Second International Conference on Chinese Language Materials Published Outside of China]. Taibei: Lianjing, 1989.

———. "Tangles and Lacunae: A Few Aspects of Ssu-ma Ch'ien's Portrayal of His Intellectual Antecedents." In Chen Jiexian 陳捷先, ed., *Chen Qilu yuanshi qizhi rongqing lunwenji* 陳奇祿院士七秩榮慶論文 [A Collection of Essays Commemorating the Seventieth Birthday of Academician Chen Qilu]. Taibei: Xuesheng, 1992.

Eno, Robert. *The Confucian Creation of Heaven*. Albany: SUNY Press, 1990.

Enoki, Kazuo. "On the Relationship Between the *Shih-chi*, Bk. 123 and the *Han-shu*, Bks. 61 and 96." *Memoirs of the Research Department of the Toyo Bunko* 41 (1983): 1–32.

Franke Otto. *Studien zur Geschichte des Konfuzianischen Dogmas und Tung Tschung-shu's Tsch'un-ts'iu fan-lu*. Hamburg: L. Friederichsen & Co., 1920.

Fung, Yu-lan. *A History of Chinese Philosophy*. 2 vols. Translated by Derk Bodde. Peiping: Henry Vetch, 1971.

Gardner, Charles S. *Chinese Traditional Historiography*. Cambridge, Mass.: Harvard University Press, 1938.

Graham, A. C., trans. *Chuang Tzu: The Inner Chapters*. London: George Allen & Unwin, 1981.

———. *Disputers of the Tao*. La Salle, Illinois: Open Court, 1989.

Hall, David and Roger Ames. *Thinking Through Confucius*. Albany: SUNY Press, 1987.

Hardy, Grant. "Can An Ancient Chinese Historian Contribute to Modern Western Theory? The Multiple Narrations of Ssu-ma Ch'ien." *History and Theory* 33.1 (1994): 20–38.

———. "The Intepretive Function of *Shih chi* 14, 'The Table by Years of the Twelve Feudal Lords.'" *Journal of the American Oriental Society* 113 (January–March 1993): 14–24.

Hart, James Pinckney, Jr. "The Philosophy of the 'Chou Yü.'" Ph.D. diss., University of Washington, 1973.

Hawkes, David. *Ch'u Tz'u: The Songs of the South*. Oxford: Clarendon, 1959.

Henderson, John B. *The Development and Decline of Chinese Cosmology.* New York: Columbia University Press, 1984.

———. *Scripture, Canon, and Commentary: A Comparison of Confucian and Western Exegesis.* Princeton: Princeton University Press, 1991.

Henry, Eric. "Motif of Recognition." *Harvard Journal of Asiatic Studies* 47.1 (June 1987): 5–30.

Hervouet, Yves. "La valeur relative des textes du Che-ki et du Han-chou." In *Mélanges de sinologie offerts à Monsieur Paul Demiéville.* Vol. 2. Paris: 1974.

Hightower, James Robert. "The Fu of T'ao Ch'ien." *Harvard Journal of Asiatic Studies* 17 (1954): 169–230.

———, trans. "The Letter to Jen An." In Cyril Birch, ed., *Anthology of Chinese Literature from Early Times to the Fourteenth Century.* New York: Grove Press, 1965.

———, trans. *Han shih wai chuan.* Harvard–Yenching Institute Monograph Series. Vol. XI. Cambridge, Mass.: Harvard University Press, 1952.

Hsiao, Kung-chuan. *A History of Chinese Political Thought.* Translated by Frederick Mote. Princeton: Princeton University Press, 1979.

Hsu, Cho-yun and Katheryn M. Linduff. *Western Chou Civilization.* New Haven and London: Yale University Press, 1988.

Hulsewé, A. F. P. "Notes on the Historiography of the Han Period." In W. G. Beasley and E. G. Pulleyblank, eds., *Historians of China and Japan.* London: School of Oriental and African Studies, 1961.

———. "The Problem of the Authenticity of *Shih-chi* Ch. 123, The Memoir on Ta Yüan." *T'oung Pao* 60.1–3 (1975): 83–147.

———. "*Shih chi.*" In Michael Loewe, ed., *Early Chinese Texts: A Bibliographic Guide.* Berkeley: The Society for the Study of Early China and the Institute of East Asian Studies, University of California, Berkeley, 1993.

Johnson, David. "The Wu Tzu-hsü Pien-wen and Its Sources." Parts 1 and 2. *Harvard Journal of Asiatic Studies* 40.1 (1980): 93–156; 40.2 (1980): 465–503.

Jones, Ernest. "The Death of Hamlet's Father." In Edith Kurzweil, ed., *Literature and Psychoanalysis.* New York: Columbia University Press, 1983.

Knoblock, John, trans. *Xunzi: A Translation and Study of the Complete Works.* Stanford: Stanford University Press, 1988.

Lau, D. C., trans. *Mencius.* Hong Kong: The University Press, 1984.

Levi, Jean. *Le Fils du ciel et son annaliste.* Paris: Gallimard, 1992.

Lewis, Mark Edward. *Sanctioned Violence in Early China.* Albany: SUNY Press, 1990.

Link, Perry. *Evening Chants in Beijing.* New York and London: W. W. Norton & Co., 1992.

Loewe, Michael. "The Campaigns of Han Wu-ti." In Frank Kierman, Jr. and John K. Fairbank, eds., *Chinese Ways in Warfare.* Cambridge, Mass.: Harvard University Press, 1974.

——. "The Former Han Dynasty." In Denis Twitchett and Michael Loewe, eds., *The Cambridge History of China, Volume 1: The Chin and Han Empires, 221 B.C.–A.D. 220.* Cambridge University Press, 1983.

Maspero, Henri. *La Chine antique.* New edition. Paris: Presses Universitaires de France, 1965.

——. "Le roman historique dans la littérature Chinoise de l'antiquité." In *Études historiques: Mélanges posthumes sur les religions et l'histoire de la Chine.* Vol. 3. Paris: Publications de Musée Guimet, 1950.

Owen, Stephen. *Traditional Chinese Poetry and Poetics.* Madison: University of Wisconsin Press, 1985.

Průšek, Jaroslav. *Chinese History and Literature.* Prague: Academia, 1970.

Rosen, Sidney. "In Search of the Historical Kuan Chung." *Journal of Asian Studies* 35.3 (May 1976): 431–40.

Schneider, Laurence A. *A Madman of Ch'u: The Chinese Myth of Loyalty and Dissent.* Berkeley: University of California Press, 1980.

Scholes, Robert and Robert Kellogg. *The Nature of Narrative.* New York: Oxford University Press, 1975.

Shaughnessy, Edward. "The Composition of *Zhouyi.*" Ph.D. diss., Stanford University, 1983.

Shigeki, Kaizuka. *Confucius.* Translated by Geoffrey Bowas. London: George Allen & Unwin, 1956.

Som, Tjan Tjoe. *The Comprehensive Discussions in the White Tiger Hall.* 2 vols. Leiden: E. J. Brill, 1949.

Sullivan, Michael. *The Arts of China.* Berkeley: University of California Press, 1984.

Tain, Tzey-yueh. "Tung Chung-shu's System of Thought, Its Sources and Its Influence on the Scholars." Ph.D. diss., University of California, Los Angeles, 1974.

Thompson, Stith. *Motif-Index of Folk Literature*. Vol. 5. Bloomington: Indiana University Press, 1957.

Tu, Wei-ming. *Confucian Thought: Selfhood as Creative Transformation*. Albany: SUNY Press, 1985.

Van Zoeren, Steven. *Poetry and Personality: Reading, Exegesis, and Hermeneutics in Traditional China*. Stanford: Stanford University Press, 1991.

Vuylsteke, Richard. "The Political Philosophy of Tung Chung-shu (179–104 B.C.). Ph.D. diss., University of Hawaii, 1982.

Wallacker, Benjamin. "Han Confucianism and Confucius in the Han." In David T. Roy and Tsuen-hsuin Tsien, ed., *Ancient China: Studies in Early Civilization*. Hong Kong: The Chinese University Press, 1978.

Wang, John C. Y. "Early Chinese Narrative: The *Tso-chuan* as Example." In Andrew Plaks edited, *Chinese Narrative*. Princeton: Princeton University Press, 1977.

Wang, Zhongshu. *Han Civilization*. Translated by K. C. Chang. New Haven and London: Yale University Press, 1982.

Watson, Burton. *Early Chinese Literature*. New York: Columbia University Press, 1962.

———. *Ssu-ma Ch'ien, Grand Historian of China*. New York: Columbia University Press, 1958.

———, trans. *Records of the Grand Historian of China*. 2 vols. New York: Columbia University Press, 1971.

———, trans. *The Tso Chuan: Selections from China's Oldest Narrative History*. New York: Columbia University Press, 1989.

Wheatley, Paul. *The Pivot of the Four Quarters: A Preliminary Inquiry into the Origins and Character of the Ancient Chinese City*. Edinburgh: Edinburgh University Press, 1971.

White, Hayden. *Metahistory*. Baltimore: Johns Hopkins University Press, 1973.

Wilhelm, Hellmut. "The Scholar's Frustration: Notes on a Type of Fu." In John K. Fairbank, ed., *Chinese Thought and Institutions*. Chicago: University of Chicago Press, 1957.

Wilhelm, Richard, trans. *The I Ching or Book of Changes*. Rendered into English by Cary F. Baynes. Bollingen Series XIX. New Edition. Princeton: Princeton University Press, 1967.

Woo Kang. *Les trois théories politiques des Tch'ouen Ts'ieou: Interprétées par Tong Tchong-chou d'après les principes de l'école de Kong-yang*.

Paris: Librairie Ernest Leroux, 1932.

Wu, Hung. *The Wu Liang Shrine: The Ideology of Early Chinese Pictorial Art*. Stanford: Stanford University Press, 1989.

Wu, Pei-yi. *The Confucian's Progress*. Princeton: Princeton University Press, 1989.

Xiao Tong. *Wen Xuan or Selections of Refined Literature. Volume 1: Rhapsodies on Metropolises and Capitals*. Translated by David Knechtges. Princeton: Princeton University Press, 1982.

Yang, Hsien-yi and Gladys Yang, trans. *Records of the Historian*. Beijing: Foreign Language Press, 1979.

Yü, Ying-shih. "The Seating Order at the Hung Men Banquet." Translated by T. C. Tang. In George Kao, ed., *The Transition of Things Past: Chinese History and Historiography*. Hong Kong: The Chinese University Press, 1982.

Chinese and Other Asian Sources

Baihua Shi ji 白話史記 [A Vernacular Translation of *Records of the Historian*]. Translated by Wu Shaozhi 吳紹志. Tainan: Xibi, 1988.

Baihua Shi ji 白話史記 [A Vernacular Translation of *Records of the Historian*] Lianjing. Translation by Long Yuchun 龍宇純 et al. 3 vols. Taibei: Lianjing, 1985.

Chun qiu fanlu 春秋繁露 [Abundant Dew of Spring and Autumn Annals]. *SBBY* edition.

Chun qiu Zuo zhuan zhu 春秋左傳注 [An Annotation of *Spring and Autumn Annals* and *Zuo Commentary*]. Edited by Yang Bojun 楊伯峻. Beijing: Zhonghua, 1981.

Cui Shi 崔適. *Shi ji tan yuan* 史記探源 [An Exploration into Sources of *Records of the Historian*]. Beijing: Zhonghua, 1986.

Cui Shu 崔述. *Kaoxin lu* 考信錄 [A Record of Investigations into Authenticity]. 2 vols. Taibei: Shijie, 1968.

Gongyang zhuan 公羊傳 [Gongyang Commentary]. *SSJZS* edition.

Gu Lisan 顧立三. *Sima Qian chuanxie Shi ji caiyong Zuo zhuan de yanjiu* 司馬遷傳寫史記採用左傳的研究 [A Study of Sima Qian's Adaptations of *Zuo Commentary* in Writing *Records of the Historian*]. Taibei: Zhongzheng, 1981.

Guliang zhuan 穀梁傳 [Guliang Commentary]. *SBBY* edition.

Guo yu 國語 [Discourses of the States]. *SBBY* edition.

Gushu diangu cidian 古書典故辭典 [A Dictionary of Allusions to Ancient Books]. Taibei: Huashi, 1987.

Hancheng xian zhi 韓城縣志 [Gazeteer of Hancheng County]. Qianlong 49 (1784).

Han shu 漢書 [Historical Records of the Han]. Beijing: Zhonghua, 1962.

Honda Shigeyuki 本田成之. *Shina keigaku shi ron.* 1927. Translated by Jiang Xi'an as *Zhongguo jingxue shi* 中國經學史 [A History of Classic Studies in China]. 1934. Reprint. Taibei: Guangwen, 1986.

Hong Yixuan 洪頤煊. *Jingdian jilin* 經典集林. *Baibu congshu* edition.

Huang Zhen 黃震. *Huang shi ri chao* 黃氏日鈔 [The Daily Copies of Mr. Huang]. *SKQS* edition.

Jia Yi 賈誼. *Xin shu* 新書 [New Documents]. *SBBY* edition.

Jin Dejian 金得建. *Sima Qian suojian shu kao* 司馬遷所見書考 [An Investigation of Books Seen by Sima Qian]. Shanghai: Renmin, 1963.

Kongzi jia yu 孔子家語 [The Family Sayings of Master Kong]. *SBBY* edition.

Lao Gan 勞榦. *Qin Han shi* 秦漢史 [A History of the Qin and Han]. Taibei: Zhongguo wenhua, 1986.

Li Changzhi 李長之. *Sima Qian zhi renge yu fengge* 司馬遷之人格與風格 [The Character and Style of Sima Qian]. 1949. Reprint. Taibei: Kaiming, 1976.

Li Shaoyong 李少雍. *Sima Qian zhuanji wenxue lun gao* 司馬遷傳記文學論稿 [Draft Essays on the Biographical Literature of Sima Qian]. Chongqing: Xinhua, 1987.

Li Weixiong 李威熊. *Dong Zhongshu yu Xi Han xueshu* 董仲舒與西漢學術 [Dong Zhongshu and Western Han Scholarship]. Taibei: Wenshizhe, 1978.

Li ji Zheng zhu 禮記鄭注 [Records of Ritual with the Zheng Commentary]. *SBBY* edition.

Liu Xiang 劉向. *Shuoyuan* 說苑 [A Garden of Sayings]. *SBCK* edition.

Liu Zhiji 劉知幾. *Shitong tongshi* 史通通釋 [A Comprehensive Explanation of *A Study of Historiography*]. Reprint. Taibei: Liren, 1980.

Lo Genze 羅根澤. "*Zhanguo ce* zuo yu Kuai Tong kao" 戰國策作於蒯通考 [An Investigation of Kuai Tong's Authorship of *Intrigues of the Warring States*]. In Gu Jiegang 顧捷剛, ed., *Gushi bian* 古史辯 [Symposium on Ancient Chinese History]. Vol. 4. Reprint. Taibei: Minglong, 1970.

Lu Jia 陸賈. *Xin yu* 新語. *SBBY* ed.

Lu Nanqiao 盧南喬. "Lun Sima Qian ji qi lishi bianzhuan xue" 論司馬遷及其歷史編撰學 [A Discussion of Sima Qian and His Compilation of History]. In Wang Guowei 王國維, et al., *Sima qian: qi ren ji qi shu* 司馬遷其人及其書 [Sima Qian: The Man and His Book]. Taibei: Chang'an, 1985.

Lu Xun 魯迅. "Han wenxue shi gangyao" 漢文學史綱要 [An Outline History of Han Literature]. In *Lu Xun quanji* 魯迅全集 [The Collected Works of Lu Xun]. Vol. 8. Beijing: Renmin, 1963.

Lun yu jijie 論語集解 [Collected Explanations of *Analects*]. *SBBY* edition.

Lü Xisheng. "Sima Qian gongxing xiyi" [A Clarification of Sima Qian's Punishment of Castration]. *Zhongguo shi yanjiu* 中國史研究 [Studies in Chinese History] 4 (1983): 68.

Lü shi chun qiu 呂氏春秋 [The Spring and Autumn Annals of Mr. Lü]. *SBBY* edition.

Mao shi Zheng jian 毛詩鄭箋 [*The Mao Odes* with the Zheng Commentary]. *SBBY* edition.

Mengzi Zhao zhu 孟子趙注 [*Mencius* with the Zhao Commentary]. *SBBY* edition.

Mozi 墨子. *SBBY* edition.

Nishijima, Sadao 西島定生. *Baihua Qin Han shi* 白話秦漢史 [A Vernacular Language History of the Qin and Han]. Translated by Huang Yaoneng 黃耀能. Taibei: Wenshizhe, 1983.

Pan Zhonggui 潘重規. "Shi ji Bo Yi lie zhuan cheng 'qi zhuan yue' kaoshi" 史記伯夷列傳稱其傳曰考試 [An Investigation into the Phrase "Their Traditions Says" in "The Traditions of Bo Yi" in *Records of the Historian*]. *Dalu zazhi* 大陸雜誌 18.5 (March 1959): 1–3.

Pi Xirui 皮希瑞. *Jingxue lishi* 經學歷史 [A History of the Study of the Classics]. With notes by Zhou Yutong 周予同. 1961. Reprint. Taibei: Hanjing wenhua shiye, 1983.

Qian Mu 錢穆. "Kongzi yu *Chun qiu* "孔子與春秋 [Confucius and *Spring and Autumn Annals*]. In Qian Mu, ed., *Liang Han jingxue jin gu wen pingyi* 兩漢經學今古文平議 [A Critical Discussion of New and Old Script Schools in Han Dynasty Classic Studies]. Taibei: Dongda, 1983, pp. 235–283.

———. "Liang Han bo shi jiafa kao" 兩漢博士家法考 [An Investigation into the School System of Academicians during the Han Dynasty]. In Qian Mu, ed., *Liang Han jingxue jin gu wen pingyi* 兩漢經學今古文平議 [A Critical Discussion of New and Old Script Schools in Han

Dynasty Classic Studies]. Taibei: Dongda, 1983, pp. 165–233.

———. *Qin Han shi* 秦漢史 [A History of the Qin and Han]. Reprint. Taibei: Dongfang, 1985.

———. *Shi ji diming kao* 史記地名考 [An Investigation of Place-names in *Records of the Historian*]. 1968. Reprint. Taibei: Sanmin, 1984.

———. *Xian Qin zhuzi xinian* 先秦諸子繫年 [Linking the Chronologies of Pre-Qin Masters]. Second edition. Hong Kong: University of Hong Kong Press, 1956.

Qu Wanli 屈萬里. *Xian Qin wen shi ziliao kao bian* 先秦文史資料考辯 [An Examination of Literary and Historical Sources for the Pre-Qin Period]. Taibei: Lianjing, 1983.

Qu Yingsheng 曲潁生. "Shi ji liezhuan yi Bo Yi ju shou zhi yuanyin" 史記列傳以伯夷居首之原因 [The Reason for Bo Yi Being Placed at the Beginning of the "Traditions" Section of *Records of the Historian*]. *Dalu zazhi* 12.3 (February 1956): 28–32.

Ruan Zhisheng 阮芝生. "Shi lun Sima Qian suoshuo de 'tong gu jin zhi bian'" 試論司馬遷所說的通古今之變 [A Preliminary Essay on Sima Qian's Statement "To Penetrate the Transformations of Ancient and Modern Times"]. In Du Weiyun 杜維運 and Huang Jinxing 黃進興, eds., *Zhongguo shixue shi lunwen xuanji* 中國史學史論文選集 [A Selected Collection of Essays on the History of Chinese Historiography]. Vol. 3. Taibei: Huashi, 1980.

———. "Tai shi gong zenyang souji he chuli shiliao" 太史公怎樣搜集和處理史料 [How Did the Gentleman Grand Historian Collect and Manage Historical Sources?]. *Shumu jikan* 書目季刊 7.4 (March 1974): 17–35.

Shang shu 尚書 [Ancient Documents]. *SSJZS* edition.

Shi Ding 施定. "Lun Sima Qian de tong gu jin zhi bian" 論司馬遷的通古今之變 [A Discussion of Sima Qian's "Penetrating the Transformations of Ancient and Modern Times"]. *Sima Qian yanjiu xinlun* 司馬遷研究新論 [New Essays on Sima Qian Studies]. Beijing: Henan Renmin, 1982.

Shi Zhimian 施之勉. *Shi ji huizhu kaozheng dingbu* 史記會注考證定補 [A Verification and Supplement to *An Examination of Collected Comments on Records of the Historian*]. Taibei: Huagang, 1976.

Shi ji 史記 [Records of the Historian]. Beijing: Zhonghua, 1959.

Shi ji 史記 [Records of the Historian]. From the Bona edition of the Twenty-Four Histories. 1937. Reprint. Taibei: Shangwu, 1981.

Shi ji cidian 史記辭典 [A Dictionary to *Records of the Historian*]. Edited by Cang Xiuliang 倉修良. Shandong: Jiaoyu chubanshe, 1991.

Shi ji pinglin 史記評林 [A Forest of Critical Comments on *Records of the Historian*]. Edited by Ling Zhilong 凌稚隆. 1576. Reprint. Taibei: Diqiu, 1992.

Shi ji quanti xinzhu 史記全體新注 [A New Commentary to the Entire *Records of the Historian*]. Edited with notes by Zhang Dake 張大可. Xi'an: Sanqin, 1990.

Shui jing zhu 水經注 [The Commentary to the Classic of Rivers]. *SBCK* edition.

Shuo wen jie zi gulin 説文解字詁林 [A Forest of Explanatory Notes on *Explaining Simple Graphs and Analyzing Compound Characters*]. Edited by Ding Fubao 丁福保. Reprint. Taibei: Shangwu, 1976.

Sun Xingyan 孫星衍. *Kongzi jiyu* 孔子集語 [The Collected Sayings of Confucius]. Taibei: Shijie, 1970.

Takikawa Kametarō 瀧川龜太郎. *Shi ki kaichū kōshō* 史記會注考證 [A Philological Examination of Collected Commentaries to *Records of the Historian*]. 1934. Reprint. Taibei: Hongshi, 1986.

Wang Anshi 王安石. "Kongzi shi jia yi" 孔子世家意 [Ideas about "The Hereditary Household of Confucius"]. *Linchuan xiansheng wenji* 臨川先生文集 [The Literary Collection of Mr. Linchuan]. Vol. 46. *SBCK* edition.

Wang Guowei 王國維. "Tai shi gong xingnian kao" 太史公行年考 [An Investigation into the Chronology of the Activities of the Duke Grand Astrologer]. *Guantang jilin* 觀堂集林. Vol. 11. Shanghai: Guji, 1983.

Wang Jia 王嘉. *Shi yi ji* 拾遺記 [A Record of Gathered Fragments]. *SKQS* edition.

Wang Li 王力. *Tongyuan zidian* 同源字典 [A Dictionary of Words of the Same Origin]. Reprint. Taibei: Wenshizhe, 1982.

Wang Ruoxu 王若虛. *Hunan yilao ji* 湖南逸老集 [The Collected Texts of a Remnant Old Man from Hunan]. *SBCK* edition.

Wang Shumin 王叔民. *Shi ji jiaozheng* 史記校證 [A Collation of *Records of the Historian*]. Taibei: Academia Sinica, 1982.

Wen Chongyi 文崇一. "Lun Sima Qian de sixiang" 論司馬遷的思想 [A Discussion of the Thought of Sima Qian]. In Huang Peirong 黃沛榮, ed., *Shi ji lunwen xuanji* 史記論文選集 [A Selection of Essays on *Records of the Historian*]. Taibei: Chang'an, 1982.

Wu Ruyu 吳汝煜. *Shi ji lun gao* 史記論稿 [Draft Essays on *Records of the Historian*]. Jiangsu: Jiaoyu chubanshe, 1986.

Wu Zhongkuang 吳忠匡. "Xian Qin xueshu sixiang de lishixing zongjie" 先

秦學術思想的歷史性總結 [A Historical Synthesis of Pre-Qin Intellectual Thought]. In Liu Naihe 劉乃和, ed., *Sima Qian he Shi ji* 司馬遷和史記 [Sima Qian and *Records of the Historian*]. Beijing: Beijing Press, 1987.

Xiao Li 肖黎. *Sima Qian pingzhuan* 司馬遷平傳 [A Critical Biography of Sima Qian]. Jilin: Jilin wenshizhe, 1986.

Xiao jing [Classic of Filial Piety] 孝經. *SBBY* edition.

Xu Fuguan 徐復觀. "Lun *Shi ji* " 論史記 [A Discussion of *Records of the Historian*]. In Du Weiyun 杜維運 and Huang Jinxing 黃進興, eds., *Zhongguo shixue shi lunwen xuanji* 中國史學史論文選集 [A Selected Collection of Essays on the History of Chinese Historiography]. Vol. 3. Taibei: Huashi, 1980.

———. "Taishi gong de sixiang beijing ji qi shixue jingshen" 太史公的思想背景及其史學精神 [The Background of the Duke Grand Astrologer's Thought and the Spirit of his Historiography]. In Huang Peirong 黃沛榮, ed., *Shiji lunwen xuanji* 史記論文選集 [A Collection of Essays on *Shiji*]. Taibei: Zhonghua, 1982.

———. "Yuan shih—you zongjiao tongxiang renwen de shixue de chengli" 原史—由宗教通向人文的史學的成立 [The Original Historian-Astrologer—The Movement from a Religious Historiography to the Establishment of a Humanistic Historiography]. In Du Weiyun 杜維運 and Huang Jinxing 黃進興, eds., *Zhongguo shixue shi lunwen xuanji* 中國史學史論文選集 [A Selected Collection of Essays on the History of Chinese Historiography], Vol. 3. Taibei: Huashi, 1980.

———. *Zhongguo jingxue shi de jichu* 中國經學史的基礎 [The Foundation of the History of Chinese Classic Studies]. Taibei: Student Bookstore, 1982.

Xunzi 荀子. *SBBY* edition.

Yang Xiong 揚雄. *Fa yan* 法言 [Model Sayings]. *SBBY* edition.

Yanzi chun qiu 晏子春秋 [The Spring and Autumn Annals of Master Yan]. *SBBY* edition.

Yu Qiding 俞啟定. *Xian Qin Liang Han rujia jiaoyu* 先秦兩漢儒家教育 [Confucian Education in the Pre-Qin and Han Period]. Beijing, 1987.

Zhanguo ce 戰國策 [Intriques of the Warring States]. *SBBY* edition.

Zhang Dake 張大可. *Shi ji yanjiu* 史記研究 [A Study of Records of the Historian]. Lanzhou: Gansu People's Press, 1985.

Zhang Xincheng 張心澂. *Weishu tongkao* 偽書通考 [A Comprehensive Investigation of Forged Books]. Shanghai: Shangwu, 1957.

Zhang Yiren 張以仁. *Guo yu Zuo zhuan lunji* 國語左傳論集 [A Collection of Essays on *Discourses of the States* and *Zuo Commentary*]. Taibei: Dongsheng, 1980.

Zhang Zhengnan 張正男. *Zhanguo ce chutan* 戰國策初探 [A Preliminary Investigation of *Intrigues of the Warring States*]. Taibei: Commercial Press, 1984.

Zhao Xingzhi 趙省之. "Sima Qian fu zuo de pingjia" 司馬遷賦作的評買 [An Evaluation of the Authorship of Sima Qian's Fu]. In Wang Guowei 王國維, et al., *Sima Qian: qi ren ji qi shu* 司馬遷其人及其書 [Sima Qian: The Man and His Book]. Taibei: Chang'an, 1985.

Zhao Yi 趙翼. *Gaiyu congkao* 陔餘叢考 [The Collected Examinations of What Remained After the Steps]. Vol. I. Reprint. Taibei: Xinwenfeng 1975.

Zheng Haosheng 鄭鶴聲. *Sima Qian nianpu* 司馬遷年譜 [A Year-by-Year Chronology of Sima Qian]. Revised Edition. Shanghai: Commercial Press, 1956.

Zheng Liangshu 鄭良樹. *Zhanguo ce yanjiu* 戰國策研究 [A Study of *Intrigues of the Warring States*]. 1972. Reprint. Taibei: Xuesheng, 1986.

Zhongguo shixue shi cidian 中國史學史辭典 [A Dictionary of the History of Chinese Historiography]. Taibei: Minwen, 1986.

Zhou Hulin 周虎林. *Sima Qian yu qi shixue* 司馬遷與其史學 [Sima Qian and His Historiography]. Taibei: Wenshizhe, 1987.

Zhou Yutong 周予同. *Jing jin gu wen xue* 經今古文學 [A Study of the Classics in New and Old Script]. 1926. Reprint. Taibei: Commercial Press, 1985.

———. *Qun jing gailun* 群經概論 [A Sketch of the Classics]. 1948. Reprint. Taibei, 1986.

Zhou li Zheng zhu 周禮鄭注 [Rituals of Zhou with the Zheng Commentary]. *SBBY* edition.

Zhu Dongrun 朱東潤. "Shi ji ben ji biao shu shi jia zhuan shuo li" 史記本紀表書世家傳說例 [Explaining the Usage of "Basic Annals," "Charts," "Essays," "Hereditary Households," and "Traditions" in *Records of the Historian*]. In Huang Peirong 黃沛榮, ed., *Shi ji lunwen xuanji* 史記論文選集 [A Selection of Essays on *Records of the Historian*]. Taibei: Chang'an, 1982.

Zhuangzi 莊子. *SBBY* edition.

Index

219

CPSIA information can be obtained
at www.ICGtesting.com
Printed in the USA
FSOW01n0958110916
24871FS